READING TUTOR

고등 독해의
절대 자신감

실력

고등 독해의 절대 자신감
리딩튜터 〈실력〉

지은이	NE능률 영어교육연구소
선임 연구원	신유승
연구원	이은주, 신이례
영문 교열	August Niederhaus, Nathaniel Galletta
디자인	박정진, 김명진
내지 일러스트	박정원, 혜란, 김영미, 홍승표
내지 사진	www.shutterstock.com, www.istockphoto.com, www.hellophoto.kr
맥편집	김재민
영업	한기영, 이경구, 박인규, 정철교, 김남준, 이우현
마케팅	박혜선, 남경진, 이지원, 김여진

READING TUTOR

고등 독해의
절대 자신감

리딩튜터 실력
어휘 암기장

NE 능률

SECTION 01 세계의 문화

□	local	지역의, 현지의; pl. 주민, 현지인
□	promote	촉진[고취]하다
□	range	다양성; 범위
□	ethnic	민족[종족]의
□	originate	비롯되다, 유래하다
□	theory	이론
□	stem from	…에서 생겨나다, 기인하다
□	term	용어, 말
□	variation	변화; 변형
□	compliment	칭찬(의 말), 찬사
□	celebrity	유명 인사, 명사
□	advertisement	광고
□	make a fist	주먹을 쥐다
□	extend	연장하다; 뻗다, 내밀다
□	pinky	새끼손가락
□	uncurl	펴다
□	palm	손바닥
□	show	표시
□	goodwill	친선, 호의
□	tremble	떨다, 떨리다
□	cliff	절벽
□	fragile	부서지기[손상되기] 쉬운
□	foundation	(건물의) 토대, 기초
□	structure	구조; 구조물, 건축물
□	construct	건설하다

□	religion	종교
□	Buddhism	불교
□	Taoism	도교
□	Confucianism	유교
□	chamber	공간, 방
□	statue	조각상
□	endanger	위험에 빠뜨리다, 위태롭게 만들다
□	spiritual	정신의, 정신적인, 영적인
□	meditate	명상하다
□	inner	내부의; 내면의
□	ironically	역설적이게도
□	tourist attraction	관광 명소
□	associate	결부[연관]짓다
□	transform	변형시키다; 완전히 바꿔 놓다
□	must-do	꼭 해야 할 일, 필수 사항
□	float	장식 차량 [꽃수레]
□	show off	…을 자랑하다, 과시하다
□	costume	의상[복장]
□	alongside	옆에, 나란히
□	toss	던지다
□	fireworks display	불꽃놀이
□	reserve	예약하다
□	range from A to B	A에서 B까지 다양하다
□	depending on	…에 따라
□	a variety of	여러 가지의
□	fabulous	기막히게 좋은[멋진]
□	carve	조각하다; 새기다, 파다
□	jack-o-lantern	호박등
□	beloved	총애받는, 인기 많은

☐	tradition	전통
☐	border	국경[경계] (지역)
☐	carving	조각(품)
☐	rather than	…보다는[대신에]
☐	radish	무
☐	celebration	기념[축하] 행사
☐	take place	개최되다, 일어나다
☐	merchant	상인
☐	attract	끌어모으다
☐	official	공식적인
☐	normal	보통의, 평범한
☐	weigh	무게가 …이다
☐	harvest	수확하다, 거둬들이다
☐	work on	…에 애쓰다[공들이다]
☐	creation	창조, 창작; 창작물

SECTION 02 역사 속 인물

☐	triangular	삼각형의
☐	play a role in	…에 역할을 하다
☐	imperial	황제의
☐	guard	호위병
☐	vertically	수직으로
☐	towering	우뚝 솟은
☐	horizontally	수평으로
☐	comparison	비교

☐	crucial	중대한
☐	examine	조사하다, 검사하다
☐	command	명령하다; 지배하다; (동정 · 존경 등을) 모으다, 일으키다
☐	end up v-ing	결국 …이 되다
☐	origin	기원
☐	portrait	초상화
☐	skilled	숙련된, 노련한
☐	statistician	통계 전문가, 통계학자
☐	statistics	통계학
☐	figure out	…을 이해하다[알아내다]
☐	effectively	효과적으로
☐	improve	개선하다, 향상시키다
☐	overworked	혹사당하는
☐	condition	상태; pl. 환경, 상황
☐	suffer	고통받다
☐	shortage	부족
☐	medicine	의학; 약
☐	significantly	상당히, 크게
☐	lower	낮추다
☐	wounded	부상을 입은
☐	unsanitary	비위생적인
☐	present	제시하다, 제출하다
☐	council	의회
☐	arrange	정리하다, 배열하다
☐	convince	납득시키다, 확신시키다
☐	sanitation	위생 시설[관리]
☐	supply	pl. 공급(량); 보급품[물자]
☐	view	견해; …라고 여기다

☐	Prime Minister	총리, 수상
☐	hold ... together	…을 단결시키다
☐	colonize	식민지로 만들다
☐	British Empire	대영제국
☐	partially	부분적으로
☐	responsible for	…에 책임이 있는
☐	region	지방, 지역
☐	rule	규칙; 통치하다
☐	famine	기근
☐	export	수출하다
☐	refuse	거절[거부]하다
☐	turn down	…을 거절[거부]하다
☐	offer	제의하다; 제의, 제안
☐	fear	공포, 두려움; …을 두려워하다
☐	approximately	거의
☐	starve to death	굶어 죽다
☐	victim	피해자, 희생자
☐	turn one's back on	…에게 등을 돌리다, …을 저버리다
☐	put A before B	A를 B보다 더 우선시하다
☐	heartless	무정한, 비정한
☐	career	직업, 직장 생활
☐	journalist	저널리스트, 기자
☐	journalism	저널리즘, 언론
☐	direct	…로 향하다[겨냥하다]
☐	dream of	…을 꿈꾸다
☐	leading	가장 중요한, 선두적인
☐	editor	편집장; 편집자
☐	investigate	조사하다

□	investigative	조사의, 수사의
□	mental	정신의, 정신적인
□	mentally	정신적으로
□	reputation	평판, 명성
□	treat	대하다
□	poorly	형편없이
□	pretend to-v	…인 척하다
□	publish	출판하다, 발행하다
□	reporting	보도
□	break the world record	세계 기록을 깨다
□	complete	완료하다, 끝마치다
□	set a record	기록을 세우다
□	fake	가짜의, 거짓된
□	female	여성의
□	pioneer	개척자, 선구자

SECTION 03 심리

□	guilt	죄책감
□	fiction	소설; 허구
□	psychologist	심리학자
□	physical	육체의, 신체의
□	unfortunately	불행하게도
□	participant	참가자
□	unethically	비윤리적으로
□	reward	보상

☐	volunteer work	자원봉사
☐	reduce	줄이다
☐	origin	기원, 근원
☐	benefit	혜택, 이득
☐	characteristic	특징, 특질
☐	lack	…이 없다[부족하다]
☐	hygiene	위생
☐	likelihood	가능성
☐	morality	도덕; 도덕성
☐	preference	선호(도)
☐	cleanliness	청결
☐	face	마주 보다; 직면하다
☐	live	살아 있는
☐	come up with	(해답 등을) 찾아내다, 내놓다
☐	catfish	메기
☐	container	그릇, 용기
☐	avoid	피하다
☐	predator	포식자, 포식 동물
☐	effect	영향; 효과, 결과
☐	apply	적용시키다
☐	field	들판; 분야
☐	motivate	동기를 부여하다
☐	employee	종업원, 고용인
☐	innovative	획기적인
☐	competitor	경쟁 상대
☐	dynamic	활발한; 역동적인
☐	survive	살아남다
☐	entire	전체의

□	pressure	압박, 압력
□	stimulation	자극; 고무, 격려
□	natural enemy	천적
□	draw	끌어당기다; 끌어내다
□	scary	무서운, 겁나는
□	control	지배하다, 통제하다
□	lucid	명쾌한; 의식이 또렷한
□	normally	보통은
□	self-aware	자기를 인식하는, 자각하는
□	explore	탐험하다
□	environment	환경
□	completely	완전히, 전적으로
□	fade	서서히 사라지다
□	exhausting	기진맥진하게 만드는
□	interrupt	방해하다, 중단시키다
□	rest	나머지; 휴식, 수면
□	addictive	중독성이 있는
□	gain	얻다
□	confidence	자신감
□	overcome	극복하다
□	unconscious	의식하지 못하는
□	behavioral	행동의, 행동에 관한
□	behavior	행동
□	experiment	실험
□	place	놓다, 두다
□	a bunch of	한 다발의
□	attract	마음을 끌다; 끌어들이다
□	scream	비명을 지르다
□	refrain from	…을 그만두다

☐	attempt to-v	…하려고 시도하다
☐	grab	붙잡다
☐	spray	뿌리다
☐	conceal	감추다, 숨기다
☐	showerhead	샤워기 꼭지
☐	ceiling	천장
☐	pull	잡아당기다
☐	similarly	비슷하게
☐	examine	조사하다, 검토하다
☐	impolite	무례한
☐	recommendable	권할 만한

SECTION 04 문화 · 예술

☐	worth	…의 가치가 있는
☐	proverb	격언, 속담
☐	arrange	정리하다, 배열하다
☐	phrase	구
☐	ideally	이상적으로
☐	publish	출판하다, 발행하다
☐	volume	용량; 양; 권; 책
☐	poem	시
☐	contain	포함하다
☐	release	발표, 개봉, 발간
☐	popular	인기 있는
☐	popularity	인기
☐	a wide range of	광범위한, 다양한

☐	labor	노동; 노고, 노력
☐	difference	차이
☐	poetry	시
☐	resemble	닮다
☐	polka dot	물방울무늬
☐	artwork	미술품
☐	have ... in common	…을 공통으로 지니다
☐	childhood	어린 시절
☐	powerful	영향력 있는; 강한, 강렬한
☐	impact	영향
☐	imagine	상상하다
☐	endless	무한한, 끝없는
☐	inspire A to-v	A가 …하도록 고무[격려]하다
☐	infinity	무한성
☐	flash	번쩍이다
☐	symbolize	상징하다
☐	enormous	막대한, 거대한
☐	universe	우주
☐	connect	연결하다
☐	connection	연결
☐	discourage	좌절시키다
☐	produce	생산하다
☐	arrange	정리하다, 배열하다
☐	fake	가짜(의); 모조품
☐	imitation	모방; 모조품
☐	imitator	모방자
☐	imitate	모방하다
☐	forgery	위조죄; 위조(품)
☐	spot	발견하다, 알아채다

☐	major	주요한
☐	expert	전문가
☐	mathematics	수학
☐	mathematical	수학적인
☐	break down	…을 분해하다
☐	method	방법
☐	compare	비교하다
☐	stroke	일격; 붓의 놀림
☐	master	훌륭한; 대가
☐	analyze	분석하다
☐	obtain	획득하다; 입수하다
☐	measurement	측정
☐	measure	측정하다; 측정(방법)
☐	genuine	진짜의
☐	embrace	껴안다; 수용하다
☐	distrust	불신하다
☐	influence	영향(력)
☐	threat	위협, 위험
☐	design	디자인하다; 만들다
☐	discourage	의욕을 꺾다, 좌절시키다
☐	legendary	전설적인, 아주 유명한
☐	involved in	…에 관여하는, 관련된
☐	comical	웃기는, 재미있는
☐	break habit	습관을 깨다
☐	go through	…을 겪다
☐	tale	이야기
☐	point out	지적하다, 언급하다
☐	amuse	즐겁게 하다

SECTION 05 유머 · 감동

☐	confident	자신감 있는
☐	employee	종업원, 고용인
☐	region	지방, 지역
☐	shift	변화; 교대 근무 (시간)
☐	salesperson	판매원
☐	skeptically	회의적으로
☐	inquire	묻다
☐	sale	판매
☐	rage	분노, 격노
☐	coworker	협력자, 동료
☐	dozens of	수십의, 많은
☐	worth	…의 가치가 있는[되는]
☐	gasp	숨이 턱 막히다, 헉 하고 숨을 쉬다
☐	astonished	깜짝 놀란
☐	fishing rod	낚싯대
☐	gear	장비
☐	inform	알리다
☐	speedboat	고속 모터보트, 쾌속정
☐	vehicle	차량, 탈것
☐	tow	끌다, 견인하다
☐	four-wheel-drive	사륜구동의
☐	purchase	구입하다
☐	convince	납득시키다, 확신시키다
☐	remedy	치료(약)
☐	effective	효과적인

☐	make a profit	이윤을 내다
☐	extremely	대단히, 몹시
☐	performance	공연
☐	present	참석한
☐	gather	모으다
☐	make a note of	…을 적어 두다
☐	be absent from	…에 결석하다
☐	envious	부러워하는
☐	sympathetic	동정심 있는
☐	grateful	감사하는
☐	faithful	충실한, 성실한
☐	humble	겸손한
☐	arrogant	오만한
☐	stubborn	완고한
☐	toss	던지다
☐	sanitation	위생 시설[관리]
☐	rescue	구하다, 구조하다
☐	headquarters	본사, 본부
☐	kind-hearted	마음씨 고운, 인정 많은
☐	public	일반 사람들, 대중
☐	lounge	라운지, 휴게실
☐	local	지역의, 현지의
☐	expand	확대시키다; 확장되다
☐	essential	필수적인
☐	community	지역 사회
☐	donate	기부[기증]하다
☐	donation	기부, 기증
☐	government	정부

□	librarian	사서
□	convert	개조하다
□	garbage	쓰레기
□	mobile	이동하는, 이동식의
□	take action	조치를 취하다
□	treasure	보물
□	single	단 하나의, 단일의
□	speed	속도; 빨리 가다[이동하다]
□	balance	균형
□	race	경주; 경주하다
□	be diagnosed with	…로 진단받다
□	fall down	넘어지다
□	interrupt	방해하다, 중단시키다
□	nerve	신경
□	properly	제대로, 적절히
□	signal	신호
□	particularly	특히
□	sense	감각; 감지하다, 느끼다
□	damage	손상을 주다
□	tissue	(세포들로 이루어진) 조직
□	bring ... back	…을 다시 가져다 주다
□	sensation	느낌; 감각
□	cure	치료법

SECTION 06 유래

☐ refer to	…을 언급하다
☐ contain	…이 들어 있다
☐ typical	전형적인, 대표적인
☐ split the bill	(비용 따위를) 각자 부담하다, 나눠 내다
☐ generous	후한
☐ agreement	협정, 합의
☐ bravery	용기, 용감
☐ confusion	혼란
☐ ruin	망치다
☐ scold	야단치다, 꾸짖다
☐ trivial	사소한
☐ compete for	…을 위해 싸우다
☐ phrase	구
☐ insult	모욕하다
☐ landmark	주요 지형지물
☐ iconic	…의 상징이 되는
☐ sandstone	사암
☐ peak	봉우리, 꼭대기
☐ be known for	…로 알려져 있다
☐ aboriginal	(오스트레일리아) 원주민의
☐ legend	전설
☐ valley	계곡, 골짜기
☐ tribe	부족
☐ fall in love with	…와 사랑에 빠지다
☐ forbidden	금지된
☐ outraged	격분한
☐ capture	포로로 잡다
☐ spark	촉발시키다, 유발하다

□	battle	전투
□	witch doctor	주술사
□	intend to-v	…하려고 의도[작정]하다
□	transform	변형시키다
□	magnificent	아주 아름다운, 훌륭한
□	pillar	기둥
□	overlook	간과하다; 바라보다, 내려다보다
□	concerning	…에 관한
□	manuscript	원고
□	publisher	출판인, 출판사
□	accompany	동반[동행]하다
□	read	읽다; (…라고) 적혀[쓰여] 있다
□	punctuation mark	구두점, 문장 부호
□	scholar	학자
□	indicate	나타내다
□	shorten	짧게 하다, 줄이다
□	lowercase	소문자의, 소문자로 인쇄한
□	atop	꼭대기에, 맨 위에
□	evolve	발달하다; 진화하다
□	as for	…에 대해서 말하자면
□	exclamation	외침, 감탄사
□	significance	중요성, 의의
□	pun	말장난
□	intentionally	의도적으로, 고의로
□	involve	수반[포함]하다
□	consonant	자음
□	vowel	모음
□	nonsense	터무니없는 생각; 뜻이 통하지 않는 말

☐	damp	축축한
☐	stealer	도둑
☐	warden	관리인; 학장
☐	peculiar	이상한, 기이한; 특유한
☐	slip	실수
☐	tongue	혀; 언어
☐	hilariously	아주 재미있게
☐	seldom	좀처럼[거의] …않는
☐	aware	…을 알고 있는
☐	blushing	얼굴이 빨개진; 부끄러워[수줍어]하는
☐	queer	기묘한, 괴상한
☐	dean	학장
☐	doubt	의심; 의문을 갖다
☐	authenticity	진실성; 진짜임
☐	quote	인용
☐	incorporate	포함하다

SECTION 07 의학 · 건강

☐	uncontrollable	제어할 수 없는
☐	desire	욕구, 충동
☐	suffer from	…을 앓다
☐	constant	끊임없는
☐	hunger	굶주림; 배고픔
☐	disorder	엉망; 장애
☐	genetic	유전적인

☐	cure	낫게 하다; 치유법
☐	take measures	조치를 취하다
☐	strict	엄격한
☐	proportion	비율
☐	flexibility	유연성
☐	suggest	제안하다; 시사[암시]하다
☐	discovery	발견
☐	acquired	후천적인
☐	depression	우울
☐	appetite	식욕
☐	obesity	비만
☐	violence	폭력
☐	operate on	…를 수술하다
☐	hum	콧노래를 부르다, 흥얼거리다
☐	unusual	특이한, 흔치 않은
☐	tumor	종양
☐	located in	…에 위치한
☐	involve	수반하다
☐	remove	제거하다, 없애다
☐	affect	영향을 미치다
☐	three-dimensional	3차원의, 입체적인
☐	perform	수행하다, 실시하다
☐	performance	공연; 연주; 실적, 성과
☐	conceal	숨기다, 감추다
☐	cautious	조심스러운, 신중한
☐	surgery	수술
☐	occasionally	가끔
☐	perfectly	완전히; 완벽하게

☐	applaud	박수치다; 박수를 보내다
☐	innovative	혁신적인
☐	treatment	치료
☐	instrument	기계; 악기
☐	combine	결합하다
☐	toothache	치통
☐	cavity	(치아에 생긴) 구멍, 충치
☐	untreated	치료를 받지 않은
☐	infected	감염된
☐	infection	감염
☐	have an impact on	…에 영향을 주다
☐	stomach	위, 복부
☐	diabetes	당뇨병
☐	highlight	강조하다
☐	severely	심하게
☐	rotten	썩은
☐	pull out	뽑다
☐	painkiller	진통제
☐	dizzy	어지러운
☐	fever	열
☐	eventually	결국
☐	collapse	무너지다; 쓰러지다
☐	figure out	이해하다, 알아내다
☐	be sure to-v	반드시 …하다
☐	end up v-ing	결국 …하게 되다
☐	operating table	수술대
☐	raise	들어 올리다; (문제 등을) 제기하다
☐	concern	우려, 걱정; 관심사

□	come across	이해되다; (우연히) 마주치다
□	emphasize	강조하다
□	safety procedure	안전수칙
□	nitrogen	질소
□	trap	가두다
□	joint	관절
□	vein	정맥
□	surface	표면; 떠오르다
□	decrease	감소, 하락
□	pressure	압박, 압력
□	expand	확대[팽창]되다
□	straighten	똑바르게 되다; (자세를) 바로 하다
□	stroke	타격; 뇌졸중
□	avoidable	막을[피할] 수 있는
□	precaution	예방책

SECTION 08 사회 · 환경

□	make a difference	영향을 주다
□	huge	막대한, 거대한
□	grateful	고마워하는, 감사하는
□	frigid	몹시 추운
□	take action	…에 대해 조치를 취하다
□	dormitory	기숙사
□	donate	기부하다, 기증하다
□	nonprofit	비영리적인

☐	organization	조직, 단체
☐	numerous	많은
☐	donor	기부자, 기증자
☐	identify	확인하다, 알아보다; 찾다, 발견하다
☐	innovative	혁신적인
☐	freezing	꽁꽁 얼게[너무나] 추운
☐	task	일, 과제
☐	complex	복잡한
☐	handle	다루다
☐	artificial	인공의
☐	intelligence	지능
☐	healthcare	건강 관리, 의료
☐	highly	매우
☐	have access to	…에 접근할 수 있다
☐	latest	최신의
☐	equipment	장비, 기구
☐	medical	의학의
☐	publish	출간하다, 발행하다
☐	estimate	…로 추정하다
☐	medication	의학, 의술
☐	fault	잘못, 책임; 결점
☐	analyze	분석하다
☐	recall	기억해 내다, 상기하다
☐	instantly	즉시, 바로
☐	recommend	추천하다
☐	treatment	치료
☐	concern	배려, 염려
☐	care	보살핌

☐	compassion	연민, 동정심
☐	replace	대체하다, 대신하다
☐	take advantage of	…를 이용하다
☐	definitely	분명히
☐	sports field	운동장
☐	running track	달리기 트랙
☐	rather	오히려, 차라리
☐	onto	…(위)로
☐	structure	구조; 구조물
☐	abandoned	버려진, 유기된
☐	tear down	파괴하다, 해체하다
☐	local	지역의, 현지의
☐	organization	단체, 조직
☐	oppose	반대하다
☐	beneficial	유익한, 이로운
☐	section	구획
☐	imagination	상상(력)
☐	demonstrate	시위하다
☐	demonstration	시위, 데모
☐	logger	벌목꾼
☐	cut down	베어 넘어뜨리다
☐	take place	일어나다, 발생하다
☐	incredible	믿을 수 없는, 믿기 힘든
☐	determination	투지
☐	bring attention to	…에 관심을 가져오다
☐	hold a record	기록을 보유하다
☐	confront	부딪치다, 마주치다
☐	official	공무상의, 공식적인; 공무원, 관리

☐	endurance	인내, 참을성
☐	quality	질, 자질
☐	deserve	…을 받을 만하다, …해야 마땅하다
☐	appreciation	감탄, 감상; 감사
☐	picky	까다로운
☐	strong-willed	의지가 강한

SECTION 09 과학 · 우주

☐	astronaut	우주 비행사
☐	accidentally	뜻하지 않게
☐	drift	떠가다, 표류하다
☐	attach A to B	A를 B에 부착하다
☐	spacesuit	우주복
☐	spacecraft	우주선
☐	spacewalk	우주 유영
☐	overboard	선체 밖으로
☐	float	떠가다, 떠돌다
☐	helplessly	어찌해 볼 수도 없이
☐	weightless	무게가 없는; 무중력의
☐	atmosphere	대기
☐	fuel	연료
☐	polar	북극[남극]의, 극지의
☐	expedition	탐험
☐	contribute	기여하다
☐	explorer	탐사자

□	use up	…을 다 써버리다
□	get rid of	…을 없애다
□	deprive of	…을 빼앗다
□	depression	우울증
□	depressed	우울한
□	disorder	엉망; 장애[이상]
□	rage	분노
□	region	지방, 지역
□	characterize	특징이 되다
□	permanent	영구[영속]적인
□	chemical	화학물질; 화학의
□	affective	정서적인
□	dung	똥
□	component	구성, 요소
□	compromise	타협, 절충
□	process	과정; 처리하다
□	extract	추출하다
□	interact	소통하다
□	recycle	재활용하다
□	remaining	남아 있는
□	fertilizer	비료
□	soil	토양
□	consumer	소비자
□	flavor	풍미, 맛
□	measure	측정하다
□	measurement	측정
□	scale	규모; 등급, 척도
□	represent	대표하다; 표현하다

□	grind up	갈아 부수다
□	sip	홀짝이다
□	solution	해법; 용액
□	dilute	희석하다
□	assign	맡기다; 부여하다
□	multiple	많은, 다수의; 배수
□	range from A to B	A에서 B까지 (범위가) 걸치다
□	rely on	…에 의존하다
□	perception	지각, 자각
□	accurately	정확하게
□	manner	방식
□	in honor of	…에게 경의를 표하여

SECTION 10 생활

□	temporary	임시의, 일시적인
□	description	서술, 기술
□	prehistoric	선사 시대의
□	fossil	화석(의)
□	exhibition	전시회, 전람회
□	take place	일어나다; 개최되다
□	enthusiastic	열성적인
□	circulate	순환하다; 돌아다니다
□	be responsible for	…에 책임이 있다
□	requirement	필요; 요건
□	outgoing	외향적인

☐	interpersonal	대인 관계의
☐	background	배경; 기초지식
☐	advantage	이점, 강점
☐	résumé	이력서
☐	candidate	후보자
☐	select	선발하다
☐	contact	연락하다
☐	personnel director	인사 관리자
☐	provide	제공하다
☐	detail	세부 사항
☐	reservation	예약
☐	available	이용 가능한
☐	additional	추가의
☐	penalty	벌금, 위약금
☐	fee	요금, 수수료
☐	refund	환불(금)
☐	commission	수수료
☐	prior to	…전[앞]에
☐	loan	빌려주다
☐	seize	잡다
☐	button	단추를 잠그다; 단추가 채워지다; 단추
☐	logical	논리적인
☐	complicated	복잡한
☐	outfit	옷(복장)
☐	upper-class	상류 계급의
☐	relatively	비교적
☐	maid	하녀, 가정부
☐	tailor	재단사

☐	custom	관습, 풍습
☐	bother	귀찮게 하다; 신경 쓰다, 애를 쓰다
☐	order	주문하다
☐	recipe	조리[요리]법
☐	flavor	풍미, 맛
☐	authentic	진짜인
☐	require	필요로 하다
☐	ingredient	(요리) 재료
☐	chopped	잘게 썬, 다진
☐	grated	(강판에) 간
☐	pepper	후추
☐	stir	젓다
☐	ground	빻은, 가루로 만든
☐	meanwhile	그동안에
☐	saucepan	냄비
☐	heat	뜨겁게 하다
☐	pour	붓다
☐	mixture	혼합물, 혼합재료
☐	drain	물을 빼내다
☐	toss	던지다
☐	raw	익히지 않은, 날것의

SECTION 11 생물·동물

☐	migrate	이주하다, 이동하다
☐	sight	시력; 광경, 모습

☐	ancient	고대의
☐	arctic	북극의
☐	apparently	분명히
☐	species	종(種)
☐	continent	대륙
☐	journey	여행, 여정
☐	make one's way to	…로 나아가다, 가다
☐	evolution	진화
☐	hump	툭 솟아 오른 곳; 혹
☐	store	저장하다
☐	frozen	얼어붙은
☐	sink	가라앉다, 빠지다
☐	feature	특징, 특성
☐	switch	바뀌다; 바꾸다
☐	habitat	서식지
☐	organism	유기체; 생물
☐	rethink	다시 생각하다, 재고하다
☐	mortality	죽음을 피할 수 없음
☐	jellyfish	해파리
☐	reproduce	복사[복제]하다; 번식하다
☐	reproduction	생식, 번식
☐	mate	짝짓기를 하다
☐	whereby	(그것에 의하여) …하는
☐	decay	부패하다, 썩다
☐	stem cell	줄기세포
☐	sperm	정자; 정액
☐	fuse	녹이다, 녹다; 융합[결합]하다
☐	egg	알; 난자

☐	literally	문자[말] 그대로
☐	indefinitely	무기한으로
☐	cave	동굴
☐	base	기슭, 맨 아래 부분
☐	border	국경, 경계
☐	furrow	고랑, 골
☐	pick	고르기, 선택; 곡괭이
☐	assume	추정하다
☐	mining	채굴; 광업
☐	observe	관찰하다
☐	plain	평원, 평지
☐	herd	무리, 떼
☐	rainforest	우림
☐	rainfall	강우
☐	wash away	…을 유실되게 하다, 쓸어가다
☐	tusk	(코끼리의) 상아
☐	chip off	떨어져 나가게 하다
☐	rough	고르지 않은
☐	risk	…의 위험을 무릅쓰다
☐	predator	포식 동물
☐	crack	(갈라져 생긴) 금
☐	in spite of	…에도 불구하고
☐	wander	돌아다니다, 헤매다
☐	reward	보상
☐	sharpen	날카롭게 하다
☐	take shelter	대피하다
☐	sardine	정어리
☐	coast	해안

☐	lay	(알을) 낳다
☐	gigantic	거대한
☐	seal	바다표범, 물개
☐	incredible	믿을 수 없는
☐	snatch	와락 붙잡다, 잡아채다
☐	take advantage of	…을 이용하다
☐	soar	솟구치다
☐	spectacle	(굉장히 인상적인) 광경
☐	equipment	장비
☐	team up	협력하다
☐	bait	미끼

SECTION 12 연예 · 스포츠

☐	stylish	멋진
☐	pose	포즈[자세]를 취하다
☐	celebrity	유명 인사
☐	street wear	길거리 패션
☐	target	목표; 대상
☐	matter	중요하다, 문제되다
☐	trendy	최신 유행의
☐	gain attention	주목을 받다
☐	typical	전형적인
☐	inspiration	영감
☐	collaborate	협력하다; 공동으로 작업하다
☐	individuality	개성, 특성

☐	display	보여 주다, 드러내다
☐	manufactured	제작된
☐	shoot	(총을) 쏘다; (사진을) 촬영하다
☐	fit	건강한, 탄탄한
☐	repetitive	반복적인
☐	wind up v-ing	…하게 되다
☐	motivated	자극받은, 동기가 부여된
☐	application	지원; 적용; 응용 프로그램
☐	progress	진전
☐	pace	속도
☐	tap	톡톡 두드리다[치다]
☐	be on track	착착 나아가다[진행 중이다]
☐	beat	이기다; 능가하다
☐	lift	들어 올리다; (기분 · 사기 등을) 좋아지게 하다
☐	boast	뽐내다, 자랑하다
☐	compatible	호환이 되는
☐	broadcast	방송하다; 널리 알리다
☐	achievement	업적, 성취한 것
☐	log	일지에 기록하다
☐	stimulate	자극[격려]하다
☐	at times	가끔은, 때때로
☐	charismatic	카리스마가 있는
☐	obstacle	장애물
☐	learning disability	학습 장애
☐	skilled	숙련된
☐	stuttering	말을 더듬는
☐	stutter	말을 더듬다; 말더듬증

□	alert	기민한
□	still	가만히 있는
□	concentration	집중력
□	tease	놀리다
□	turn out	…인 것으로 드러나다[밝혀지다]
□	dyslexia	난독증
□	defeat	물리치다, 이기다
□	make a deal	거래[타협]하다
□	counterclockwise	시계 반대 방향으로; 시계 반대 방향의
□	track and field	육상경기
□	understandably	당연히
□	specifically	분명히, 구체적으로
□	vital	필수적인
□	organ	장기[기관]
□	slightly	약간, 조금
□	encounter	맞닥뜨리다, 부딪히다
□	blood circulation	혈액순환
□	motion	운동, 움직임
□	athletics	육상경기
□	clockwise	시계 방향의
□	stiff	뻣뻣한
□	fatal	죽음을 초래하는, 치명적인

고등 독해의 절대 자신감

READING TUTOR

READING TUTOR의 특징

Fun & Interesting 지루한 독해는 그만! 우린 재미있게 공부한다

High Quality 최신 학습 경향을 반영한 양질의 문제로 독해 실력을 키운다

New & Informative 새로운 정보로 가득한 지문을 통해 배경지식을 넓힌다

The future belongs to those who believe in the beauty of their dreams.

미래는 꿈의 아름다움을 믿는 사람의 것이다.

– 엘리너 루즈벨트 (Eleanor Roosevelt) –

영어를 잘하고 싶은데, 지루하고 어렵게 느껴지나요?

다양한 주제의 흥미로운 글을 영어로 읽어 보세요. 문법, 문장구조, 어려운 어휘, 이런 것들에 너무 얽매이지 말고, 전체적인 내용에만 집중하세요. 그렇게 읽다 보면, 조금 더 자세히, 정확히 알고 싶은 부분이 생기고, 그런 것들을 알기 위해 공부하고자 하는 마음이 들 것입니다. 완벽하게 해석이 되지 않는다고 스트레스받지 마세요. 글을 읽으며 자신에게 필요한 학습 요소가 무엇인지 파악하고 차근차근 더해 나가면 됩니다.

이렇게 영어 공부에 대한 스트레스는 줄이고, 재미와 상식을 더하는 영어 독해!

리딩튜터 시리즈와 함께 하면 됩니다.

새로운 정보와 흥미로운 이야기가 담긴 지문들을 읽으면서 재미있게 공부할 수 있고, 자연스럽게 다양한 분야와 주제에 대한 배경지식을 넓힐 수 있을 것입니다. 또한 글을 꼼꼼하게 이해하고 파악하는 데 도움이 되는 양질의 문제들을 풀면서 독해 실력도 향상시킬 수 있을 것입니다.

리딩튜터를 통해 여러분이 목표하는 영어 실력을 얻고, 나아가 여러분이 이루고자 하는 꿈에 조금 더 가까이 다가갈 수 있기를 바랍니다.

저자 일동

영어 독해가 재미있어지는 리딩튜터만의 매력

Welcome to Reading Tutor

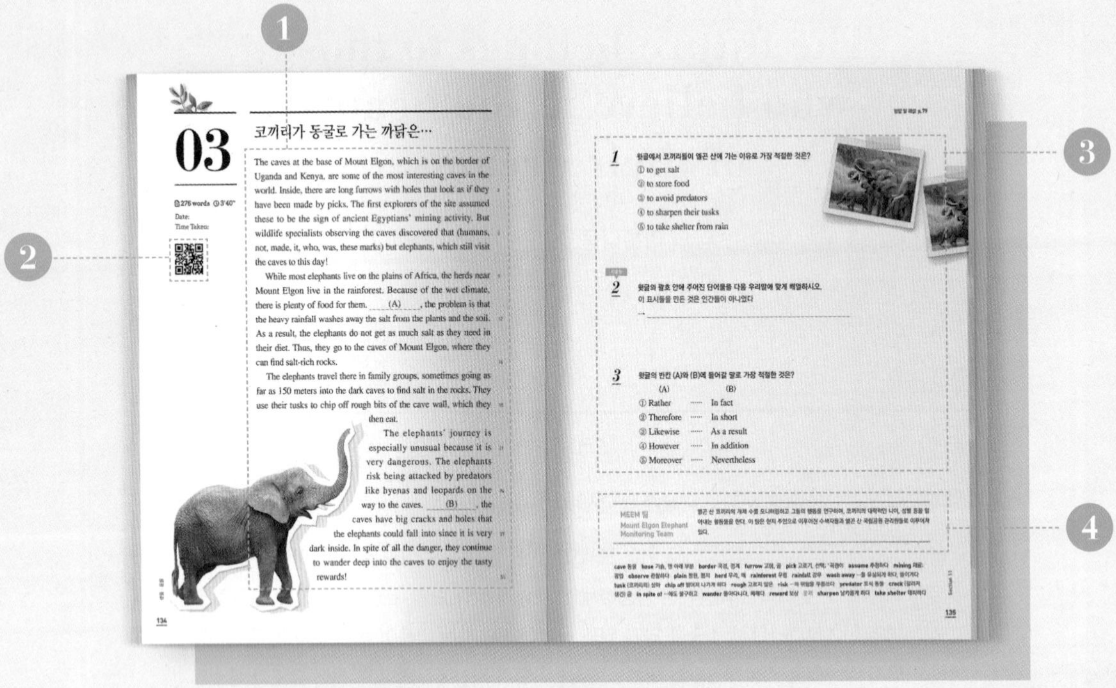

❶ New & Informative

새롭고 흥미로우면서도 논리적인 지문들을 수록하였습니다. 영어 독해 실력은 물론 상식을 넓히고 사고력도 길러 보세요!

❷ Smart Learning

원어민이 녹음한 지문 MP3 파일을 QR 코드 스캔 한 번으로 바로 들을 수 있게 하였습니다.

❸ 최신 경향의 문제

수능, 내신 대비용, 서술형 주관식, 어휘 문제 등 최신 경향의 다양한 문제를 수록하였습니다.

❹ 배경지식

지문 내용과 관련된 배경지식을 수록하여, 지문을 보다 흥미롭고 깊이 있게 읽을 수 있게 하였습니다.

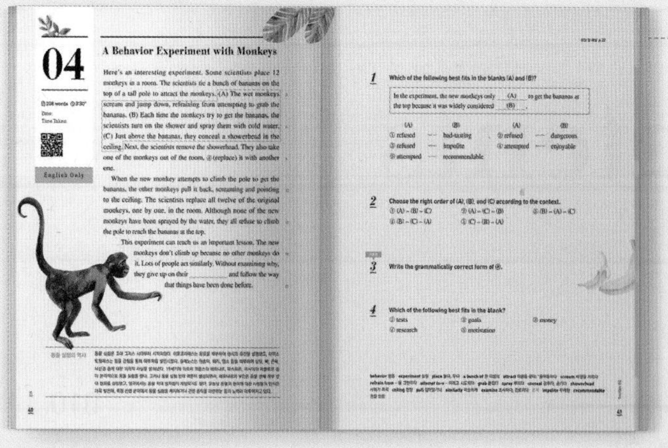

English Only

모든 문제를 영어로 제시하는 English Only.
섹션마다 한 개씩 제공되며, 독해 실력을 한층 업그레이드 할 수 있도록 도와줍니다.

Review Test

각 섹션에서 배운 단어와 숙어, 주요 구문들을 다양한 유형의 문제를 통해 확인하고 정리해 보세요.

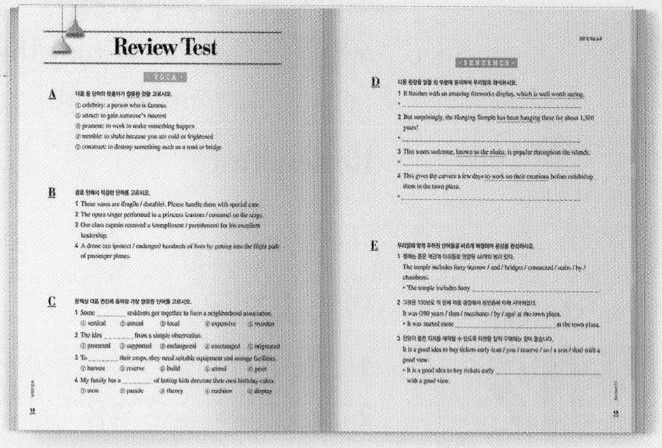

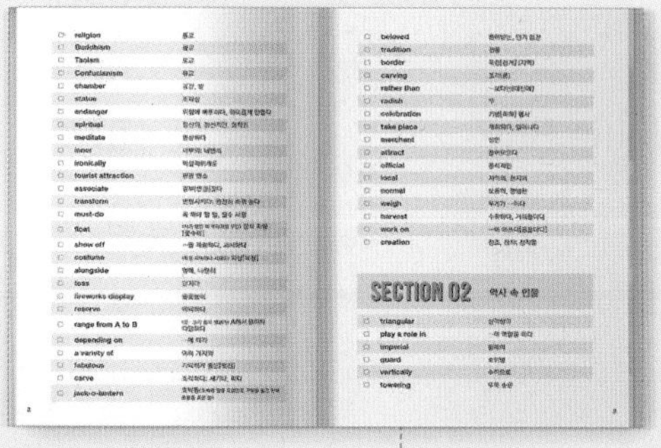

어휘 암기장

본문에서 쓰인 주요 어휘들을 부록으로 별도 제공하여
휴대하면서 틈틈이 어휘 학습을 할 수 있도록 하였습니다.

Special Corners

표현의 유래와 세계의 다양한 공익 캠페인을 소개하는 재미있는 쉬어가기 코너를 준비하였습니다. 공부에 지친 몸과 마음에 잠시 휴식을 주는 건 어떨까요?

Contents

SECTION 12

연예 · 스포츠

표현의 유래

CAMPAIGN IN THE WORLD

SECTION 01

세계의 문화

1 손을 들어 모두, 샤카!
2 보기만 해도 아찔해요!
3 니스 카니발로의 초대장
4 Let's Enjoy the Night of the Radishes in Mexico!

01

손을 들어 모두, 샤카!

198 words 3'00"
Date:
Time Taken:

If you ever visit Hawaii, the locals will probably greet you with an unusual hand gesture and the words "shaka brah." This warm welcome, known as the *shaka*, is popular throughout the islands. From bankers and businessmen to surfers, everyone uses this friendly gesture. (①) It helps to promote peace and harmony among the wide range of ethnic groups living there. (②)

No one is sure where the *shaka* first originated, but the most common theory is that it stems from beach culture. (③) The term *shaka* itself is probably a variation on the common expression "shark eye," a compliment paid to show respect. (④) The *shaka* gesture became popular in the 1960s thanks to local celebrity Lippy Espinda, who used it in television advertisements. (⑤)

Here's how to make a *shaka* sign. The first step is to make a fist. Then extend your thumb and pinky, but be sure not to uncurl your middle fingers. Then, (so that, your palm, you, is facing towards, turn, your hand). Finally, move it as if writing the letter "J." That's it. Now you are ready to greet people the Hawaiian way!

1 **샤카에 관한 윗글의 내용과 일치하지 않는 것은?**

① 하와이의 원주민들 사이에서만 사용되는 제스처이다.
② 평화와 조화를 증진시킨다고 여겨진다.
③ 명확한 기원은 밝혀지지 않았다.
④ 용어 자체는 'shark eye'에서 비롯되었다고 여겨진다.
⑤ 주먹을 쥔 후에 엄지와 새끼손가락을 펴서 만든다.

2 **윗글의 흐름으로 보아, 주어진 문장이 들어가기에 가장 적절한 곳은?**

From then on, everyone began using the *shaka* as a friendly show of goodwill.

서술형

3 **윗글의 괄호 안에 주어진 단어들을 다음 우리말에 맞게 배열하시오.**
당신의 손바닥이 당신 쪽을 향하도록 손을 돌려라

→ ______________________________

알로하 Aloha 하와이에서 만나거나 헤어질 때 하는 인사말 '알로하'는 철자 하나하나에 의미가 숨어 있다.
A – Akahai (아카하이: 친절, 부드러움)
L – Lokahi (로카히: 통합, 조화로움)
O – Olu'olu (올루올루: 화합, 기쁨)
H – Ha'aha'a (하아하아: 겸허, 겸손)
A – Ahonui (아호누이: 참을성, 인내)

local 지역의, 현지의; (*pl.*) *주민, 현지인 **promote** 촉진[고취]하다 **range** 다양성; 범위 **ethnic** 민족[종족]의 **originate** 비롯되다, 유래하다 **theory** 이론 **stem from** …에서 생겨나다, 기인하다 **term** 용어, 말 **variation** 변화; *변형 **compliment** 칭찬(의 말), 찬사 **celebrity** 유명 인사, 명사 **advertisement** 광고 **make a fist** 주먹을 쥐다 **extend** 연장하다; *뻗다, 내밀다 **pinky** 새끼손가락 **uncurl** 펴다 **palm** 손바닥 문제 **show** 표시 **goodwill** 친선, 호의

02

212 words 3'10"

Date:

Time Taken:

보기만 해도 아찔해요!

Your legs tremble and your palms sweat as you walk. Where are you? You are climbing to Xuan Kong Si, also called the Hanging Temple, in China.

The temple is famous for its location. It is built into a cliff, more than 75 meters above the ground. It looks very fragile. But surprisingly, the Hanging Temple has been "hanging" there for about 1,500 years!

The secret is in its ① unique building design. Its long, thin wooden poles were built into the rock as the foundation. They seem to support the structure. But it was actually constructed in a way that lets the rock in back ② carry most of the weight.

The temple is not only special outside. The inside is also unique. It is a place for three different traditional religions: Buddhism, Taoism, and Confucianism. The temple includes forty chambers ③ connected by narrow stairs and bridges. There are eighty-seven statues from all three religions inside as well.

Do you think why the temple was built like this? One reason is that the location ④ endangers the temple from the nearby river's floods. The other reason is spiritual. The quiet location is ⑤ ideal for meditating and searching for inner peace. Ironically, the temple is now a busy tourist attraction. Would you like to go?

정답 및 해설 p.3

1 윗글의 제목으로 가장 적절한 것은?

① China's Oldest Temple
② The History of Xuan Kong Si
③ How to Search for Inner Peace
④ Three Traditional Religions of China
⑤ Xuan Kong Si: A Temple Built on A Cliff

서술형

2 윗글의 밑줄 친 문장에서 어법상 틀린 부분을 찾아 바르게 고쳐 쓰시오. (1개)

VOCA

3 윗글의 밑줄 친 ①~⑤ 중, 문맥상 낱말의 쓰임이 적절하지 않은 것은?

4 윗글의 내용과 일치하면 T에, 일치하지 않으면 F에 표시하시오.

	T	F
(1) Xuan Kong Si was constructed 75 meters above a cliff.	☐	☐
(2) Three different religions are associated with the temple.	☐	☐
(3) Because of its location, few tourists visit the temple.	☐	☐

현공사(悬空寺, 하늘에 매달린 절)

현공사는 중국 다퉁에서 65km가량 떨어진 헝산산(恒山)의 협곡에 위치해 있다. 약 1,500년 전 승려 랴오란(了然)이 세운 것으로 알려져 있으며, 공사를 시작한 이후 여러 차례 증축과 보수를 거쳤다. 전해지는 바에 따르면, 당시 이 일대 산기슭은 비가 올 때마다 홍수가 났고, 사람들은 이것이 용(龍)의 짓이라고 생각해 절을 세워 그 용을 누르고자 했다. 또한, 당시 절 밑에 있는 길의 통행을 방해하지 않기 위해 공중에 지었다는 설도 있다. 오랜 세월에도 불구하고 이 절이 비교적 온전한 형태를 유지하는 이유 중 하나는, 절 주위의 산봉우리들이 건물을 햇빛으로부터 가려주기 때문이다.

tremble 떨다, 떨리다 **cliff** 절벽 **fragile** 부서지기[손상되기] 쉬운 **foundation** (건물의) 토대, 기초 **structure** 구조; *구조물, 건축물 **construct** 건설하다 **religion** 종교 **Buddhism** 불교 **Taoism** 도교 **Confucianism** 유교 **chamber** 공간, 방 **statue** 조각상 **endanger** 위험에 빠뜨리다, 위태롭게 만들다 **spiritual** 정신의, 정신적인, 영적인 **meditate** 명상하다 **inner** 내부의; *내면의 **ironically** 역설적이게도 **tourist attraction** 관광 명소 문제 **associate** 결부[연관]짓다

03

241 words 3'20"

Date:

Time Taken:

Invitation to the Nice Carnival

In February, Nice, in France, is transformed into an exciting city (A) crowded / crowding with people looking for fun. That's because February is the month of the city's biggest annual event, the Nice Carnival. Everyone gets into the party spirit during this month, (B) enjoyed / enjoying the parades, fireworks and other delightful activities during the day and at night. You can also enjoy this amazing experience. Here's some travel information that will help you.

· *Things To Do*

Attending the parades is a must-do activity. The most incredible are the Flower Parades, where you can see 20 floats (C) covered / covering in flowers parade along the *Promenade des Anglais*. These show off all of the French *Riviera's most beautiful flowers. At the same time, men and women in costume walk alongside the floats and toss 100,000 flowers into the audience. The other great event is the Grand Parade at the end of the festival. It finishes with an amazing fireworks display, which is well worth seeing.

· *Getting Tickets*

Many of the events are free, though there is a charge for the Parades. It is a good idea to buy tickets early so that you can reserve a seat with a good view. The fee ranges from 10 to 25 euros, depending on whether you want to stand or sit.

· *Dining*

Nice is home to a wide variety of fabulous restaurants. The main streets (many countries, have, serving, from, restaurants, traditional food), such as France, Italy, Turkey, and China.

*Riviera 《지명》 (프랑스의) 리비에라 (지방)

1 윗글의 내용과 일치하지 않는 것은?

① 니스 카니발은 매년 2월에 열린다.
② 플라워 퍼레이드에서는 약 10만 송이의 꽃이 뿌려진다.
③ 그랜드 퍼레이드에서 불꽃놀이를 볼 수 있다.
④ 티켓은 미리 구매할 수 있다.
⑤ 퍼레이드의 모든 관람 티켓 가격은 동일하다.

수능 어법

2 윗글의 (A), (B), (C)의 각 네모 안에서 어법에 맞는 표현으로 가장 적절한 것은?

	(A)		(B)		(C)
①	crowded	……	enjoyed	……	covered
②	crowded	……	enjoying	……	covering
③	crowded	……	enjoying	……	covered
④	crowding	……	enjoying	……	covering
⑤	crowding	……	enjoyed	……	covered

서술형

3 윗글의 괄호 안에 주어진 단어들을 다음 우리말에 맞게 배열하시오.

중심가에는 많은 나라들의 전통 음식을 제공하는 식당들이 있다

→ The main streets ______________________________

영국인의 산책로 Promenade des Anglais

프랑스의 니스는 18세기 무렵 따뜻한 지중해를 동경하는 영국 상류층의 휴가지로 인기가 있었다. 산책을 즐기는 영국인들이 니스의 해변가에 있던 폭 2m에 불과한 산책로를 넓히기 시작했고, 길 가운데 꽃밭을 가꾸고 종려나무를 심으면서 이 길에는 Promenade des Anglais(영국인의 산책로)라는 이름이 붙여졌다. 3.5km에 이르는 이 해변 산책로는 꾸준히 사랑받고 있다.

transform 변형시키다; *완전히 바꿔 놓다 **must-do** 꼭 해야 할 일, 필수 사항 **float** (시가 행진 때 무대처럼 꾸민) 장식 차량[꽃수레] **show off** …을 자랑하다, 과시하다 **costume** (특정 지역이나 시대의) 의상[복장] **alongside** 옆에, 나란히 **toss** 던지다 **fireworks display** 불꽃놀이 **reserve** 예약하다 **range from A to B** (양 · 크기 등의 범위가) A에서 B까지 다양하다 **depending on** …에 따라 **a variety of** 여러 가지의 **fabulous** 기막히게 좋은[멋진]

04

Let's Enjoy the Night of the Radishes in Mexico!

220 words 3'30"

Date:

Time Taken:

English Only

On Halloween, people in the United States carve scary faces into pumpkins. These jack-o-lanterns are a beloved Halloween tradition. But south of the border, in Oaxaca, Mexico, there is a different carving tradition. It happens around Christmas instead of Halloween. And rather than pumpkins, people carve radishes!

The celebration is called Noche de Rabanos, or Night of the Radishes, and it takes place on December 23. (①) It was started more than 100 years ago by merchants at the town plaza. (②) Hoping to attract Christmas shoppers, they would carve designs into the bright red skin of radishes. (③) People loved them! (④) In 1897, Noche de Rabanos became an official holiday in Oaxaca. (⑤)

Today, the carvings are made by local artists and amateurs. ⓐ They use special radishes whose are larger than normal and not used for food. These radishes, which can weigh as much as three kilograms, are harvested on December 18. This gives the carvers a few days to work on their creations before ⓑ exhibiting them in the town plaza. The person who carves the best radish wins a grand prize of 15,000 pesos.

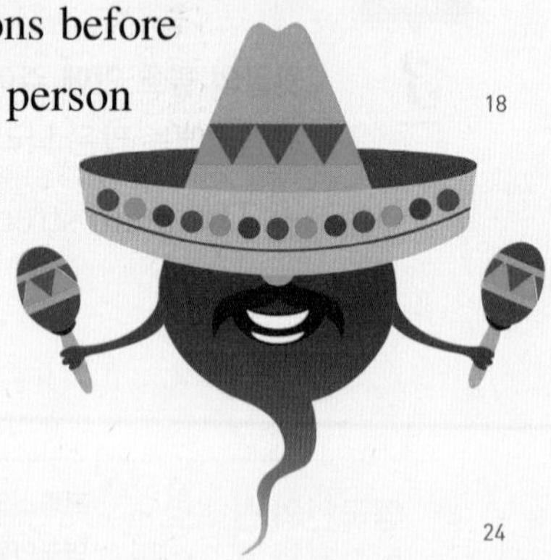

If you're ever in Mexico during the holiday season, you should head to Oaxaca and check out these wonderful Christmas radishes!

멕시코의 크리스마스

멕시코의 크리스마스는 12월 25일 하루가 아니라, 12월 초부터 1월 초까지 다양한 행사를 거치며 이어진다. 멕시코의 크리스마스 문화는 멕시코의 주요 종교인 가톨릭과 다양한 토착 문화의 영향으로 비롯되었다고 할 수 있다. 대표적인 행사로는 12월 12일에 열리는 '과달루페 성모 발현 축일'이 있다. 이날은 원주민 '성 후안 디에고'에게 갈색 피부의 과달루페 성모가 출연했던 것을 기념하는 날로, 매년 수백만의 가톨릭 신자들이 멕시코시티의 과달루페 대성당으로 모여든다. 뒤이어 12월 16일부터 24일까지는, 포사다(Las Posadas)라는 행진과 파티가 벌어진다. 성경에서 요셉이 마리아와 함께 출산할 장소를 찾는 부분을 기념하는 행사로, 9일 동안 매일 밤 아이들은 이웃집에서 게임과 음식, 폭죽과 함께 파티를 즐긴다.

정답 및 해설 p.6

1

What is NOT mentioned in the passage?

① when Oaxaca's carving tradition started
② why people started carving radishes
③ who participates in the festival as carvers these days
④ what the carved radishes look like
⑤ what the best radish-carver gets as a prize

2

Where would the given sentence best fit among ①~⑤?

> They bought the carved radishes and placed them in the center of the table at Christmas dinner.

서술형

3

Find the grammatically incorrect part in the underlined sentence ⓐ and correct it.

VOCA

4

Which is the closest in meaning to the underlined word ⓑ"exhibiting"?

① displaying ② selling ③ disguising
④ transporting ⑤ promoting

carve *조각하다; 새기다, 파다 **jack-o-lantern** 호박등(호박에 얼굴 모양으로 구멍을 뚫고 안에 촛불을 꽂은 등) **beloved** 총애받는, 인기 많은 **tradition** 전통 **border** 국경[경계] (지역) **carving** 조각(품) **rather than** … 보다는[대신에] **radish** 무 **celebration** 기념[축하] 행사 **take place** 개최되다, 일어나다 **merchant** 상인 **attract** 끌어모으다 **official** 공식적인 **local** 지역의, 현지의 **normal** 보통의, 평범한 **weigh** 무게가 …이다 **harvest** 수확하다, 거둬들이다 **work on** …에 애쓰다[공들이다] **creation** 창조, 창작; *창작물

Review Test

· VOCA ·

A 다음 중 단어의 뜻풀이가 잘못된 것을 고르시오.

① celebrity: a person who is famous

② attract: to gain someone's interest

③ promote: to work to make something happen

④ tremble: to shake because you are cold or frightened

⑤ construct: to destroy something such as a road or bridge

B 괄호 안에서 적절한 단어를 고르시오.

1 These vases are (fragile / durable). Please handle them with special care.

2 The opera singer performed in a princess (custom / costume) on the stage.

3 Our class captain received a (compliment / punishment) for his excellent leadership.

4 A drone can (protect / endanger) hundreds of lives by getting into the flight path of passenger planes.

C 문맥상 다음 빈칸에 들어갈 가장 알맞은 단어를 고르시오.

1 Some __________ residents got together to form a neighborhood association.

① vertical ② annual ③ local ④ expensive ⑤ wooden

2 The idea __________ from a simple observation.

① protected ② supported ③ endangered ④ encouraged ⑤ originated

3 To __________ their crops, they need suitable equipment and storage facilities.

① harvest ② reserve ③ build ④ attend ⑤ greet

4 My family has a __________ of letting kids decorate their own birthday cakes.

① term ② parade ③ theory ④ tradition ⑤ display

정답 및 해설 p.8

• SENTENCE •

D

다음 문장을 밑줄 친 부분에 유의하여 우리말로 해석하시오.

1 It finishes with an amazing fireworks display, which is well worth seeing.

▶ ______________________________

2 But surprisingly, the Hanging Temple has been hanging there for about 1,500 years!

▶ ______________________________

3 This warm welcome, known as the *shaka*, is popular throughout the islands.

▶ ______________________________

4 This gives the carvers a few days to work on their creations before exhibiting them in the town plaza.

▶ ______________________________

E

우리말에 맞게 주어진 단어들을 바르게 배열하여 문장을 완성하시오.

1 절에는 좁은 계단과 다리들로 연결된 40개의 방이 있다.

The temple includes forty (narrow / and / bridges / connected / stairs / by / chambers).

▶ The temple includes forty ______________________________.

2 그것은 100년도 더 전에 마을 광장에서 상인들에 의해 시작되었다.

It was started more (100 years / than / merchants / by / ago) at the town plaza.

▶ It was started more ______________________________ at the town plaza.

3 전망이 좋은 자리를 예약할 수 있도록 티켓을 일찍 구매하는 것이 좋습니다.

It is a good idea to buy tickets early (can / you / reserve / so / a seat / that) with a good view.

▶ It is a good idea to buy tickets early ______________________________ with a good view.

1

BLACK SHEEP

검은 양(black sheep)은 사람들에게 환영받지 못하는 동물이었다. 목동들은 특히 검은 양을 싫어했는데, 검은 양털은 다른 색으로 염색이 되지 않아서 상업적 가치가 낮았기 때문이다. 여기서 유래한 black sheep은 오늘날 '가족 중에서 수치로 여겨지거나 별로 환영받지 못하는 말썽꾸러기' 혹은 '어떤 집단에서 튀거나 기준에서 벗어난 사람'을 지칭하는 말로 쓰인다.

내 동생은 우리 집안의 골칫거리야. / 항상 말썽을 일으키나 보구나!

SECTION 02

역사 속 인물

01

165 words 2'30"

Date:

Time Taken:

그에 관한 진실

Everyone thinks that Napoleon Bonaparte was a very short man. Actually, the triangular hat he loved to wear played a role in making him look so short. The hats used by Napoleon's Imperial Guards were worn vertically, making the towering men look even taller. ___________, Napoleon liked to wear his hat horizontally, making him look short in comparison.

Another crucial reason why Napoleon has become the symbol of the short man is that the doctor who examined him upon his death recorded his height as 5 feet 2 inches, or 158 cm. ___________, Napoleon was actually 169 cm, about the average height for European men at the time. The 11cm difference resulted from the fact (A) [that / which] the French unit of "feet" and the British unit of "feet" were different. (B) [Because / Due to] this error, the French emperor Napoleon Bonaparte, whose name commanded respect and fear throughout all of Europe, lost 11cm of his height and ended up (C) [to become / becoming] a hero for short men everywhere.

나폴레옹 나폴레옹(1769-1821)은 지중해 섬 코르시카 출신으로, 프랑스 혁명 당시 이탈리아, 이집트 등에서 장교로 활약하여 무공을 세웠다. 지지 세력을 등에 업고 1799년 쿠데타를 일으켜 정부를 수립하고 제1통령 자리에 오르게 된다. 1804년에는 프랑스 초대 황제로 즉위, 조세 · 행정 · 교육 제도 및 교통망을 정비하고 도량형을 통일하여 근대적 기준을 마련했다. 특히 그가 편찬한 『나폴레옹 법전』은 법 앞의 평등, 국가와 종교의 분리, 소유권 인정 등 근대 헌법의 모델이 되었다. 전 유럽을 통치하고자 하는 야심으로, 오스트리아 빈을 함락시키고 신성 로마 제국을 와해시켰으나 1812년 러시아 원정에서 실패한 후 몰락의 길을 걷기 시작한다. 1815년 100여 일간 잠깐 다시 정권을 장악하지만, 워털루 전투에서 대패하여 세인트 헬레나 섬으로 유배되어 결국 거기서 사망하게 된다.

1 윗글의 제목으로 가장 적절한 것은?

① The Last Days of Napoleon
② The Origin of Napoleon's Hat
③ Napoleon and His Imperial Guards
④ Was Napoleon Really a Short Man?
⑤ The Secret in the Portrait of Napoleon

2 윗글의 빈칸에 공통으로 들어갈 말로 가장 적절한 것은?

① Therefore ② However ③ Furthermore
④ For example ⑤ As a result

수능어법

3 윗글의 (A), (B), (C)의 각 네모 안에서 어법에 맞는 표현으로 가장 적절한 것은?

	(A)		(B)		(C)
①	that	……	Because	……	to become
②	that	……	Due to	……	becoming
③	that	……	Due to	……	to become
④	which	……	Because	……	becoming
⑤	which	……	Due to	……	to become

서술형

4 윗글의 내용과 일치하도록 빈칸에 알맞은 말을 본문에서 찾아 쓰시오.

Napoleon has been thought to be a short man for two reasons: he wore his hat __________, and the French and British units of feet were __________.

triangular 삼각형의 **play a role in** …에 역할을 하다 **imperial** 황제의 **guard** 호위병 **vertically** 수직으로 **towering** 우뚝 솟은 **horizontally** 수평으로 **comparison** 비교 **crucial** 중대한 **examine** 조사하다, 검사하다 **command** 명령하다; 지배하다; *(동정 · 존경 등을) 모으다, 일으키다 **end up v-ing** 결국 …이 되다 문제 **origin** 기원 **portrait** 초상화

02

크림 전쟁의 숨은 영웅

241 words 3'30"

Date:

Time Taken:

Although Florence Nightingale is best known as the founder of modern nursing, she was also a skilled statistician. Nightingale used statistics to figure out why so many people died in the Crimean War. She then used this information effectively to change public opinion.

Nightingale was sent to a British hospital in Turkey in 1854 in order to improve its conditions. Many injured soldiers were dying in the hospital, which suffered from shortages of food and medicine, an overworked staff, and unclean conditions. By the time the war ended in 1856, Nightingale and her team had successfully improved the hospital, significantly lowering the death rates of wounded soldiers.

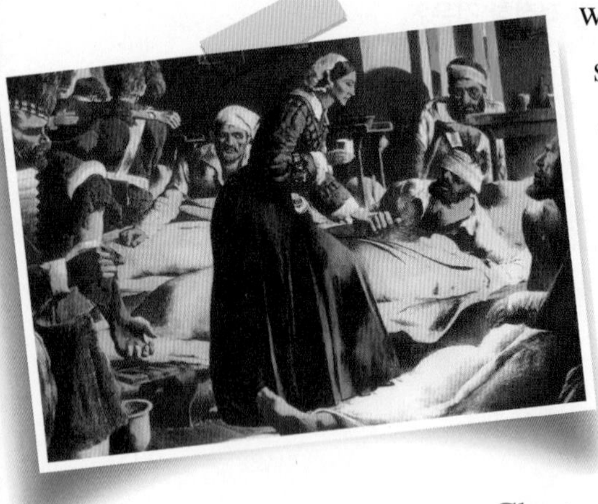

Despite this success, Nightingale worried that similar situations would occur in the future. So she used her abilities as a statistician to ______________________. It was commonly believed that most of the deaths were due to shortages of food and medicine. However, Nightingale found that the real cause was unsanitary conditions. Nightingale was asked to present this information to the queen and her council. She knew that simply reading a list of numbers weren't enough. So she arranged the numbers into charts to make them clearer.

Charts weren't commonly used in those days, but they had a powerful impact. They convinced many people that something had to be done. Thanks to Florence Nightingale's statistical skills, public sanitation and the British hospital system were improved, saving countless lives.

크림 전쟁 1853년부터 1856년에 걸쳐, 크림 반도와 흑해에서의 주도권을 두고 러시아와 오스만투르크 · 프랑스 · 영국 · 사르데냐 연합군이 벌인 전쟁이다. 전쟁의 직접적 계기는 오스만투르크 내의 기독교 성지에 대한 권리를 둘러싸고 프랑스와 러시아가 대립한 데 있다. 프랑스가 먼저 오스만투르크 정부로부터 성지에 대한 가톨릭의 권리를 인정받자, 그리스 정교가 국교였던 러시아는 이에 강력히 반발한다. 이에 러시아의 지중해 진출을 경계하던 서유럽 열강이 오스만투르크에 가세해 러시아에 선전포고를 함으로써 전쟁이 발발했다. 결국 이 전쟁은 1856년 연합군의 승리로 종결된다.

1 윗글의 주제로 가장 적절한 것은?

① the effect of using numbers and charts
② Nightingale's contribution as a statistician
③ the poor conditions in 19th-century hospitals
④ the history of public sanitation in Great Britain
⑤ the real cause of soldiers' deaths in the Crimean War

2 윗글의 빈칸에 들어갈 말로 가장 적절한 것은?

① predict and prevent serious diseases
② help hospitals train nurses effectively
③ support soldiers who suffered during the war
④ provide the armies with enough medical supplies
⑤ analyze the cause of hospital deaths during the war

3 윗글의 내용과 일치하지 않는 것은?

① 나이팅게일은 현대 간호학의 창시자로 잘 알려져 있다.
② 나이팅게일의 노력으로 영국군 병원 환경이 개선되었다.
③ 전쟁 당시 음식과 약 부족이 환자 사망의 실제 원인이었다.
④ 나이팅게일은 여왕과 의회에 병원의 실상을 보고했다.
⑤ 나이팅게일은 차트를 이용하여 병원의 실상을 효과적으로 알릴 수 있었다.

서술형

4 윗글의 밑줄 친 문장에서 어법상 틀린 부분을 찾아 바르게 고쳐 쓰시오. (1개)

skilled 숙련된, 노련한 **statistician** 통계 전문가, 통계학자 ※ **statistics** 통계학 **figure out** …을 이해하다[알아내다] **effectively** 효과적으로 **improve** 개선하다, 향상시키다 **overworked** 혹사당하는 **condition** 상태; *(*pl.*) 환경, 상황 **suffer** 고통받다 **shortage** 부족 **medicine** 의학; *약 **significantly** 상당히, 크게 **lower** 낮추다 **wounded** 부상을 입은 **unsanitary** 비위생적인 **present** 제시하다, 제출하다 **council** 의회 **arrange** 정리하다, 배열하다 **convince** 납득시키다, 확신시키다 **sanitation** 위생 시설[관리] 문제 **supply** (*pl.*) 공급(량); *보급품[물자]

03

전쟁 속의 또 다른 비극

225 words 3'10"

Date:

Time Taken:

Many people view Winston Churchill as one of the greatest leaders of World War II. As the Prime Minister of the United Kingdom, he held his country together during difficult times and helped to lead *the Allied Forces to victory.

But not everyone saw Churchill as a great man, especially not those living in areas colonized by the British Empire. In fact, he is considered to be partially ① responsible for millions of deaths in Bengal, a region in northeastern India. In 1943, Bengal was ruled by Britain and was suffering from a serious famine. There was plenty of rice being grown in other parts of India, but most of it was being exported to feed British soldiers. Not only did Churchill ② refuse to send some of this rice to Bengal, but he also turned down ③ offers from the United States and Canada to provide food. His reason was that he ④ feared enemy soldiers who were near Bengal would take the food. In the end, approximately 3 million people starved to death in Bengal.

Although Churchill had no way of preventing the famine, (could, victims, he, reduced, the number of, have). Instead, he turned his back on the people of Bengal and let them ⑤ survive. Because he coldly decided to put his country before human lives, some people view him as a heartless and cruel man.

*the Allied Forces 연합군

정답 및 해설 p.12

1 윗글의 내용과 일치하는 것은?

① The whole world showed respect for Churchill.
② The region of Bengal wasn't ruled by the British Empire.
③ There was no rice being grown in India.
④ People in Bengal received food aid from the U.S.
⑤ Churchill let the hungry Indians starve to death.

VOCA

2 윗글의 밑줄 친 ①~⑤ 중, 문맥상 낱말의 쓰임이 적절하지 않은 것은?

서술형

3 윗글의 괄호 안에 주어진 단어들을 다음 우리말에 맞게 배열하시오.
그는 희생자의 수를 줄일 수도 있었다

→ ____

윈스턴 처칠 윈스턴 처칠(1874-1965)은 영국의 귀족 가문 출신으로, 어린 시절 학교에서 '품행이 나쁘고 의욕이 없으며 다른 학생들과 자주 다투고 상습적으로 지각하는' 말썽꾸러기 학생이었다. 성적도 하위권이었지만, 샌드허스트 사관학교에 입학한 후 차츰 변모하여 우수한 성적으로 졸업한다. 그 후, 종군기자로 활동하다 1900년 하원의원에 당선되면서 정치가로서의 활동을 시작하였다. 정치 경력 이외에도 처칠은 수준급의 화가였으며 수많은 명연설과 에세이, 역사서 등을 집필한 작가로, 1953년에는 노벨 문학상을 수상했다.

view 견해; *…라고 여기다 **Prime Minister** 총리, 수상 **hold ... together** …을 단결시키다 **colonize** 식민지로 만들다 **British Empire** 대영제국 **partially** 부분적으로 **responsible for** …에 책임이 있는 **region** 지방, 지역 **rule** 규칙; *통치하다 **famine** 기근 **export** 수출하다 **refuse** 거절[거부]하다 **turn down** …을 거절[거부]하다 **offer** 제의하다; *제의, 제안 **fear** 공포, 두려움; *…을 두려워하다 **approximately** 거의 **starve to death** 굶어 죽다 **victim** 피해자, 희생자 **turn one's back on** …에게 등을 돌리다, …을 저버리다 **put A before B** A를 B보다 더 우선시하다 **heartless** 무정한, 비정한

04

202 words 3'20"

Date:

Time Taken:

English Only

Do You Know of Nellie Bly?

In 1887, 23-year-old Nellie Bly already had a career as a journalist in the small city of Pittsburgh. However, most of the stories she was asked to write were directed only at women. Bly dreamed of writing important stories for all readers, so she moved to New York and tried to find work at the *New York World*, which was one of the nation's leading newspapers at that time.

The editor of the newspaper offered her a ______________. He asked her to investigate a local mental hospital with a bad reputation for treating patients poorly. In order to get inside, Bly pretended to be mentally ill for 10 days. The story she wrote about her experience was published as a six-part series, and it made her one of America's most famous journalists. It also helped start a new style of reporting called investigative journalism.

Later, after reading the famous book *Around the World in 80 Days*, Bly decided to break the world record for the fastest trip around the world. Completing the trip in just 72 days, she set the record and then wrote a book about the experience. Today, Bly is remembered as both an important journalist and a brave woman.

조지프 퓰리처 조지프 퓰리처(Joseph Pulitzer)는 현대 저널리즘의 창시자로, 1847년 헝가리에서 출생했다. 1864년 미국 세인트루이스로 건너가 1868년 한 독일어 신문사에서 기자로서 첫 발을 내딛는다. 뛰어난 독일어 실력과 수준 높은 교양으로 기자로서 크게 성공한 그는 『포스트 디스패치』를 창간한다. 이후 뉴욕으로 진출해 『뉴욕 월드』를 인수, 선정적이고도 흥미진진한 기사로 신문의 패러다임을 바꾼다. 이전에는 없었던 스포츠 뉴스, 여성 독자들을 타깃으로 한 기사 등은 대중들의 관심을 한눈에 받았다. 당시 넬리 블라이도 이 신문사에서 활약하게 된다. 언론인으로서 퓰리처는 권력에 굴하지 않는 언론의 독립을 강조하였으며, 유언을 통해 퓰리처상을 제정하였다.

정답 및 해설 p.14

1 Which of the following is the best title for the passage?

① What Is Investigative Journalism?

② Getting a Job at the *New York World*

③ A Fake Patient in a Mental Hospital

④ Amazing American Travel Writers

⑤ Nellie Bly: A Female Pioneer in Journalism

2 What is NOT mentioned about Bly in the passage?

① who inspired her to become a journalist

② why she wanted to work at the *New York World*

③ what she did to get inside the mental hospital

④ what the effects of her story about the mental hospital were

⑤ why she went on the 72-day trip around the world

3 Which of the following best fits in the blank?

① raise ② promotion ③ challenge

④ compliment ⑤ settlement

서술형

4 Write what the underlined "It" refers to using words from the passage. (7 words)

career 직업, 직장 생활 **journalist** 저널리스트, 기자 ※ **journalism** 저널리즘, 언론 **direct** …로 향하다[겨냥하다] **dream of** …을 꿈꾸다 **leading** 가장 중요한, 선두적인 **editor** *편집장; 편집자 **investigate** 조사하다 ※ **investigative** 조사의, 수사의 **mental** 정신의, 정신적인 ※ **mentally** 정신적으로 **reputation** 평판, 명성 **treat** 대하다 **poorly** 형편없이 **pretend to-v** …인 척하다 **publish** 출판하다, 발행하다 **reporting** 보도 **break the world record** 세계 기록을 깨다 **complete** 완료하다, 끝마치다 **set a record** 기록을 세우다 문제 **fake** 가짜의, 거짓된 **female** 여성의 **pioneer** 개척자, 선구자

Review Test

• VOCA •

A

다음 단어의 영영풀이를 바르게 연결하시오.

1 pretend •	• ⓐ to have power over a country
2 rule •	• ⓑ to act in an untruthful way
3 command •	• ⓒ to send a product to another country for sale
4 export •	• ⓓ to feel pain
5 suffer •	• ⓔ to get or receive attention

B

괄호 안에서 적절한 단어를 고르시오.

1 He painted the stripe on the wall (horizontally / vertically) from ceiling to floor.

2 He (confused / refused) to answer the questions of the police officer.

3 A (comparison / variation) of the two products showed that one was much better than the other.

4 The (abundance / shortage) of water has led to poor crop yields in the area.

C

다음 밑줄 친 부분의 의미로 가장 적절한 것은?

1 Steven has played a <u>crucial</u> role in dealing with the issue.
① basic ② political ③ important ④ weak ⑤ constant

2 I came to the conclusion that I should accept their <u>offer</u>.
① conflict ② change ③ evidence ④ knowledge ⑤ proposal

3 The doctor recommended changing my diet to <u>lower</u> my blood pressure.
① raise ② lengthen ③ treat ④ reduce ⑤ enhance

4 The professor is a <u>leading</u> figure in the field of biotechnology.
① tall ② top ③ final ④ responsible ⑤ minor

정답 및 해설 p.16

• SENTENCE •

D

다음 문장을 밑줄 친 부분에 유의하여 우리말로 해석하시오.

1 Most of the stories she was asked to write were directed only at women.

▸ ______________________________

2 Despite this success, Nightingale worried that similar situations would occur in the future.

▸ ______________________________

3 The triangular hat he loved to wear played a role in making him look so short.

▸ ______________________________

4 Not everyone saw Churchill as a great man, especially not those living in areas colonized by the British Empire.

▸ ______________________________

E

우리말에 맞게 주어진 단어들을 바르게 배열하여 문장을 완성하시오.

1 나이팅게일은 왜 그렇게 많은 사람들이 크림 전쟁에서 죽었는지 알아내기 위해 통계학을 활용했다.

Nightingale used statistics (died / why / figure out / many / to / so / people) in the Crimean War.

▸ Nightingale used statistics ______________________________ in the Crimean War.

2 블라이는 영향력이 큰 기자이자 용감한 여성으로 기억된다.

Bly is remembered as (woman / journalist / and / brave / an / a / important / both).

▸ Bly is remembered as ______________________________.

3 그는 벵골 근처에 있는 적군이 그 식량을 빼앗을 것을 두려워했다.

He feared (the food / enemy soldiers / were / near / would / Bengal / take / who).

▸ He feared ______________________________.

CAMPAIGN IN THE WORLD

• 아동인권 •

MAKE-A-WISH FOUNDATION

꿈을 이루어 드립니다!

메이크어위시 재단은 1980년 미국 애리조나 경찰이 백혈병에 걸린 한 소년의 소망을 들어 준 일에서 시작되었다. 크리스라는 소년의 꿈은 경찰관이 되는 것이었고, 지역 경찰들은 소년을 명예 경찰관으로 임명하여 하루 동안 경찰 체험을 하게 해 주었다. 이 일을 계기로 경찰관 샘크위츠와 주변 사람들은 난치병에 걸린 어린이들의 소원을 이루어 주는 일을 시작했다. 이후 1993년에는 국제메이크어위시 재단이 설립되었고, 현재 50여 개 국가에 지부를 두고 있다. 설립 이래 약 45만 명의 어린이들이 재단을 통해 소원을 이루었다. 메이크어위시 재단은 자원봉사와 기부를 통해 운영된다.

MAKANI CENTER

난민 어린이들을 위한 교육 센터

마카니 센터는 시리아 내전으로 발생한 난민 어린이들을 교육하고 보호하기 위해 유니세프가 요르단의 도시와 난민 캠프에 세운 무료 교육 센터이다. 요르단 정부가 받아들인 60만여 명의 시리아 난민들 중 취학 연령 아동의 수는 1/3에 달하며, 요르단 공교육을 받는 어린이는 그중 약 60%밖에 되지 않는다. 이에 유니세프에서는 'I am safe, I Learn, I connect(나는 안전하고, 나는 배우고, 나는 연결되어 있어요)'라는 모토하에 마카니 센터를 설립하였다. Makani는 아랍어로 'my space'를 의미한다. 이 센터에서 어린이들은 학습 기회뿐 아니라 건강 지원 서비스도 제공받을 수 있다.

SECTION 03

심리

01

손을 씻으면 사라져요

223 words 3'20"

Date:

Time Taken:

In the famous Shakespeare play *Macbeth*, Lady Macbeth encourages her husband to kill the king but begins to feel terrible guilt after he actually does. She imagines there is blood on her hands and tries to wash it off. Although this is just fiction, some psychologists believe it really is possible to wash away guilt through physical washing. They call it the "Lady Macbeth Effect," and, unfortunately, it's not always a good thing.

In a study, the psychologists asked certain participants to think about times they had behaved unethically in the past. They then thanked everyone for participating and allowed each person to choose a reward. The rewards they offered were small, everyday items, including pens, kitchen tools, and cleaning products. After ⓐ (think) about their bad behavior, people were much more likely to choose a cleaning product, such as soap or hand wipes, than any of the other products.

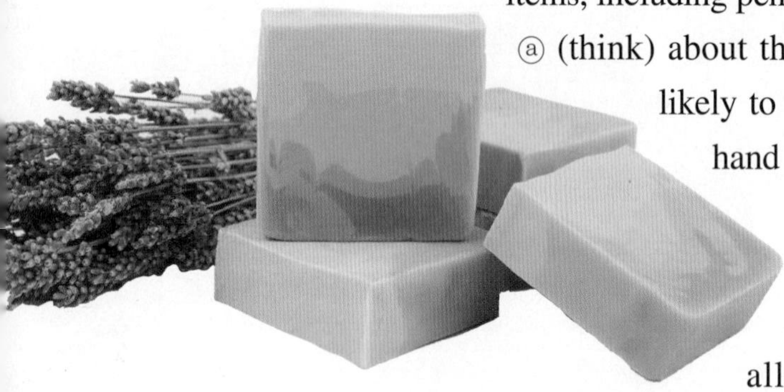

Researchers in a similar study also asked people to think about bad things they had done. But this time half of them were allowed ⓑ (wash) their hands afterwards, while the others were not. The researchers found that those who had washed their hands felt less guilt and were less likely to do volunteer work later. This suggests that washing one's hands can reduce bad feelings, but it can also reduce ____________________.

맥베스 『맥베스』는 『햄릿』, 『리어 왕』, 『오셀로』와 함께 셰익스피어의 4대 비극 중 하나로, 한 인간의 탐욕이 초래하는 비극을 그렸다. 스코틀랜드의 장군인 맥베스는 자신이 왕이 될 것이라는 마녀들의 예언을 듣고 왕위를 탐하게 된다. 아내마저 왕을 죽이라고 부추기자 그는 사촌이자 국왕인 던컨을 시해하고 왕위에 오르지만, 점점 많은 사람들을 죽이는 폭군이 된다. 마침내, 죄책감에 시달리던 맥베스 부인은 몽유병 발작을 일으켜 절벽에서 떨어져 죽는다. 그리고 던컨의 아들인 맬컴 왕자와 맥더프 장군이 반란을 일으켜 맥베스는 맥더프의 칼에 죽게 되고, 맬컴 왕자가 왕위에 오르게 된다.

1 윗글의 제목으로 가장 적절한 것은?

① Different Views about *Macbeth*
② The Origin of the Lady Macbeth Effect
③ The Lady Macbeth Effect: What It Is and Its Dark Side
④ The Physical and Mental Benefits of Washing
⑤ The Characteristics of People Who Lack a Sense of Guilt

2 윗글의 빈칸에 들어갈 말로 가장 적절한 것은?

① trust in others
② one's sense of hygiene
③ the likelihood of disease
④ emotions related to morality
⑤ one's preference for cleanliness

서술형

3 윗글의 ⓐ와 ⓑ에 주어진 동사를 어법에 알맞은 형태로 쓰시오.

ⓐ ________________ ⓑ ________________

4 윗글의 내용과 일치하면 T에, 일치하지 않으면 F에 표시하시오.

	T	F
(1) In Shakespeare's *Macbeth*, Lady Macbeth kills the king.	□	□
(2) Those who don't feel guilty about their past are more likely to wash their hands frequently than those who do.	□	□

guilt 죄책감 **fiction** 소설; *허구 **psychologist** 심리학자 **physical** 육체의, 신체의 **unfortunately** 불행하게도 **participant** 참가자 **unethically** 비윤리적으로 **reward** 보상 **volunteer work** 자원봉사 **reduce** 줄이다 문제 **origin** 기원, 근원 **benefit** 혜택, 이득 **characteristic** 특징, 특질 **lack** …이 없다[부족하다] **hygiene** 위생 **likelihood** 가능성 **morality** 도덕; 도덕성 **preference** 선호(도) **cleanliness** 청결

02

메기가 나타나면…

168 words 2'30"

Date:

Time Taken:

*Sardine fishermen were facing a problem. The fish would die quickly after being caught in their nets. But live sardines could be sold at a higher price. So one fisherman ⓐ <u>came up with</u> a great idea. He put a catfish into each container of sardines. To avoid ⓑ <u>this predator</u>, the sardines had to keep (A) [swim / swimming] around and around. This kept them alive longer.

This is called the "catfish effect." It can be applied to situations in many fields. In sports, for example, coaches know that bringing a new, talented player onto a team makes the other players better. This is because they start trying harder to avoid (B) [losing / to lose] their position on the team. Businesses can use this effect to motivate their employees, too. In economics, it explains how companies become creative and innovative. When strong competitors enter the market, other companies have to become more dynamic to survive. This makes the entire economy stronger. In short, pressure and stimulation from competitors can make people and businesses (C) [work / to work] harder.

*sardine 정어리 (청어과의 바닷물고기)

과학 저널 『사이언스』 지의 메뚜기 연구

미국 『사이언스』 지에 실린 연구에 따르면, 포식자의 존재가 항상 피식자를 강하게 만드는 것은 아니다. 메뚜기 사육장 한 곳에 메뚜기의 천적인 거미를 입을 막은 채 풀어놓았다. 거미의 입을 막아 메뚜기를 먹지 못하게 했음에도 불구하고, 거미와 같은 사육장에 있던 메뚜기들은 공포에 휩싸여 스트레스를 받았다. 그 결과 메뚜기 몸속 에너지 소비가 증가하여 영양 성분인 질소 함량이 줄어들었고, 이는 메뚜기의 사체가 분해될 때 토양에도 영향을 미쳐 미생물의 활동을 방해했다.

정답 및 해설 p.19

1 윗글의 주제로 가장 적절한 것은?

① a natural enemy of sardines
② how to avoid a risky situation
③ what draws out one's best ability
④ how to keep fish alive for a long time
⑤ the meaning of competition in business

VOCA

2 윗글의 밑줄 친 ⓐ came up with와 바꿔 쓸 수 있는 말로 가장 적절한 것은?

① turned on
② thought of
③ pointed out
④ looked forward to
⑤ came together

수능 어법

3 윗글의 (A), (B), (C)의 각 네모 안에서 어법에 맞는 표현으로 가장 적절한 것은?

	(A)		(B)		(C)
①	swim	……	losing	……	work
②	swim	……	to lose	……	to work
③	swim	……	losing	……	to work
④	swimming	……	to lose	……	to work
⑤	swimming	……	losing	……	work

서술형

4 윗글의 밑줄 친 ⓑ this predator가 가리키는 것을 본문에서 찾아 쓰시오.

face 마주 보다; *직면하다 **live** 살아 있는 **come up with** (해답 등을) 찾아내다, 내놓다 **catfish** 메기 **container** 그릇, 용기 **avoid** 피하다 **predator** 포식자, 포식 동물 **effect** 영향; *효과, 결과 **apply** 적용시키다 **field** 들판; *분야 **motivate** 동기를 부여하다 **employee** 종업원, 고용인 **innovative** 획기적인 **competitor** 경쟁 상대 **dynamic** 활발한; 역동적인 **survive** 살아남다 **entire** 전체의 **pressure** 압박, 압력 **stimulation** 자극; 고무, 격려 문제 **natural enemy** 천적 **draw** 끌어당기다; *끌어내다

03

꿈을 꾸고 있어요

208 words 3'00"

Date:

Time Taken:

Dreams can be fun, exciting, or even scary. Most of the time we can't control them at all. But sometimes we have special dreams. Not only (we, do, dreaming, we, realize, that, are), but we can also control what happens! These are called "lucid dreams."

Normally, when we dream, we are no longer self-aware. But in a lucid dream, it is as if the brain wakes up while we are dreaming. This allows us to move around and explore our dream environment as though we were completely awake. What's more, normal dreams usually fade as soon as we wake up. So we can only remember them for a short time. But lucid dreams can be remembered long after we have woken up! However, there are some problems with lucid dreams. First of all, they can be exhausting. They interrupt normal sleep patterns, preventing us from getting enough rest. Also, they can be addictive.

But there are some people who believe that lucid dreams are more than just an interesting experience. They say these dreams can lead to ____________________. People can use them to gain confidence and overcome their fears. If there's something they're afraid to try in real life, they can experience it in their dreams instead!

1 윗글의 내용과 일치하지 않는 것은?

① We can control our dreams while lucid dreaming.
② In a normal dream, we are unconscious of what's happening.
③ It is harder to remember lucid dreams than normal dreams.
④ Lucid dreaming can make us very tired.
⑤ Some people think lucid dreams are more than an interesting experience.

서술형

2 윗글의 괄호 안에 주어진 단어들을 다음 우리말에 맞게 배열하시오.

우리가 꿈을 꾸는 중이라는 것을 깨달을 뿐만 아니라

→ Not only ______________________________

3 윗글의 빈칸에 들어갈 말로 가장 적절한 것은?

① physical fitness
② mental depression
③ behavioral problems
④ personal development
⑤ better sleeping patterns

몽유병 Sleepwalking

몽유병은 수면 중 이상행동을 보이는 것을 말한다. 몽유병 환자는 자는 도중 의미를 알 수 없는 말을 하거나, 벌떡 일어나 걸어 다니고 운동을 하기도 한다. 몽유병은 대개 어린 시절에 겪는 경우가 많으며 성장하면서 차차 없어지는데, 일부는 성인이 되어서도 이를 겪는다. 몽유병에 걸리면 수면 중에 한 행동을 잠에서 깬 뒤 기억하지 못한다고 한다. 원인은 정확히 알려지지 않았으며, 특별한 치료법 역시 아직 알려진 바 없다.

scary 무서운, 겁나는 **control** 지배하다, 통제하다 **lucid** 명쾌한; *의식이 또렷한 **normally** 보통은 **self-aware** 자기를 인식하는, 자각하는 **explore** 탐험하다 **environment** 환경 **completely** 완전히, 전적으로 **fade** 서서히 사라지다 **exhausting** 기진맥진하게 만드는 **interrupt** 방해하다, 중단시키다 **rest** 나머지; *휴식, 수면 **addictive** 중독성이 있는 **gain** 얻다 **confidence** 자신감 **overcome** 극복하다
문제 **unconscious** 의식하지 못하는 **behavioral** 행동의, 행동에 관한

04

208 words 3'30"

Date:

Time Taken:

English Only

A Behavior Experiment with Monkeys

Here's an interesting experiment. Some scientists place 12 monkeys in a room. The scientists tie a bunch of bananas on the top of a tall pole to attract the monkeys. (A) The wet monkeys scream and jump down, refraining from attempting to grab the bananas. (B) Each time the monkeys try to get the bananas, the scientists turn on the shower and spray them with cold water. (C) Just above the bananas, they conceal a showerhead in the ceiling. Next, the scientists remove the showerhead. They also take one of the monkeys out of the room, ⓐ (replace) it with another one.

When the new monkey attempts to climb the pole to get the bananas, the other monkeys pull it back, screaming and pointing to the ceiling. The scientists replace all twelve of the original monkeys, one by one, in the room. Although none of the new monkeys have been sprayed by the water, they all refuse to climb the pole to reach the bananas at the top.

This experiment can teach us an important lesson. The new monkeys don't climb up because no other monkeys do it. Lots of people act similarly. Without examining why, they give up on their ____________ and follow the way that things have been done before.

동물 실험의 역사

동물 실험은 고대 그리스 시대부터 시작되었다. 히포크라테스는 동물을 해부하여 생식과 유전을 설명했고, 아리스토텔레스는 동물 관찰을 통해 해부학을 발전시켰다. 갈레노스는 원숭이, 돼지, 염소 등을 해부하여 심장, 뼈, 근육, 뇌신경 등에 대한 의학적 사실을 밝혀냈다. 19세기에 이르러 프랑스의 베르나르, 파스퇴르, 러시아의 파블로프 등이 본격적으로 동물 실험을 했다. 그러나 동물 실험 반대 여론이 형성되면서, 베르나르의 부인은 동물 생체 해부 반대 협회를 설립했고, 영국에서는 동물 학대 방지법이 제정되기도 했다. 오늘날 동물의 권리에 대한 사람들의 인식은 더욱 발전해, 특정 산업 분야에서 동물 실험을 폐지하거나 관련 원칙을 마련하는 등의 노력이 이루어지고 있다.

정답 및 해설 p.22

1 Which of the following best fits in the blanks (A) and (B)?

> In the experiment, the new monkeys only ____(A)____ to get the bananas at the top because it was widely considered ____(B)____.

(A)		(B)	(A)		(B)
① refused	……	bad-tasting	② refused	……	dangerous
③ refused	……	impolite	④ attempted	……	enjoyable
⑤ attempted	……	recommendable			

2 Choose the right order of (A), (B), and (C) according to the context.

① (A) – (B) – (C)　② (A) – (C) – (B)　③ (B) – (A) – (C)
④ (B) – (C) – (A)　⑤ (C) – (B) – (A)

서술형

3 Write the grammatically correct form of ⓐ.

4 Which of the following best fits in the blank?

① tests　② goals　③ money
④ research　⑤ motivation

behavior 행동 **experiment** 실험 **place** 놓다, 두다 **a bunch of** 한 다발의 **attract** 마음을 끌다; *끌어들이다 **scream** 비명을 지르다 **refrain from** …을 그만두다 **attempt to-v** …하려고 시도하다 **grab** 붙잡다 **spray** 뿌리다 **conceal** 감추다, 숨기다 **showerhead** 샤워기 꼭지 **ceiling** 천장 **pull** 잡아당기다 **similarly** 비슷하게 **examine** 조사하다, 검토하다 문제 **impolite** 무례한 **recommendable** 권할 만한

Review Test

· VOCA ·

A 다음 중 단어의 뜻풀이가 잘못된 것을 고르시오.

① fade: to disappear suddenly
② exhausting: making someone feel very tired
③ innovative: doing something in a new and better way
④ dynamic: always active or showing a lot of energy
⑤ predator: an animal that hunts and eats other animals

B 괄호 안에서 적절한 것을 고르시오.

1 You will get stronger by (facing / racing) many challenges in your life.
2 The police officer found a microphone (concealed / revealed) under the table.
3 The employee received a cash bonus as a (loss / reward) for her hard work.
4 The railway service was temporarily (advanced / interrupted) by the accident.

C 문맥상 다음 빈칸에 들어갈 가장 알맞은 단어를 고르시오.

1 I __________ to trim my cat's claws but failed.
① attempted ② refrained ③ avoided ④ applied ⑤ explored

2 You can __________ yourself by visualizing your goals.
① argue ② punish ③ offend ④ motivate ⑤ refuse

3 Research found that sugar is far more __________ than cigarettes or caffeine.
① relative ② addictive ③ creative ④ supportive ⑤ alternative

4 Taking a nap can help relieve your __________ fatigue.
① original ② unethical ③ similar ④ impolite ⑤ physical

정답 및 해설 p.23

· SENTENCE ·

D

다음 문장을 밑줄 친 부분에 유의하여 우리말로 해석하시오.

1 What's more, normal dreams usually fade as soon as we wake up.

▸ ______________________________

2 This is because they start trying harder to avoid losing their position on the team.

▸ ______________________________

3 They also take one of the monkeys out of the room, replacing it with another one.

▸ ______________________________

4 Researchers in a similar study also asked people to think about bad things they had done.

▸ ______________________________

E

우리말에 맞게 주어진 단어들을 바르게 배열하여 문장을 완성하시오.

1 물고기는 그물에 잡힌 후에 빨리 죽곤 했다.

The fish would die quickly (in / being / the nets / after / caught).

▸ The fish would die quickly ______________________________.

2 자각몽에서는, 꿈을 꾸는 동안 마치 두뇌가 깨어나는 것 같다.

In a lucid dream, it is (up / the / as if / wakes / brain) while we are dreaming.

▸ In a lucid dream, it is ______________________________ while we are dreaming.

3 하지만 이번에는 그들 중 절반이 그들의 손을 씻는 것이 허용된 반면에, 나머지 사람들은 허용되지 않았다.

But this time half of them (hands / allowed / their / wash / were / to), while the others were not.

▸ But this time half of them ______________________________, while the others were not.

2

ON CLOUD NINE

세계기상기구에서 간행한 국제구름도감에 따르면, 구름은 외형에 따라 10종으로 분류된다. 그중 cloud nine인 적란운(cumulonimbus)은 솜털처럼 보이는, 수직으로 발달한 큰 구름이다. 이 구름은 지상에서 10킬로미터까지도 올라간다. 만약 누군가가 cloud nine 위에 있다고 하면 그는 아주 높은 곳에 있게 된다. 따라서 be on cloud nine은 '더할 나위 없이 행복하고 기쁘다'라는 뜻이 되었다.

너 오늘 기분이 좋네. /
응, 기분 최고야. 제이크가 나한테 데이트 신청을 했거든.

SECTION 04

문화 · 예술

01

그림일까 글씨일까

214 words 3'10"

Date:
Time Taken:

"A picture is worth a thousand words" is a common proverb, but calligrams are both words and pictures. They are created by arranging letters, words, or phrases into an image. Ideally, a calligram's image expresses the meaning of its words.

The most famous calligram artist was Guillaume Apollinaire, who was born in Rome in 1880. (①) He published a volume of poems called *Calligrammes* in 1918. (②) All of the poems ⓐ (contain) in the book form images. (③) After the release of the book, he, as well as calligrams, became popular around the world. (④)

Calligrams are even more popular today. (⑤) (A) It is also easier for people to share their calligrams today, and they do so on blogs, Web sites, and online galleries. (B) But now they can be made using computer programs, so they are easier to make and can include a wide range of colors. (C) In the past, they were created by hand, which took a lot of time and labor, and were usually black-and-white, since people made them with ink and paper. Why don't you join in the fun by creating a calligram yourself?

기욤 아폴리네르 기욤 아폴리네르(Guillaume Apollinaire, 1880-1918)는 프랑스에서 활동한 시인이자 작가로, 로마에서 태어났으며 1899년 파리로 가서 유럽 여러 나라를 여행하였다. 그의 초기 작품에는 여행에서 받은 인상과 다른 나라의 전설이나 민화를 주제로 한 시나 단편 소설이 많다. 또한 피카소, 앙리 루소, 앙드레 브르통, 마르크 샤갈과 같은 당대의 유명 예술가들과 어울리며 미술과 문학에 심취하였다. 글의 시각적 측면을 매우 중시하여, 자신의 시가 그 의미에 맞도록 배열되어야 한다고 생각했으며 이는 시집 『칼리그람(1918)』에 잘 나타나 있다. 그 밖의 대표적 시집으로는 『알코올(1913)』이 있다.

정답 및 해설 p.24

1

윗글의 주제로 가장 적절한 것은?

① the popularity of calligrams in the past
② the life of a French artist named Apollinaire
③ how to make and share your own calligrams
④ the difference between calligrams and poetry
⑤ what calligrams are and how they have changed

2

윗글의 흐름으로 보아, 주어진 문장이 들어가기에 가장 적절한 곳은?

For example, "La Tour Eiffel" is shaped like the Eiffel Tower, and "Cheval" resembles a horse.

서술형

3

윗글의 ⓐ에 주어진 동사를 어법에 알맞은 형태로 쓰시오.

4

윗글의 (A) ~ (C)를 글의 흐름에 맞게 배열한 것으로 가장 적절한 것은?

① (A) – (B) – (C)　② (A) – (C) – (B)　③ (B) – (C) – (A)
④ (C) – (A) – (B)　⑤ (C) – (B) – (A)

worth …의 가치가 있는 **proverb** 격언, 속담 **arrange** 정리하다, 배열하다 **phrase** 구 **ideally** 이상적으로 **publish** 출판하다, 발행하다 **volume** 용량; 양; 권; *책 **poem** (한 편의) 시 **contain** 포함하다 **release** 발표, 개봉, 발간 **popular** 인기 있는 ※ **popularity** 인기 **a wide range of** 광범위한, 다양한 **labor** 노동; *노고, 노력 문제 **difference** 차이 **poetry** 시 **resemble** 닮다

02

물방울무늬의 여왕

234 words 3'20"

Date:
Time Taken:

A Japanese artist named Yayoi Kusama is often called "the princess of polka dots." This is because all of her artwork has one thing in common — it is covered in dots.

It started with a strange experience in childhood that had a powerful impact on her. As she was standing in the middle of a large field of flowers, she imagined she could hear the flowers (A) [talking / to talk] to her. Looking around, it seemed as though she were standing in a field of endless dots. This inspired her to become an artist. Later, in the 1950s, she moved to New York and became part of the city's art scene, meeting such famous artists as Andy Warhol.

Yayoi is best known for her special *Infinity Rooms*, which allow people (B) [experience / to experience] the same feeling she had as a child standing in the field of flowers. When people enter one of these dark rooms filled with mirrors and small flashing lights, they feel as though they were standing in the middle of an endless space.

Besides these rooms, Yayoi also creates paintings, drawings, clothes, and other objects, all of which she covers in dots. She does this to symbolize the fact (C) [that / which] the earth is just one small dot in our enormous universe. By covering her artwork in dots, she is connecting it to the rest of the universe.

야요이 쿠사마 미술관
Yayoi Kusama Museum

야요이 쿠사마 본인이 2017년 1월 도쿄 신주쿠에 설립하고 야요이 쿠사마 재단이 운영하는 미술관이다. 쿠사마의 작품들은 전 세계 여러 미술관에도 이미 전시되어 있으나, 이 미술관은 쿠사마의 작품을 전시하는 데서 나아가 그녀의 예술에 관한 강연을 열고 기록물을 출간하여 쿠사마의 작품 세계와 삶을 널리 알리는 데 목적을 둔다. 미술관에서는 성인 관람객을 위한 '갤러리 토크', 아동 관람객을 위한 '미술관 탐험 투어' 등의 프로그램을 제공한다.

1 **야요이 쿠사마에 관한 윗글의 내용과 일치하지 않는 것은?**

① 작품의 공통점은 물방울무늬의 사용이다.
② 어린 시절의 특별한 체험을 계기로 예술가가 되었다.
③ 뉴욕 예술계에서 활동한 경험이 있다.
④ 〈인피니티 룸〉은 그녀의 대표 회화 작품이다.
⑤ 활동 분야는 그림에만 국한되어 있지 않다.

수능어법

2 **윗글의 (A), (B), (C)의 각 네모 안에서 어법에 맞는 표현으로 가장 적절한 것은?**

	(A)		(B)		(C)
①	talking	……	experience	……	that
②	talking	……	experience	……	which
③	talking	……	to experience	……	that
④	to talk	……	experience	……	that
⑤	to talk	……	to experience	……	which

VOCA

3 **윗글의 밑줄 친 inspired와 바꿔 쓸 수 있는 말로 가장 적절한 것은?**

① motivated ② discouraged ③ shaped
④ produced ⑤ arranged

서술형

4 **주어진 질문에 대한 답을 할 때, 빈칸에 들어갈 알맞은 말을 본문에서 찾아 쓰시오.**

Why does Yayoi Kusama fill her artwork with dots?
→ Because she wants to show that the __________ is just one small dot in our universe and that the dots in her artwork are a connection to the rest of the __________.

polka dot 물방울무늬 **artwork** 미술품 **have ... in common** …을 공통으로 지니다 **childhood** 어린 시절 **powerful** 영향력 있는; *강한, 강렬한 **impact** 영향 **imagine** 상상하다 **endless** 무한한, 끝없는 **inspire A to-v** A가 …하도록 고무[격려]하다 **infinity** 무한성 **flash** 번쩍이다 **symbolize** 상징하다 **enormous** 막대한, 거대한 **universe** 우주 **connect** 연결하다 ※ **connection** 연결 문제 **discourage** 좌절시키다 **produce** 생산하다 **arrange** 정리하다, 배열하다

03

쉽게 속일 수 없을걸?

187 words 2'50"

Date:

Time Taken:

Real or fake? In the world of art, this is an important question. Famous paintings by well-known artists can sell for millions of dollars. So people often try to sell paintings that are imitations of the real thing. When the forgeries are done well, ① spotting them can be a major challenge, even for experts.

Now, researchers say they ② have found a new way to tell the real from the fake ③ using mathematics. They start with a digital image. Then they use a mathematical technique ④ to break the image down into a collection of smaller, more basic images. This method is especially useful for comparing brush strokes. When an imitator ⑤ will try to copy a master artist, his or her brush strokes will most surely be different.

A team of researchers used this new technique to analyze eight drawings by a 16th-century artist named Pieter Brueghel the Elder. They then compared the data obtained from these drawings with measurements from five imitations. The team found that the genuine Brueghel drawings all had similar patterns. By the same measure, the fakes were different from each other and from the original drawings.

정답 및 해설 p.28

1 윗글의 주제로 가장 적절한 것은?

① how to imitate famous paintings
② how difficult it is to spot fake paintings
③ the most copied masterpieces in history
④ a new technique for finding imitation art
⑤ a famous artist whose work has many imitations

수능 어법

2 윗글의 밑줄 친 ①~⑤ 중, 어법상 <u>틀린</u> 것은?

서술형

3 다음은 윗글의 밑줄 친 <u>this new technique</u>이 의미하는 바를 나타낸 것이다. 빈칸에 들어갈 알맞은 말을 본문에서 찾아 쓰시오.

After a(n) __________ image of an imitation is broken down into smaller images, its __________ __________ are compared with those of the original painting.

대 피터르 브뤼헐 대 피터르 브뤼헐(Pieter Brueghel the Elder)은 16세기의 네덜란드 출신 화가로, 순수 풍경화를 회화 장르의 새로운 분야로 개척했다. 브뤼헐 집안은 4대에 걸쳐 많은 화가들을 배출했으며, 그의 아들들과 구별하기 위해 대(the Elder) 피터르 브뤼헐이라 불린다. 초기에는 주로 민간 전설, 미신 등을 주제로 삼았고, 후에는 소박한 농민의 모습과 농촌의 풍경을 많이 그렸다. 대표 작품으로 〈바벨탑〉, 〈눈 속의 사냥꾼〉 등이 있다.

fake 가짜(의); 모조품 **imitation** 모방; *모조품 ※**imitator** 모방자 ※**imitate** 모방하다 **forgery** 위조죄; *위조(품) **spot** 발견하다, 알아채다 **major** 주요한 **expert** 전문가 **mathematics** 수학 ※ **mathematical** 수학적인 **break down** …을 분해하다 **method** 방법 **compare** 비교하다 **stroke** 일격; *붓의 놀림 **master** *훌륭한; 대가 **analyze** 분석하다 **obtain** 획득하다; 입수하다 **measurement** 측정 ※**measure** 측정하다; *측정(방법) **genuine** 진짜의

04

238 words 3'40"

Date:

Time Taken:

English Only

Let's Play Music for Coffee

Although most of Europe had embraced the habit of drinking coffee by the 17th century, it wasn't until the second half of the 18th century that it was accepted in Germany. Before that time, many Germans, who distrusted foreign influences on their culture, saw coffee as a threat to their preferred local drink, beer. As a result, there were laws and taxes designed to discourage coffee drinking.

In 1732, the legendary composer Johann Sebastian Bach became involved in these "coffee wars" with his *Coffee Cantata*. (①) It was a comical *operetta about a traditional father and his modern, coffee-drinking daughter. (②) He tries to break her habit by telling her that she has to choose between getting married and drinking coffee. (③) Despite this threat, she sings "Ah, how sweet coffee tastes — lovelier than a thousand kisses, far sweeter than *muscatel." (④) But as much as she loves coffee, the daughter does not want to go through life unmarried. (⑤) However, she secretly explains to the men her father introduces that she won't marry anyone who tries to keep her away from coffee.

The *Coffee Cantata*, which was originally performed at a popular German coffee shop, had a simple message for its audiences: there's nothing wrong with drinking coffee. By telling a tale that pointed out the generational differences of the time in a humorous way, Bach's work amused and entertained both coffee-loving and coffee-hating Germans.

*operetta 오페레타 (내용이 가볍고 감상적인 오페라의 대중적 장르)
*muscatel 백포도주 (머스캣 포도로 만듬)

정답 및 해설 p.29

1 What is NOT mentioned in the passage?

① why Germans hated drinking coffee
② what Germans did to discourage drinking coffee
③ who composed the *Coffee Cantata*
④ where the *Coffee Cantata* was first performed
⑤ how the *Coffee Cantata* changed Germans' views toward coffee

2 Where would the given sentence best fit among ①~⑤?

Therefore, she agrees to stop drinking coffee.

서술형

3 The following sentence is the summary of the passage. Fill in the blanks using appropriate words from the passage.

The *Coffee Cantata* shows a(n) __________ gap between a traditional father and a modern daughter about drinking __________.

라이프치히 커피 박물관

독일 작센 주에 위치한 '아라비아의 커피나무'라는 카페에 속해 있는 박물관으로, 300년이 넘는 역사를 지녔다. '아라비아의 커피나무'는 1711년부터 커피를 판매하기 시작해 유럽에서 두 번째로 오래된 커피 하우스로, 괴테, 바흐, 슈만, 바그너 등의 당대 문인과 예술가들이 즐겨 찾는 명소이기도 했다. 1층은 커피숍, 2층은 레스토랑, 3층은 박물관으로 사용되고 있으며, 이곳에서 커피가 독일에 전해진 역사를 볼 수 있다. 박물관에는 바흐의 '커피 칸타타'로 알려진 〈bwv 211〉 악보도 전시되어 있다.

embrace 껴안다; *(생각 등을) 수용하다 **distrust** 불신하다 **influence** 영향(력) **threat** 위협, 위험 **design** 디자인하다; *만들다 **discourage** 의욕을 꺾다, 좌절시키다 **legendary** 전설적인, 아주 유명한 **involved in** …에 관여하는, 관련된 **comical** 웃기는, 재미있는 **break habit** 습관을 깨다 **go through** …을 겪다 **tale** 이야기 **point out** (주의를 기울이도록) 지적하다, 언급하다 **amuse** 즐겁게 하다

Review Test

· VOCA ·

A 다음 단어의 영영풀이를 바르게 연결하시오.

1 popular •	• ⓐ actual, real or true
2 enormous •	• ⓑ having great power or influence
3 legendary •	• ⓒ greatly large in amount or size
4 powerful •	• ⓓ liked or enjoyed by a lot of people
5 genuine •	• ⓔ very famous or well-known

B 괄호 안에서 적절한 단어를 고르시오.

1 The singer hopes her music will (inspire / admire) children to have dreams.

2 A healthy diet can make a big (similarity / difference) to your everyday life.

3 Scientists warn that plastic materials pose a serious (relief / threat) to the marine environment.

4 Melanie (observed / obtained) the photographer's permission to use his pictures in her book.

C 문맥상 다음 빈칸에 들어갈 가장 알맞은 단어를 고르시오.

1 He prefers not to become __________ in politics.

① contained ② involved ③ published ④ arranged ⑤ released

2 My friends and I talked about teachers who had had a positive __________ on us.

① advice ② proverb ③ attraction ④ influence ⑤ weakness

3 Parrots are the only animal that can __________ human speech.

① lead ② protect ③ imitate ④ symbolize ⑤ embrace

4 The Internet seems to have a big __________ on our lives in many ways.

① volume ② infinity ③ tale ④ result ⑤ impact

· SENTENCE ·

D

다음 문장을 밑줄 친 부분에 유의하여 우리말로 해석하시오.

1 By covering her artwork in dots, she is connecting it to the rest of the universe.

▸ ______________________________

2 Looking around, it seemed as though she were standing in a field of endless dots.

▸ ______________________________

3 After the release of the book, he, as well as calligrams, became popular around the world.

▸ ______________________________

4 Calligrams can be made using computer programs, so they are easier to make and can include a wide range of colors.

▸ ______________________________

E

우리말에 맞게 주어진 단어들을 바르게 배열하여 문장을 완성하시오.

1 이는 그녀의 모든 예술 작품이 점으로 덮여 있다는 한 가지 공통점이 있기 때문이다.

This is because all of her artwork (thing / in / common / one / has) — it is covered in dots.

▸ This is because all of her artwork ______________________ — it is covered in dots.

2 그래서 종종 사람들은 진짜 그림의 모조품을 팔려고 한다.

So people often try to sell paintings (that / the real thing / imitations / are / of).

▸ So people often try to sell paintings ______________________.

3 결과적으로, 커피 마시는 것을 자제시키려 만들어진 법과 세금이 있었다.

As a result, there were laws and taxes (to / coffee drinking / designed / discourage).

▸ As a result, there were laws and taxes ______________________.

CAMPAIGN IN THE WORLD

• 기부와 공유 •

SHARETHEMEAL

식사를 나눠요

ShareTheMeal은 식사 기부 애플리케이션으로, 제로 헝거(Zero Hunger) 즉, 굶주림으로 고통받는 전 세계 아이들의 수를 0(zero)로 만드는 것을 목표로 하는 WFP(World Food Programme, 유엔세계식량계획)의 공식 프로젝트이다. 이 애플리케이션의 사용자들은 스마트폰을 한 번 탭하기만 하면 굶주리는 어린이들에게 건강한 식사를 기부할 수 있다. 이 프로젝트의 핵심 가치는 투명성, 효율성, 지속 가능성으로, 기부자는 끼니당 500원인 기부금이 어떻게 쓰이는지를 바로 확인할 수 있다. 참여가 쉽고 기부 효과가 즉각적이라는 특성 덕분에 이 애플리케이션은 금세 인기를 끌었고, 현재까지 수천만 끼니가 기부되었다.

#GIVEASHIT

똥 이모지를 활용한 이색 캠페인

전 세계 인구의 1/3이나 되는 많은 이들이 비위생적인 화장실 환경으로 고통받고 있다는 것을 알고 있는 이는 많지 않을 것이다. 이러한 사실을 사람들에게 알리고 대중의 관심을 촉구하고자 비영리 단체인 워터에이드(WaterAid)는 아주 이색적인 캠페인을 펼쳤다. 바로 #GIVEASHIT 캠페인으로, 사람들이 Wateraid Emoji Creator 라는 무료 애플리케이션을 이용해 똥 모양 이모지를 직접 디자인하고, 그 이모지를 #GIVEASHIT이라는 해시태그를 통해 공유할 수 있게 하였다. 이 캠페인은 인스타그램이나 트위터 등의 SNS에서 유명 인사와 그 팔로워들을 통해 퍼져 나갔으며, 워터에이드는 1만여 명의 신규 후원자를 확보할 수 있었다.

SECTION 05

유머 · 감동

01 딱 한 번만 팔았을 뿐인데…

204 words 3'00"

Date:
Time Taken:

A confident new employee at the region's largest department store told his manager at the beginning of his first shift, "I'm the world's greatest salesperson." The manager laughed skeptically and replied, "We shall see."

At closing time, when the manager inquired how many sales the man had made, he replied that he had made a single sale. The manager turned red with rage and shouted that most of his coworkers had made dozens of sales worth hundreds of dollars. The man winked and explained that his one sale was worth $50,000.

"Fifty thousand dollars?" gasped the astonished manager. "How is that possible?"

"Well, first I sold the customer a fishing rod, along with some expensive fishing gear. Then, after I informed him that the biggest fish are in the middle of the lake, I sold him a new speedboat. And since he was ⓐ(worry) that his vehicle wasn't powerful enough to tow the boat, I sold him a new four-wheel-drive SUV."

"You're kidding! A customer wanted to purchase a fishing rod, and you sold him all that?" asked the manager.

"Actually, he came in to buy some aspirin, and I convinced him that fishing is the best ⓑ<u>remedy</u> for a headache," answered the employee.

성공하는 세일즈맨의 전략

데일 카네기의 『인간관계론』에서 제시하는 설득 방법 중 하나는, 자신과 의견이 다른 상대방의 말에 반박하지 말고 그대로 들어주라는 것이다. 구체적인 사례로 화이트 모터 사의 최우수 판매원이었던 패트릭 J. 오헤어의 이야기가 실려 있다. 고객이 화이트 사의 트럭보다 경쟁사의 트럭을 더 좋아한다고 말하면, 이 판매원은 고객의 말에 우선 동의하며 경쟁사 제품의 장점을 늘어놓기 시작했다. 그러면 고객은 곧 기세가 꺾이고, 경쟁사 트럭에 관해 말하기를 그만두게 된다. 이때 자사 트럭만의 장점을 부각시켜 고객의 마음을 돌리는 것이 이 판매원의 영업 비밀이었다.

정답 및 해설 p.32

1 윗글의 제목으로 가장 적절한 것은?

① A Valuable Lesson from a Failure
② Dealing with an Angry Customer
③ How an Amazing Salesperson Works
④ The Most Effective Way to Treat a Headache
⑤ A Manager Who Makes a Profit of $50,000 a Day

2 윗글의 영업 사원이 고객에게 사라고 권하지 않은 것은?

① 아스피린 ② 낚싯대 ③ 낚시 장비
④ 고속 모터보트 ⑤ 자동차

서술형

3 윗글의 ⓐ에 주어진 동사를 어법에 알맞은 형태로 쓰시오.

VOCA

4 윗글의 밑줄 친 ⓑremedy와 바꿔 쓸 수 있는 말로 가장 적절한 것은?

① cure ② care ③ injury
④ reason ⑤ result

confident 자신감 있는 **employee** 종업원, 고용인 **region** 지방, 지역 **shift** 변화; *교대 근무 (시간) **salesperson** 판매원 **skeptically** 회의적으로 **inquire** 묻다 **sale** 판매 **rage** 분노, 격노 **coworker** 협력자, 동료 **dozens of** 수십의, 많은 **worth** …의 가치가 있는[되는] **gasp** 숨이 턱 막히다, 헉 하고 숨을 쉬다 **astonished** 깜짝 놀란 **fishing rod** 낚싯대 **gear** 장비 **inform** 알리다 **speedboat** 고속 모터보트, 쾌속정 **vehicle** 차량, 탈것 **tow** 끌다, 견인하다 **four-wheel-drive** 사륜구동의 **purchase** 구입하다 **convince** 납득시키다, 확신시키다 **remedy** 치료(약) 문제 **effective** 효과적인 **make a profit** 이윤을 내다

02

공연하기 참 힘드네

166 words 2'40"

Date:

Time Taken:

The leader of a rock band (difficult, it, get, extremely, ready, to, was finding) for an important performance because the members of the band were never all present at any of the rehearsals. Then the final rehearsal before the show came, and again one of the band members was not there. At the end of the rehearsal, the leader gathered all the members of the band who were present and said, "I have been making a note of everyone who has been absent from our rehearsals. Here it is." He took a piece of paper out of his pocket and looked at it carefully. "I see that there is only one member who has been hard-working and ____________ enough to be present at every rehearsal. That person is Billy, our drummer." The drummer's face suddenly went very red. He slowly stood up and answered, "Well, I thought it was the right thing to do... since I won't be able to come to the concert tomorrow night."

rock band

록 음악 Rock Music

록 음악은 1950년대 초 미국에서 생겨난 대중음악의 한 장르로, 강렬한 기타 혹은 드럼 소리가 특징이다. 록 밴드는 일반적으로 보컬리스트, 리드 기타리스트, 리듬 기타리스트, 베이시스트, 드러머 등의 멤버로 구성되며, 이 형태는 비틀즈가 확립했다. 록 음악은 처음 등장하자마자 전 세계 젊은 층을 중심으로 급속도로 퍼져나가 그들의 문화를 대변하는 상징으로 자리잡았다. 기성 세대들은 이런 현상을 일시적인 유행으로 생각해 무시하거나 사회에 대한 도전이라고 비난했다. 하지만, 1960년대 중반, 록 음악은 음악 형식의 하나로 확고히 자리잡으며 폭넓은 인기와 관심을 끌게 되고, 이후 음반 사업뿐 아니라 영화, 패션 트렌드에까지 그 영향력을 미치며 오늘날까지 계속 발전해오고 있다.

정답 및 해설 p.33

1 빌리의 대답을 듣고 난 후, 록 밴드 리더의 심경 변화로 가장 적절한 것은?

① sad → happy ② jealous → upset
③ angry → envious ④ satisfied → sympathetic
⑤ grateful → disappointed

서술형

2 윗글의 괄호 안에 주어진 단어들을 다음 우리말에 맞게 배열하시오.

준비를 하는 것이 매우 어렵다는 것을 알았다

→ ______________________________

3 윗글의 빈칸에 들어갈 말로 가장 적절한 것은?

① rude ② faithful ③ humble
④ arrogant ⑤ stubborn

4 윗글의 내용과 일치하면 T에, 일치하지 않으면 F에 표시하시오.

	T	F
(1) The leader of the band has been making a note of who has been absent from the rehearsals.	□	□
(2) The drummer of the band didn't take part in most of the rehearsals.	□	□

extremely 대단히, 몹시 **performance** 공연 **present** 참석한 **gather** 모으다 **make a note of** …을 적어 두다 **be absent from** …에 결석하다 **문제** **envious** 부러워하는 **sympathetic** 동정심 있는 **grateful** 감사하는 **faithful** 충실한, 성실한 **humble** 겸손한 **arrogant** 오만한 **stubborn** 완고한

03

앙카라의 헌책 도서관

241 words 3'20"

Date:

Time Taken:

What happens to old books when their owners don't want them anymore? Sadly, many of them are tossed into the trash. Sanitation workers in Ankara, Turkey, noticed this, so they began to rescue the books and bring them back to the sanitation department's headquarters. As their collection grew larger and larger, these kind-hearted workers decided to put the books to good use.

(A) [Working / Worked] together, they created their own library. At first it was only used by their friends and families, but soon they opened it to the public. The library is located in their headquarters, and it includes more than 6,000 books. There are textbooks, comic books, children's books, science fiction novels, and more! The library even includes a lounge, (B) [which / where] local people can drink tea, play chess, or just sit back and enjoy a good book.

Today, the library continues to expand. It has become an essential part of the local community. People now donate their unwanted books directly to the library. And thanks to the local government, it now has a full-time librarian. There are even plans to convert an old garbage truck into a mobile library, which will be driven around the city and to nearby villages, bringing books to people who need them.

All of this began with some sanitation workers who didn't want to see books (C) [go / to go] to waste. Together, they showed the world that anyone can take action and make their community a better place.

터키의 공공 도서관

터키의 인구는 약 7천만 명으로, 유럽에서는 러시아와 독일 다음으로 인구가 많은 반면, 인구 대비 공공 도서관의 수는 턱없이 부족한 것으로 드러났다. 2017년 국제 도서관 협회(IFLA)가 조사한 결과에 따르면 유럽 연합(EU) 국가 국민들은 평균 6,200명당 하나의 도서관을 공유하는 반면, 터키의 공공 도서관은 총 1,143개로 국민 70,000 명이 하나의 도서관을 공유하고 있다. 아울러 터키는 도서관 이용자 수, 도서관 직원의 수 또한 유럽 최하위이다. 이에 터키 내에서도 체계적이고 장기적인 도서관 설립 사업의 필요성이 꾸준히 제기되고 있다. 앙카라의 헌책 도서관은 이처럼 열악한 터키의 공공 도서관 이용에 작게나마 활력을 불어넣을 것으로 기대되고 있다.

정답 및 해설 p.35

1

윗글의 제목으로 가장 적절한 것은?

① The Oldest Library in Turkey
② Sanitation Workers Turn Trash into Treasure
③ A Library Building in Ankara Built from Junk
④ A Single Simple Idea That Made a City Clean
⑤ Read One, Give One: A New Donation Culture

2

도서관에 관한 윗글의 내용과 일치하지 <u>않는</u> 것은?

① 터키 환경미화원들의 아이디어로 탄생했다.
② 처음에는 환경미화원들의 지인과 가족들만 이용했다.
③ 공중 위생부 본부에 위치해 있다.
④ 수천 권의 책뿐만 아니라 편의 시설도 갖추고 있다.
⑤ 오래된 트럭을 개조한 이동 도서관도 운영 중이다.

수능 어법

3

윗글의 (A), (B), (C)의 각 네모 안에서 어법에 맞는 표현으로 가장 적절한 것은?

	(A)		(B)		(C)
①	Working	……	which	……	go
②	Working	……	where	……	go
③	Working	……	where	……	to go
④	Worked	……	which	……	go
⑤	Worked	……	where	……	to go

toss 던지다 **sanitation** 위생 시설[관리] **rescue** 구하다, 구조하다 **headquarters** 본사, 본부 **kind-hearted** 마음씨 고운, 인정 많은 **public** 일반 사람들, 대중 **lounge** 라운지, 휴게실 **local** 지역의, 현지의 **expand** 확대시키다; *확장되다 **essential** 필수적인 **community** 지역 사회 **donate** 기부[기증]하다 ※ **donation** 기부, 기증 **government** 정부 **librarian** 사서 **convert** 개조하다 **garbage** 쓰레기 **mobile** 이동하는, 이동식의 **take action** (…에 대해) 조치를 취하다 문제 **treasure** 보물 **single** 단 하나의, 단일의

04

253 words 3'50"

Date:

Time Taken:

English Only

Never Stop Running!

As a group of girls speeds across the finish line, one girl seems to be having trouble. Her legs begin shaking, making her lose her balance. A moment later, she falls into her coach's waiting arms. The same thing happens every time she races.

Her name is Kayla Montgomery, and she was diagnosed with *multiple sclerosis at age fifteen. Once, during a soccer game, she started to feel something wrong on her legs and back and suddenly fell down. After months of tests, Kayla learned that she had multiple sclerosis. Known as MS, it is a disease that interrupts communication between the brain and other body parts. Because MS blocks her nerves from properly sending signals, particularly when she's warm, she cannot sense the pain that other runners feel.

This makes running dangerous for her because she can't feel her legs by the end of the race. So, she could fall and hurt herself. In addition, she damages tissues in her body when she keeps running. Kayla gets help at every finish line, where her coach catches her and her parents put ice on her legs to bring the sensation back.

Kayla won the North Carolina state title in March 2014. Her next goal is winning the national title. She has said she was scared that she might not be able to run much longer. Nevertheless, she has decided to focus on what she's able to do now. MS may not have a cure, but that isn't going to stop her from running.

*multiple sclerosis 다발성 경화증

정답 및 해설 p.36

1 What is the third paragraph of the passage mainly about?

① how to cure MS patients
② what Kayla's coach does for her
③ how Kayla got MS and what it is
④ the athletic advantages of having MS
⑤ dangers an MS patient faces when running

VOCA

2 Which is the closest in meaning to the underlined word "interrupts"?

① intends ② disturbs ③ supports
④ interprets ⑤ distinguishes

서술형

3 Fill in the blanks using appropriate words from the passage.

Kayla can't feel the __________ in her legs when she runs because MS stops her nerves from sending __________ properly.

다발성 경화증
Multiple Sclerosis

다발성 경화증이란 신경세포를 둘러싸고 있는 껍질이 벗겨져 염증이 생기는 질환이다. 이 병에 걸리면 중추신경에 이상이 생겨 신경 신호가 정상적으로 전달되지 않고, 신경세포는 점차 죽게 된다. 감각이 무뎌지거나 상황에 맞지 않는 갑작스러운 이상감각을 느끼고, 몸의 일부분이나 팔다리가 마비되는 등의 증상을 보인다. 정확한 원인은 밝혀지지 않았으며, 증상을 완화시킬 수는 있지만 완치 방법은 아직 발견되지 않았다.

speed 속도; *빨리 가다[이동하다] **balance** 균형 **race** 경주; *경주하다 **be diagnosed with** …로 진단받다 **fall down** 넘어지다 **interrupt** 방해하다, 중단시키다 **nerve** 신경 **properly** 제대로, 적절히 **signal** 신호 **particularly** 특히 **sense** 감각; *감지하다, 느끼다 **damage** 손상을 주다 **tissue** (세포들로 이루어진) 조직 **bring ... back** …을 다시 가져다 주다 **sensation** 느낌; *감각 **cure** 치료법

Review Test

• VOCA •

A 다음 중 단어의 뜻풀이가 잘못된 것을 고르시오.

① local: belonging to the area where you live
② mobile: able to travel or move from place to place
③ confident: being sure about one's own abilities or ideas
④ present: not in the place where you are supposed to be
⑤ cure: a medical treatment that makes a sick person healthy

B 괄호 안에서 적절한 단어를 고르시오.

1 The fire fighter (endangered / rescued) a kid from the burning building.
2 Do you have any medicine that is (attractive / effective) for headaches?
3 I (required / inquired) whether the plane would arrive on time.
4 You need to (convince / consider) Mr. Brown that he should see a doctor.

C 문맥상 다음 빈칸에 들어갈 가장 알맞은 단어를 고르시오.

1 It's rude to __________ when another person is speaking.
① sense ② involve ③ damage ④ interrupt ⑤ imagine

2 We were __________ by the loud noise and went outside to see where it came from.
① diagnosed ② expanded ③ bored ④ tossed ⑤ astonished

3 All of them are going to work the morning __________ next month.
① part ② shift ③ balance ④ coworker ⑤ employee

4 My daughter wants to save the money and __________ it to an animal rescue center.
① gather ② release ③ purchase ④ donate ⑤ convert

정답 및 해설 p.38

• SENTENCE •

D

다음 문장을 밑줄 친 부분에 유의하여 우리말로 해석하시오.

1 Her legs begin shaking, making her lose her balance.

▸ ______________________________

2 He was worried that his vehicle wasn't powerful enough to tow the boat.

▸ ______________________________

3 As their collection grew larger and larger, they decided to put the books to good use.

▸ ______________________________

4 I have been making a note of everyone who has been absent from our rehearsals.

▸ ______________________________

E

우리말에 맞게 주어진 단어들을 바르게 배열하여 문장을 완성하시오.

1 그럼에도 불구하고, 그녀는 지금 할 수 있는 것에 집중하기로 결심했다.

Nevertheless, she has decided to (to / she's / now / on / do / able / what / focus).

▸ Nevertheless, she has decided to ______________________.

2 이 모든 것은 책이 쓰레기가 되는 것을 보고 싶지 않았던 환경미화원들 몇 명으로 시작되었다.

All of this began with some sanitation workers (to see / to / want / books / didn't / waste / who / go).

▸ All of this began with some sanitation workers ______________________.

3 관리자는 그의 동료 대부분이 수백 달러어치의 판매 수십 건을 성사시켰다고 큰 소리로 말했다.

The manager shouted that most of his coworkers had made (sales / dollars / worth / dozens of / hundreds of).

▸ The manager shouted that most of his coworkers had made ______________________.

표현의 유래

3

RAIN CHECK

rain check는 문자 그대로 '우천 교환권'이라는 뜻으로, 1870년대부터 미국의 야구장에서 시행되던 관행과 관련이 있다. 비가 오면 야구 경기를 할 수 없었기 때문에, 비가 올 경우 구단은 관중들에게 'rain check'라는 표를 지급했다. 관중들은 이 표를 가지고 나중에 비로 연기된 경기를 다시 관람할 수 있었다. 이후 어떤 일에 당장 응할 수 없어서 적당한 때로 미루거나 미래를 기약하는 말을 할 때 사용하는 표현으로 굳어지게 되었다.

오늘 밤에 영화 보러 갈래? /
미안하지만 이미 계획이 있어. 다음 기회로 미룰게.

SECTION 06

유래

01

Dutch가 대체 뭘 어쨌길래

168 words 2'40"
Date:
Time Taken:

When ① <u>referred</u> to people or things from the Netherlands, we use the word "Dutch." But did you ever notice that many expressions ② <u>containing</u> the word "Dutch" have ____________? A typical example is "Dutch treat," also known as "Dutch pay." It is used when you eat with someone at a restaurant and split the bill. The expression makes it ③ <u>seem</u> as if the Dutch are not generous, even among friends. There are many other examples. A "Dutch bargain" is an agreement made after ④ <u>drinking</u> alcohol. "Dutch courage" is bravery people show when drunk. "Dutch concert" means a lot of noise or confusion. And a "Dutch uncle" is a person who ruins others' fun by ⑤ <u>scolding them over</u> trivial matters.

Where did these expressions come from? It is believed that most of them were made by the English in the 17th century. At that time, the English and Dutch were competing for power on the seas. So English sailors would make up these phrases to insult their rivals.

영국-네덜란드 전쟁
Anglo-Dutch Wars

17세기 중반, 영국과 네덜란드가 동방 무역권을 두고 세 차례에 걸쳐 벌인 해상 전쟁이다. 당시 네덜란드는 동방 무역으로 막대한 수익을 올리고 있었다. 이에 위기를 느낀 영국이 1651년 영국이 점령한 항구에 영국 선박을 통해서만 상품을 들일 수 있다는 항해 조례를 선포함으로써, 1652년 1차 전쟁이 발발했다. 2차 전쟁은 1665년 영국이 네덜란드 식민지를 점령하여 발발하였고, 3차 전쟁은 1672년 프랑스 루이 14세와 연합한 영국이 네덜란드를 공격하여 일어났다. 영국에 비해 해군의 조직력이 약했던 네덜란드는 해상 지배권을 차츰 영국에게 내주게 되었고, 영국은 이를 계기로 본격적인 동방 무역에 진출할 수 있었다.

정답 및 해설 p.39

1 윗글의 빈칸에 들어갈 말로 가장 적절한 것은?

① a negative feeling
② a historical lesson
③ a way to split the bill
④ information about the Dutch
⑤ ideas on how to make friends

2 윗글에서 언급된 표현과 그 의미가 바르게 연결되지 않은 것은?

① Dutch treat: 식사 후 각자 계산하는 것
② Dutch bargain: 술을 마신 후에 맺은 합의
③ Dutch courage: 술에 취했을 때 생기는 용기
④ Dutch concert: 지루하고 따분한 콘서트
⑤ Dutch uncle: 잔소리로 분위기를 깨는 사람

수능어법

3 윗글의 밑줄 친 ①~⑤ 중, 어법상 틀린 것은?

서술형

4 윗글의 내용과 일치하도록 빈칸에 알맞은 말을 본문에서 찾아 쓰시오.

To __________ the Dutch, the __________ made up bad expressions about the Dutch because they were rivals in the 17th century.

refer to …을 언급하다 **contain** …이 들어 있다 **typical** 전형적인, 대표적인 **split the bill** (비용 따위를) 각자 부담하다, 나눠 내다 **generous** 후한 **agreement** 협정, 합의 **bravery** 용기, 용감 **confusion** 혼란 **ruin** 망치다 **scold** 야단치다, 꾸짖다 **trivial** 사소한 **compete for** …을 위해 싸우다 **phrase** 구(句) **insult** 모욕하다

02

마법에 걸린 세 자매

163 words 2'30"

Date:

Time Taken:

Among the many beautiful landmarks in Australia's Blue Mountains, the most iconic place is the Three Sisters. These sandstone peaks are known for their great beauty. But why are they called the Three sisters?

According to aboriginal legends, there were three sisters named Meehni, Wimlah, and Gunnedoo who lived in the Jamison Valley as members of the Katoomba tribe. These beautiful young ladies fell in love with three brothers from the Nepean tribe, but marriage between the two tribes was forbidden. The outraged brothers decided to capture the three sisters, (A) [sparked / sparking] a great battle between the tribes.

In order to protect the three sisters from all of the fighting, a witch doctor from the Katoomba tribe turned them into stone. He (B) [has intended / had intended] to transform them back into humans when the battle was over, but he was killed during the fighting. Since there was no one (C) [changed / to change] the sisters back, they remain to this day as magnificent stone pillars overlooking the valley.

블루 마운틴즈
Blue Mountains

시드니에서 서쪽으로 약 100km 떨어진 곳에 있는 블루 마운틴즈는 웅장한 산악 지대이다. 산을 뒤덮고 있는 유칼립투스 나무의 잎에서 나오는 유액이 태양열에 의해 증발하면서 푸른 안개를 발생시키는 현상 때문에 '블루 마운틴즈'라는 이름이 붙었다. 약 5억 년 전에 형성된 것으로 추정되며, 국토 전체가 평평한 호주에서는 드물게 1,000m급의 구릉이 이어지는 곳이다. 협곡, 폭포, 기암 등 다양한 지형이 자아내는 경관이 수려하여 등산이나 관광, 드라이브 코스, 휴양지로 사랑받는다.

정답 및 해설 p.41

1 윗글의 제목으로 가장 적절한 것은?

① Great Places to Go on Vacation
② Australia's Most Famous Legend
③ Why the Three Sisters Are So Popular
④ How the Three Sisters Got Its Name
⑤ A Symbol of Beauty: The Three Sisters

수능어법

2 윗글의 (A), (B), (C)의 각 네모 안에서 어법에 맞는 표현으로 가장 적절한 것은?

	(A)		(B)		(C)
①	sparked	……	has intended	……	changed
②	sparked	……	had intended	……	changed
③	sparked	……	had intended	……	to change
④	sparking	……	has intended	……	changed
⑤	sparking	……	had intended	……	to change

서술형

3 주어진 질문에 대한 답을 할 때, 빈칸에 들어갈 알맞은 말을 본문에서 찾아 쓰시오.

Why did the witch doctor turn the three sisters into stone?
→ In order to __________ them from all of the __________.

landmark 주요 지형지물 **iconic** …의 상징이 되는 **sandstone** 사암(沙巖) **peak** (산의) 봉우리, 꼭대기 **be known for** …로 알려져 있다 **aboriginal** (오스트레일리아) 원주민의 **legend** 전설 **valley** 계곡, 골짜기 **tribe** 부족 **fall in love with** …와 사랑에 빠지다 **forbidden** 금지된 **outraged** 격분한 **capture** 포로로 잡다 **spark** 촉발시키다, 유발하다 **battle** 전투 **witch doctor** 주술사 **intend to-v** …하려고 의도[작정]하다 **transform** 변형시키다 **magnificent** 아주 아름다운, 훌륭한 **pillar** 기둥 **overlook** 간과하다; *바라보다, 내려다보다

03

199 words 3'00"

Date:

Time Taken:

물음표? 느낌표!

There is a famous story concerning the great author Victor Hugo. In 1862, after completing *Les Misérables*, Hugo sent the manuscript to his publishers. It was accompanied by a note that simply read, "?". The publishers understood that Hugo was asking what they thought of his latest work. After reading it, they sent a note in reply. It read, "!".

It's a funny story, but did you ever wonder about the origin of those two common punctuation marks? No one is exactly sure where they came from, but (that, created, is, the question mark, it, by, believed, was, early scholars). When writing in Latin, they would write *questio* at the end of sentences to indicate that they were questions. This was eventually shortened to *qo* to save space. The lowercase *q* was written atop the *o* and over time the two letters evolved into the question mark.

As for the exclamation mark, it is thought to have been created through a similar process. The Latin word *io* means "an exclamation of joy." The word was written with one letter above the other at the end of sentences, and it was slowly transformed into the punctuation mark we know today.

쉼표, 마침표. Comma, Period.

기원전 3세기, 알렉산드리아 도서관 사서인 아리스토파네스는 문장부호 없이 글자들이 이어진 그리스어 연설문을 읽을 때 의미를 더 정확하게 전달할 수 있도록 단어들 사이에 점 찍기를 제안했다. 점의 위치는 위, 가운데, 아래의 세 곳으로 높이에 따라 쉬는 간격을 달리했다. 그러나 이 방식은 로마 시대에 들어 버려졌다가 6세기의 기독교 문헌에서 다시 나타난다. 이때 맨 위의 점은 문장을 끝내는 역할을, 맨 아래의 점은 쉬어 가는 역할로 정해졌다. 그러나 점을 찍는 위치에 따른 구별은 서서히 흐려졌고, 12세기 이탈리아의 학자가 제안한 부호 /(slash)가 맨 아래 점의 기능을 대체하고 모양이 변형된 결과 ,(comma)가 되었으며, 아리스토파네스의 점은 .(period)의 형태로만 남게 되었다.

정답 및 해설 p.42

1 **윗글의 주제로 가장 적절한 것은?**

① a strange habit of Victor Hugo
② the history of punctuation marks
③ various ways of asking questions
④ the most valuable ancient invention
⑤ the significance of the Latin language

서술형

2 **윗글의 괄호 안에 주어진 단어들을 다음 우리말에 맞게 배열하시오.**

물음표는 고대 학자들에 의해 만들어졌다고 여겨진다

→ ______________________________

VOCA

3 **윗글의 밑줄 친 transformed의 의미로 가장 적절한 것은?**

① gone ② made ③ fallen
④ changed ⑤ transferred

4 **윗글의 내용과 일치하면 T에, 일치하지 않으면 F에 표시하시오.**

	T	F
(1) 라틴어에서는 문장 끝에 *qo*를 붙여서 의문문이라는 것을 나타냈다.	□	□
(2) *io*는 라틴어로 '놀라서 지르는 외침'을 의미한다.	□	□

concerning …에 관한 **manuscript** (책 · 악보 등의) 원고 **publisher** 출판인, 출판사 **accompany** 동반[동행]하다 **read** 읽다; *(…라고) 적혀[쓰여] 있다 **punctuation mark** 구두점, 문장 부호 **scholar** 학자 **indicate** 나타내다 **shorten** 짧게 하다, 줄이다 **lowercase** 소문자의, 소문자로 인쇄한 **atop** 꼭대기에, 맨 위에 **evolve** 발달하다; *진화하다 **as for** …에 대해서 말하자면 **exclamation** 외침, 감탄사
문제 **significance** 중요성, 의의

04

223 words 3'30"

Date:

Time Taken:

English Only

What Did You Just Say?

Those who enjoy puns and word games will also have fun with "spoonerisms." A spoonerism is the mixing of sounds in a phrase that makes the phrase itself sound funny, either intentionally or by mistake. Some spoonerisms involve confusion of consonant sounds, as in saying "fight a liar" rather than "① light a fire." Others occur when the vowel sounds are mixed up, like when "feel like a fool" becomes "② fool like a feel." Spoonerisms often result in nonsense, but the funniest are those that change the meaning altogether, such as saying "I'm a damp stealer" instead of "③ I'm a stamp dealer."

Spoonerisms are named after *Rev. William A. Spooner, warden of New College in Oxford around the turn of the 20th century. Popular, kind, and intelligent, Spooner was famous for these peculiar slips of the tongue. Hilariously, he was seldom aware that he was making such mistakes.

It is thought that Spooner's classic mistakes included "you've tasted two worms" instead of "you've wasted two terms," "a blushing crow" for "④ a crushing blow," and "our queer old Dean" when he meant "⑤ our dear old Queen." Although some doubted the authenticity of these quotes, the Spooner legend grew bigger and bigger. The term "spoonerism" was officially incorporated into the English language while he was still in his fifties, marking his amusing place in history forever.

*Rev. 선생, 목사 (= Reverend)

1 **Which of the following is NOT true about spoonerism?**

① It is made by switching sounds in a phrase.

② It can be created on purpose or by accident.

③ Mixed up phrases can mean totally different things.

④ It was named after a warden of Oxford.

⑤ This term became an official word after Spooner died.

2 **Which is an example of a spoonerism among ①~⑤?**

서술형

3 **Write what the underlined "such mistakes" refers to using words from the passage. (4 words)**

It refers to the strange ______________________ Spooner made when speaking.

말장난 Pun 동음이의어나 다의어를 이용해 말장난하는 것을 pun이라고 한다. 예를 들어, Q: What do you call a deer with no eyes? (눈이 없는 사슴을 뭐라고 부를까?) A: No idea. 라는 pun이 있다. 여기서 No idea는 '모른다'를 의미하는 동시에, 'No eye deer'와 발음이 같다는 점을 노린 말장난이다. pun은 단순히 농담뿐만 아니라, 문학 속에서 인물의 성격이나 주제를 드러내는 장치로 쓰이기도 한다. 셰익스피어는 pun을 여러 작품 속에 적극적으로 사용했으며, 루이스 캐럴의 『이상한 나라의 앨리스』도 다양한 pun이 쓰인 것으로 유명하다.

pun 말장난 **intentionally** 의도적으로, 고의로 **involve** 수반[포함]하다 **consonant** 자음 **vowel** 모음 **nonsense** 터무니 없는 생각; *뜻이 통하지 않는 말 **damp** 축축한 **stealer** 도둑 **warden** 관리인; *학장 **peculiar** 이상한, 기이한; 특유한 **slip** (작은) 실수 **tongue** 혀; *언어 **hilariously** 아주 재미있게 **seldom** 좀처럼[거의] …않는 **aware** …을 알고 있는 **blushing** 얼굴이 빨개진; *부끄러워[수줍어]하는 **queer** 기묘한, 괴상한 **dean** 학장 **doubt** 의심; 의문을 갖다 **authenticity** 진실성; 진짜임 **quote** 인용 **incorporate** 포함하다

Review Test

• VOCA •

A

다음 단어의 영영풀이를 바르게 연결하시오.

1 quote •		• ⓐ to think something is not true
2 scold •		• ⓑ to spoil or destroy something completely
3 doubt •		• ⓒ a building or place that is easily recognized
4 ruin •		• ⓓ to criticize someone because of his or her behavior
5 landmark •		• ⓔ something said or written by someone else

B

괄호 안에서 적절한 단어를 고르시오.

1 They are going to (perform / transform) this basement into a gallery.

2 It is believed that birds (evolved / involved) from dinosaurs.

3 You can see (magnetic / magnificent) buildings in European countries.

4 The house is on the hill, (overlooking / overtaking) the whole town.

C

문맥상 다음 빈칸에 들어갈 가장 알맞은 단어를 고르시오.

1 Although he didn't __________ to hurt Susan's feeling, she felt bad.

① doubt ② matter ③ intend ④ bother ⑤ recognize

2 Brian is an American, but he speaks Korean as if it were his mother __________.

① religion ② tongue ③ tradition ④ phrase ⑤ vocabulary

3 Jack __________ me several times, but I tried to forgive him.

① pulled ② admitted ③ wondered ④ insulted ⑤ responded

4 I asked Mori to __________ me on a trip to Spain next month.

① split ② compete ③ capture ④ recommend ⑤ accompany

정답 및 해설 p.45

• SENTENCE •

D

다음 문장을 밑줄 친 부분에 유의하여 우리말로 해석하시오.

1 These sandstone peaks are known for their great beauty.

▸ ______________________________

2 Hilariously, he was seldom aware that he was making such mistakes.

▸ ______________________________

3 The expression makes it seem as if the Dutch are not generous, even among friends.

▸ ______________________________

4 The publishers understood that Hugo was asking what they thought of his latest work.

▸ ______________________________

E

우리말에 맞게 주어진 단어들을 바르게 배열하여 문장을 완성하시오.

1 그것은 어구를 재미있게 들리게 만드는 어구 내에서의 소리들의 혼합이다.

It is the mixing of sounds in a phrase (sound / makes / that / funny / the phrase).

▸ It is the mixing of sounds in a phrase ______________.

2 그는 전투가 끝나면 그들을 다시 사람으로 되돌려놓을 작정이었다.

He had intended to (them / transform / humans / into / back) when the battle was over.

▸ He had intended to ______________ when the battle was over.

3 '더치 엉클'은 사소한 일로 사람들을 꾸짖음으로써 다른 사람들의 즐거움을 망치는 사람이다.

A "Dutch uncle" is a person who ruins others' fun (scolding / over / them / by) trivial matters.

▸ A "Dutch uncle" is a person who ruins others' fun ______________ trivial matters.

CAMPAIGN IN THE WORLD

• 장애인 •

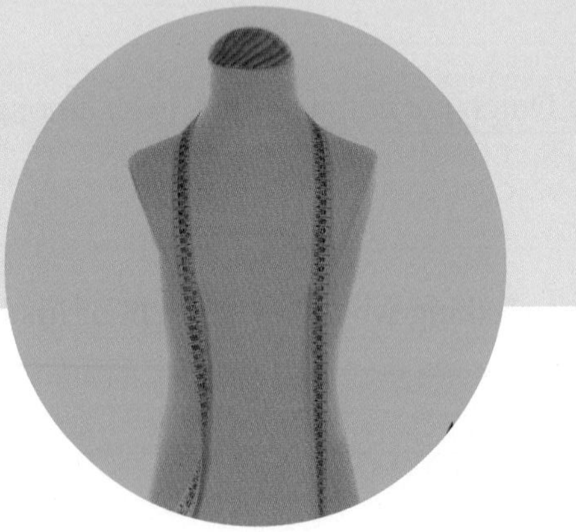

BECAUSE WHO IS PERFECT?

장애인 마네킹

상점의 쇼윈도를 보면 비율이 완벽한 인체를 형상화한 마네킹이 서 있다. 스위스의 장애인 복지단체 Pro Infirmis에서는 이런 쇼윈도 안에 한쪽 다리가 짧거나, 허리가 굽거나 휠체어를 타고 있는 마네킹을 진열하는 캠페인을 벌였다. 장애인도 비장애인과 마찬가지로 옷을 구매해 입는다. 하지만 옷, 신발 등의 제품은 대부분 비장애인을 기준으로 만들어지고 마케팅 역시 비장애인을 기준으로만 이루어진다. 이 캠페인은 쇼윈도에 진열된 마네킹을 바꾸는 간단한 방법으로 장애인에 대한 사회적 편견을 꼬집으며 전체 사회에 메시지를 보냈다.

EMPLOY THE DISABLED

장애인 고용 촉진을 위한 캠페인

브라질의 장애인 스포츠협회에서 제작한 공익광고는 어느 회사의 주차장을 계속 보여 준다. 그 영상 안에서 한참의 시간이 흐르고 여러 차들이 오가는 와중에도 그 누구도 장애인용 주차 공간에는 차를 주차하지 않는다. 아마 대부분의 사람들은 이 영상을 보고, '장애인에 대한 인식이 많이 높아졌구나.'하고 생각할 것이다. 하지만 이 영상은 장애인용 주차 공간에 주차를 하지 말자는 의도로 제작된 것이 아니라 장애인이 이 회사에 다니지 않는다는 것을 보여 주기 위한 것이다. 장애인에 대한 인식을 높이고 배려하는 것을 넘어, 장애인 고용 차별을 그만두어야 한다는 메시지를 전달하였다.

SECTION 07

의학 · 건강

01

먹어도 먹어도 또 먹고 싶은

180 words 2'50"

Date:

Time Taken:

When we feel hungry, a good meal soon leaves us full and satisfied. But imagine if, (how, no, much, matter, ate, you), the uncontrollable desire to eat never left you. Children with Prader-Willi syndrome (PWS) actually suffer from this constant hunger. Sometimes it even causes them to eat soil, paper, or almost anything they can put into their mouths.

PWS is caused by a disorder in a part of the brain called the *hypothalamus, which controls ____(A)____. As PWS is a genetic disease, it cannot be cured. The greatest risk of PWS is ____(B)____. Since children with PWS are always hungry, it can be particularly difficult to control their weight. They will do anything to get food whenever they can. So parents are advised to take strict measures to prevent overeating.

Recent research has shown that certain growth hormones can help to reduce the proportion of body fat and improve the physical strength and flexibility of PWS sufferers. This does not suggest a cure of the syndrome, but it is certainly an encouraging discovery for PWS patients and their families.

*hypothalamus 시상하부

안젤만 증후군 Angelman Syndrome

인간은 한 쌍의 15번 염색체를 가진다. 하나는 아버지로부터, 다른 하나는 어머니로부터 받는데, 아버지에게 받은 15번 염색체에 이상이 생기면 프라더 윌리 증후군이 나타나고, 어머니에게 받은 15번 염색체에 이상이 생기면 안젤만 증후군이 나타난다. 안젤만 증후군에 걸리면 머리카락이 가늘어지고, 웃음을 조절할 수 없으며, 발작, 지능 저하 등의 증상을 보인다. 직접적인 치료 방법은 아직 알려지지 않았다.

정답 및 해설 p.46

1 프라더 윌리 증후군(PWS)에 관한 윗글의 내용과 일치하는 것은?

① People with PWS cannot feel hunger at all.
② PWS is an acquired disease.
③ It is not hard for PWS patients to control their weight.
④ Parents of patients shouldn't take strict measures to control overeating.
⑤ A certain growth hormone can be helpful for patients with PWS.

서술형

2 윗글의 괄호 안에 주어진 단어들을 다음 우리말에 맞게 배열하시오.

당신이 아무리 많이 먹어도

→ ______________________________

3 윗글의 빈칸 (A)와 (B)에 들어갈 말로 가장 적절한 것은?

	(A)		(B)
①	hunger	……	depression
②	appetite	……	obesity
③	stress	……	obesity
④	desire	……	depression
⑤	appetite	……	violence

uncontrollable 제어할 수 없는 **desire** 욕구, 충동 **suffer from** …을 앓다 **constant** 끊임없는 **hunger** 굶주림; *배고픔 **disorder** 엉망; *(신체 기능) 장애 **genetic** 유전적인 **cure** 낫게 하다; 치유법 **take measures** 조치를 취하다 **strict** 엄격한 **proportion** 비율 **flexibility** 유연성 **suggest** 제안하다; *시사[암시]하다 **discovery** 발견 문제 **acquired** 후천적인 **depression** 우울 **appetite** 식욕 **obesity** 비만 **violence** 폭력

02

수술실에 울려 퍼진 음악 소리

201 words 3'10"

Date:

Time Taken:

While a team of doctors operates on his brain, a patient hums songs and plays the saxophone. This ① <u>unusual</u> situation actually happened in 2016. The patient was a 25-year-old musician named Dan Fabbio.

Fabbio had a tumor located in the part of the brain (A) [involving / involved] in making and listening to music. Doctors hoped to remove it without affecting Fabbio's musical abilities. They spent months making a three-dimensional map of his brain. Fabbio would listen to songs and then hum them while the doctors performed MRI scans on his brain. This helped the doctors ② <u>conceal</u> the parts of his brain related to music.

Although the map was useful, the ③ <u>cautious</u> doctors decided to keep Fabbio awake during the surgery, asking him to hum songs occasionally. This activity showed the doctors exactly which areas of the brain to avoid. Toward the end of the operation, they decided to give Fabbio a test. They brought his saxophone into the operating room and had him (B) [play / played] a song on it. He played the song perfectly, and the doctors and nurses happily ④ <u>applauded</u> his performance.

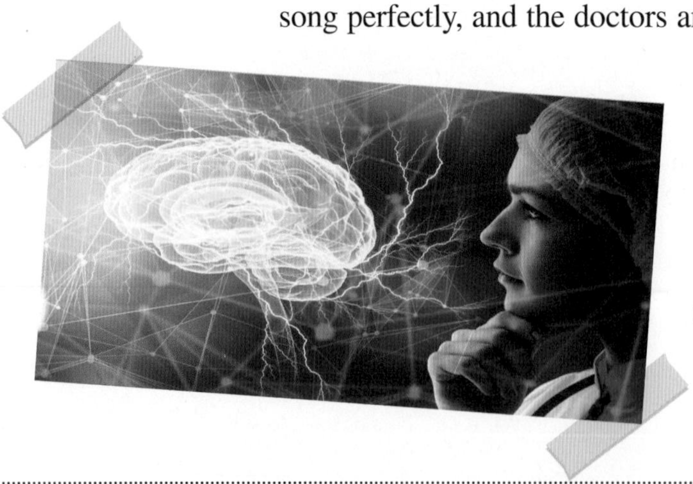

In the end, the surgery was a great success. The tumor (C) [removed / was removed], and Fabbio didn't ⑤ <u>lose</u> his musical talent!

로봇 수술
Robotic Surgery

의료 분야에서 첨단 기술을 활용하는 대표적 사례로는 로봇을 이용한 내시경 및 복강경 수술이 있다. 환자의 몸에 구멍을 뚫고 기존의 수술 기구 대신 로봇 팔과 수술용 카메라를 삽입하여, 보다 정밀하고 정확한 수술을 진행할 수 있다. 이때 의사는 콘솔에서 로봇 팔과 수술용 카메라를 원격 조종하며, 3D 확대 카메라 영상을 통해 환자의 몸 내부를 볼 수 있다. 상용화된 수술 로봇 중 가장 널리 쓰이는 것은 1999년 미국의 인튜이티브 서지컬(Intuitive Surgical) 사가 출시한 다 빈치(Da Vinci) 수술 시스템이다.

정답 및 해설 p.48

1 윗글의 제목으로 가장 적절한 것은?

① Innovative Ways to Find Brain Tumors
② How to Develop Your Brain with Music
③ Unique Surgery to Preserve a Patient's Talent
④ A New Brain Treatment Using Musical Instruments
⑤ Dangerous Technology Combining Medicine and Art

수능어법

2 윗글의 (A), (B), (C)의 각 네모 안에서 어법에 맞는 표현으로 가장 적절한 것은?

	(A)		(B)		(C)
①	involving	……	play	……	removed
②	involving	……	played	……	was removed
③	involving	……	played	……	removed
④	involved	……	play	……	removed
⑤	involved	……	play	……	was removed

VOCA

3 윗글의 밑줄 친 ①~⑤ 중, 문맥상 낱말의 쓰임이 적절하지 않은 것은?

서술형

4 주어진 질문에 대한 답을 할 때, 빈칸에 들어갈 알맞은 말을 본문에서 찾아 쓰시오.

What did the doctors do to remove a tumor without affecting the area of the patient's brain related to music?

→ They kept the patient __________ while he was undergoing the surgery and made him __________ __________ from time to time.

operate on …를 수술하다 **hum** 콧노래를 부르다, (노래를) 흥얼거리다 **unusual** 특이한, 흔치 않은 **tumor** 종양 **located in** …에 위치한 **involve** 수반하다 **remove** 제거하다, 없애다 **affect** 영향을 미치다 **three-dimensional** 3차원의, 입체적인 **perform** 수행하다, 실시하다 ※ **performance** 공연; *연주; 실적, 성과 **conceal** 숨기다, 감추다 **cautious** 조심스러운, 신중한 **surgery** 수술 **occasionally** 가끔 **perfectly** 완전히; *완벽하게 **applaud** 박수치다; *박수를 보내다 문제 **innovative** 혁신적인 **treatment** 치료 **instrument** 기계; *악기 **combine** 결합하다

03

충치가 무서워!

198 words 3'00"

Date:

Time Taken:

If you ever feel a pain in your mouth, don't ignore it. A toothache can be a sign that you have a cavity. And if cavities are left ① untreated for too long, they can become infected. The problem is that this kind of infection doesn't just affect your teeth. It can have a serious impact on your health, ② leading to stomach problems, heart disease, diabetes, and brain disease.

A recent story of a man highlights the danger of ignoring a cavity. The man had a severely rotten tooth, but he was too scared ③ going to the dentist to have it pulled out. So, he just kept ④ taking painkillers. After some time, he began feeling dizzy, developed a fever, and eventually collapsed. He was taken to a hospital, but the doctors couldn't figure out what was wrong with him. Finally, they realized that his rotten tooth had become infected. Bacteria from the infection had entered his brain, ⑤ causing cancer to form.

So even if you're afraid of getting into the dentist's chair, be sure to make an appointment if you think you have a cavity. If you don't, you could end up lying down on an operating table instead!

충치의 원인과 예방

입안의 세균이 당분을 분해할 때 나오는 산 성분은 치아의 법랑질(에나멜질)을 녹여 충치를 유발하며, 이러한 질환을 치아 우식증이라고 한다. 법랑질은 산에 취약하며 한번 마모되면 재생되지 않는다. 법랑질 속에는 치신경이 분포한 상아질이 있어, 충치가 상아질까지 침범하면 이가 시리고 통증을 느끼게 된다. 따라서 치아 우식이 시작되는 초기에 치료를 받는 것이 중요하다. 충치를 예방하려면 단 음식이나 치아에 달라붙는 음식 섭취를 피해야 한다.

1 윗글의 제목으로 가장 적절한 것은?

① Why We Fear the Dentist
② How to Find a Good Dentist
③ A Sign That You Have a Cavity
④ What Causes Cavities in Adults
⑤ The Danger of Ignoring a Cavity

수능어법

2 윗글의 밑줄 친 ①~⑤ 중, 어법상 틀린 것은?

3 윗글의 밑줄 친 you could end up lying down on an operating table instead가 의미하는 바로 가장 적절한 것은?

① 충치 치료가 불가능한 상황이 될 수 있다.
② 충치를 방치하면 심각한 질병에 걸릴 수 있다.
③ 충치가 심한 부위를 수술 받아야 할 수도 있다.
④ 치통으로 인해 입원 치료를 받아야 할 수 있다.
⑤ 충치 치료를 받는 중에 다른 질병에 걸릴 수 있다.

서술형

4 윗글의 내용과 일치하도록 빈칸에 들어갈 알맞은 말을 본문에서 찾아 쓰시오.

The man's __________ tooth was __________ with bacteria, and it led to brain cancer.

toothache 치통 **cavity** (치아에 생긴) 구멍, 충치 **untreated** 치료를 받지 않은 **infected** 감염된 ※**infection** 감염 **have an impact on** …에 영향을 주다 **stomach** 위, 복부 **diabetes** 당뇨병 **highlight** 강조하다 **severely** 심하게 **rotten** 썩은 **pull out** 뽑다 **painkiller** 진통제 **dizzy** 어지러운 **fever** 열 **eventually** 결국 **collapse** 무너지다; *(의식을 잃고) 쓰러지다 **figure out** 이해하다, 알아내다 **be sure to-v** 반드시 …하다 **end up v-ing** 결국 …하게 되다 **operating table** 수술대

04

219 words 3'20"

Date:

Time Taken:

English Only

Is Scuba Diving Dangerous?

www.askme.com

Q I've always wanted to try scuba diving, but I've heard scary stories about *decompression sickness. Can you tell me what this is and how dangerous it is?

A Thanks for raising this important concern. As a professional scuba instructor based in Cebu, Philippines, I have come across other divers who have experienced decompression sickness. ____(A)____, I must emphasize that it is rare, and it only occurs when divers ignore basic safety procedures.

The condition itself involves nitrogen bubbles becoming trapped in a diver's body, normally in the joints or veins. This happens when divers don't surface properly or surface too quickly. When this happens, the sudden decrease in pressure causes tiny nitrogen bubbles to expand into big ones and get stuck inside the body. When these bubbles are in the joints, it becomes incredibly painful to divers to straighten their arms and legs — the reason why decompression sickness is commonly called "the bends." ____(B)____, if the bubbles are in the veins, they can travel to the brain and cause a stroke.

As you can see, decompression sickness can be very serious. The good news is, though, that it is easily avoidable. If you follow the safety precautions and stay calm, you will have no such problems! Please feel free to contact me if you have any further questions.

*decompression sickness 감압병, 잠수병

1 According to the passage, which of the following is NOT true?

① Some divers have experienced decompression sickness.

② Decompression sickness occurs when divers ignore basic safety procedures.

③ Nitrogen bubbles trapped in a diver's body cause decompression sickness.

④ When divers surface improperly, nitrogen bubbles become smaller inside the body.

⑤ If nitrogen bubbles are in the veins, they can travel to the brain and cause a stroke.

서술형

2 Find the grammatically incorrect part in the underlined phrase and correct it.

3 Which of the following best fits in the blanks (A) and (B)?

	(A)		(B)
①	Instead	......	Similarly
②	However	......	Moreover
③	Eventually	......	Hence
④	Therefore	......	Otherwise
⑤	Likewise	......	Besides

고산병 우리가 일반적으로 생활하는 공간은 일정한 대기압을 유지한다. 이런 대기압이 급격히 증가하거나 감소하면 우리의 신체에도 이상 증상이 나타나는데, 가장 대표적인 두 가지 경우가 심해에서 나타나는 잠수병과 고산지대에서 나타나는 고산병이다. 저지대에서 생활하던 사람이 갑자기 해발 고도 2,000m 이상의 고지대로 이동하면 희박한 산소 때문에 두통, 구토, 저체온증 등의 증상이 나타난다.

raise 들어 올리다; *(문제 등을) 제기하다 **concern** 우려, 걱정; 관심사 **come across** 이해되다; *(우연히) 마주치다 **emphasize** 강조하다 **safety procedure** 안전수칙 **involve** 수반[포함]하다 **nitrogen** 질소 **trap** 가두다 **joint** 관절 **vein** 정맥 **surface** 표면; (물 위에) 떠오르다 **decrease** 감소, 하락 **pressure** 압박, 압력 **expand** 확대[팽창]되다 **straighten** 똑바르게 되다; *(자세를) 바로 하다 **stroke** 타격; *뇌졸중 **avoidable** 막을[피할] 수 있는 **precaution** 예방책

Review Test

• VOCA •

A

다음 중 단어의 뜻풀이가 잘못된 것을 고르시오.

① constant: happening all the time or very often

② affect: to make it easy for someone to succeed

③ cautious: careful to avoid risks

④ infection: a disease caused by bacteria or a virus

⑤ painkiller: a medicine that relieves pain

B

괄호 안에서 적절한 단어를 고르시오.

1 Mastering a musical (instrument / amusement) takes time and effort.

2 The villagers felt (attention / concern) about the severe drought.

3 They attempted to destroy the cancer cells by using (innocent / innovative) therapies.

4 A high (proportion / promotion) of students at this school enter top universities.

C

문맥상 다음 빈칸에 들어갈 가장 알맞은 단어를 고르시오.

1 One __________ potato damages all the potatoes in the sack.

① fresh ② green ③ sweet ④ rotten ⑤ burnt

2 Stress can be a cause of a sleeping __________.

① appetite ② obesity ③ disorder ④ surgery ⑤ stomach

3 Doctors __________ the importance of regular check-ups.

① remove ② emphasize ③ criticize ④ organize ⑤ combine

4 The soprano received a big applause for her __________.

① desire ② discovery ③ violence ④ performance ⑤ error

· SENTENCE ·

D

다음 문장을 밑줄 친 부분에 유의하여 우리말로 해석하시오.

1 Be sure to make an appointment if you think you have a cavity.

▸ ____________________

2 It even causes them to eat soil or almost anything they can put into their mouths.

▸ ____________________

3 This activity showed the doctors exactly which areas of the brain to avoid.

▸ ____________________

4 They brought his saxophone into the operating room and had him play a song on it.

▸ ____________________

E

우리말에 맞게 주어진 단어들을 바르게 배열하여 문장을 완성하시오.

1 당신은 대신 수술대 위에 누워 있게 될 수도 있다.

You (lying down / up / could / on / end) an operating table instead.

▸ You ____________________ an operating table instead.

2 그는 너무 겁이 나서 그것을 뽑으러 치과에 갈 수가 없었다.

He (too / go / to / was / scared) to the dentist to have it pulled out.

▸ He ____________________ to the dentist to have it pulled out.

3 부모들은 과식을 막기 위해 엄격한 조치를 취하라는 조언을 받는다.

Parents (take / to / strict measures / advised / are) to prevent overeating.

▸ Parents ____________________ to prevent overeating.

4

WORTH ONE'S SALT

소금(salt)은 고대로부터 귀한 조미료였다. 고대 로마 병사들은 급료(salary)에 소금 구입을 위한 비용이 따로 포함되어 있었다. 여기에서 비롯되어 worth one's salt라는 표현은 '급료에 상응하는 일을 하는', '제구실하는'이라는 의미를 가지게 되었다.

그는 현재 리그에서 최고의 투수야. /
그래, 그는 틀림없이 제구실을 하지.

SECTION 08

사회 · 환경

01

215 words 3'10"

Date:

Time Taken:

똑똑! 양말 한 켤레만 주세요

Socks are just something we pull onto our feet every morning, so they may not seem important to you and me. But they can make a huge difference in the lives of some people. Adina Lichtman learned this when she was a college student.

(①) She had decided to help homeless people in New York City and was distributing free sandwiches on the street. (②) One grateful man thanked her for the sandwich, but then he mentioned that winter was coming. (③) When the weather turns frigid, he told her, homeless people need socks more than anything else. (④) That night, after deciding to take action, Lichtman started knocking on doors in her dormitory, asking her classmates to donate one pair of socks. (⑤)

Today she runs a nonprofit organization, called Knock Knock, Give a Sock (KKGS), that has donated more than 350,000 pairs of socks to homeless people all across America. There are numerous organizations that work to help the homeless, but Lichtman explains why KKGS is special: "While many people donate clothing, nine out of every ten clothing donors have never donated socks." Lichtman identified an important need and found a way to fill it. Thanks to her innovative thinking, thousands of people will have warm feet this winter.

커뮤니티 솔루션즈 Community Solutions

미국에는 노숙자를 지원하는 자선 단체나 캠페인이 많은데, 로잔느 허거티가 설립한 비정부 기구인 커뮤니티 솔루션즈가 대표적인 예이다. 이곳에서는 노숙자 문제 해결을 위해 '10만 가구 캠페인'을 펼쳤다. 이 캠페인은 2010년부터 2014년에 걸쳐 대대적으로 이루어졌으며, 자원 봉사자들이 전국에 조직적 네트워크를 갖추어 10만 인의 노숙자들에게 영구 주택을 마련해 주고 필요 기금을 모으는 데 성공했다. 이 캠페인은 2013년에 세계 해비타트 어워드를 수상했으며, 이후 미국 정부의 노숙자 관련 정책에도 영감을 주었다.

정답 및 해설 p.53

1 윗글의 제목으로 가장 적절한 것은?

① Give Homeless People a Home
② A Small Idea That Had a Big Effect
③ The Freezing Cold in New York City
④ Your Old Socks Can Make Big Money
⑤ How a Homeless Girl Became a Success

VOCA

2 윗글의 밑줄 친 distributing과 바꿔 쓸 수 있는 말로 가장 적절한 것은?

① handing out ② showing off ③ throwing away
④ setting up ⑤ giving up

3 윗글의 흐름으로 보아, 주어진 문장이 들어가기에 가장 적절한 곳은?

By the next morning, she had collected 40 pairs.

4 윗글의 내용과 일치하면 T에, 일치하지 않으면 F에 표시하시오.

	T	F
(1) Lichtman got her idea for KKGS from a college friend.	□	□
(2) KKGS has helped many homeless people throughout the country so far.	□	□
(3) KKGS's founder considers the organization special because few people have thought about donating socks before.	□	□

make a difference (…에) 영향을 주다 **huge** 막대한, 거대한 **grateful** 고마워하는, 감사하는 **frigid** 몹시 추운 **take action** …에 대해 조치를 취하다[행동에 옮기다] **dormitory** 기숙사 **donate** 기부하다, 기증하다 **nonprofit** 비영리적인 **organization** 조직, 단체 **numerous** 많은 **donor** 기부자, 기증자 **identify** 확인하다, 알아보다; *찾다, 발견하다 **innovative** 혁신적인 문제 **freezing** 꽁꽁 얼게[너무나] 추운

02

AI: The Smartest Doctor of All Time

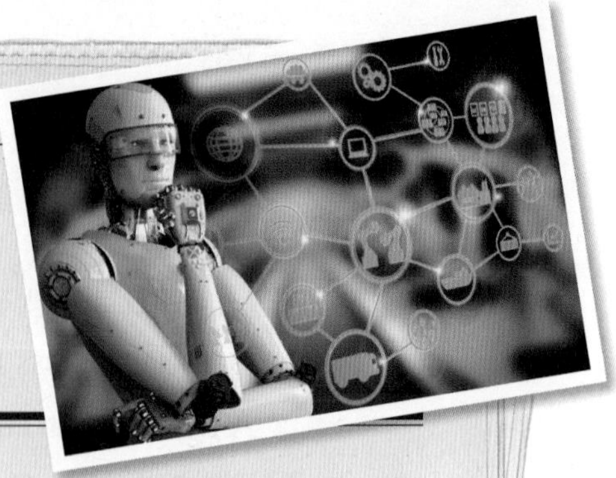

220 words 3'10"

Date:

Time Taken:

The human brain is an amazing thing. ______(A)______, there are some tasks that are simply too complex for our brains to handle well. That's why artificial intelligence, also known as AI, plays many important roles, especially in the field of healthcare.

Doctors in the US are ① highly trained and have access to all the latest equipment. (A) If you wanted to read every new medical paper that was published, you would need 160 hours of free time every week. (B) Despite this, it is estimated that American doctors make about 1.5 million medication mistakes every year. (C) This isn't always the doctors' fault. In reality, most doctors spend five hours a month or less reading medical papers.

AI, ______(B)______, has the ability to ② analyze and understand every medical paper ever written. All of these details can be stored in a database and recalled instantly. Using this information, it can ③ recommend medications and treatments just as well as the best doctors, and it is less likely to make mistakes.

Of course, there is a ④ benefit. AI cannot show concern and care as a human can. Patients need proper treatments and medications, but they also need compassion. For this reason, AI will never completely replace human doctors. However, we should still take advantage of AI to ⑤ reduce errors within the healthcare system.

인공지능(AI)의 부정적인 측면

최근 다양한 분야에서 AI가 활용되면서 그 위험성에 관한 우려도 높아지고 있다. 스티븐 호킹 박사는 스스로 사고할 수 있는 AI의 위험성을 경고했는데, 그 이유는 인공지능은 스스로를 재창조해나가며 급속도로 발전하는 것이 가능하지만 인간은 그 발전 속도를 따라잡을 수 없어, 결국 인간이 인공지능으로 대체될 수 있다는 것이다. 또한, 테슬라 모터스의 최고경영자인 엘론 머스크는 AI가 개발 의도와 달리 인간에게 악영향을 미칠 가능성을 제시하며, 강력한 규제의 필요성을 주장했다. 2015년 국제 인공지능 컨퍼런스에서는 AI 연구자들이 인공지능 무기에 반대하는 성명에 동참하기도 했다.

1 윗글의 빈칸 (A)와 (B)에 들어갈 말로 가장 적절한 것은?

(A)		(B)
① Therefore	……	however
② Nevertheless	……	as a result
③ Likewise	……	nonetheless
④ Moreover	……	on the contrary
⑤ However	……	on the other hand

2 윗글의 (A) ~ (C)를 글의 흐름에 맞게 배열한 것으로 가장 적절한 것은?

① (A) – (B) – (C) ② (A) – (C) – (B) ③ (B) – (C) – (A)
④ (C) – (A) – (B) ⑤ (C) – (B) – (A)

VOCA

3 윗글의 밑줄 친 ① ~ ⑤ 중, 문맥상 낱말의 쓰임이 적절하지 않은 것은?

서술형

4 〈보기〉에 주어진 단어를 바르게 배열하여 윗글의 요지를 완성하시오.

〈보기〉 dealing with in the healthcare system medical data humans in

AI has some weak points compared to humans, but it is definitely very useful and works better than ______________________________.

task 일, 과제 **complex** 복잡한 **handle** 다루다 **artificial** 인공의 **intelligence** 지능 **healthcare** 건강 관리, 의료 **highly** 매우 **have access to** …에 접근할 수 있다 **latest** 최신의 **equipment** 장비, 기구 **medical** 의학의 **publish** 출간하다, 발행하다 **estimate** …로 추정하다 **medication** 의학, 의술 **fault** *잘못, 책임; 결점 **analyze** 분석하다 **recall** 기억해 내다, 상기하다 **instantly** 즉시, 바로 **recommend** 추천하다 **treatment** 치료 **concern** 배려, 염려 **care** 보살핌 **compassion** 연민, 동정심 **replace** 대체하다, 대신하다 **take advantage of** …를 이용하다 문제 **definitely** 분명히

03

254 words 3'40"

Date:

Time Taken:

도심 속 작은 오아시스

Unlike most parks, the High Line in New York City does not have sports fields, playgrounds, or a running track. It is not even (A) [found / finding] at street level; rather, it is located high above the streets, and passes between buildings.

The High Line was originally a train line in Manhattan. The street it ran along became known as "Death Avenue" because a number of people (B) [was / were] hit by passing trains there. To stop this, the tracks were moved onto a structure that was 10 meters high. Over time, however, the line was used less and less, and in 1980 trains stopped (C) [using / to use] it altogether.

Some people complained about the abandoned structure, so the city decided to tear it down. (①) But Robert Hammond, a local designer, wanted to keep it. (②) So he started an organization called Friends of the High Line. (③) One day Hammond climbed onto it and saw that it was covered in beautiful wildflowers. (④) At that moment, he decided to turn it into a park. (⑤)

At first, people opposed his idea, because the park would cost a lot of money to build. But Hammond explained that the park would be beneficial to the city. The city government finally decided to support the project. The park's first section opened to the public in 2009. The next year, more than two million people visited it. With a little imagination and some hard work, an old train line was turned into a unique public space.

정답 및 해설 p.57

1 하이라인 공원에 관한 윗글의 내용과 일치하지 않는 것은?

① 운동장이나 놀이터 같은 시설이 없다.
② 과거에는 철길로 이용되었다.
③ 지상에서 10미터 높이에 위치한다.
④ 정부의 도심 녹색화 정책의 일환으로 조성되었다.
⑤ 2009년에 시민들에게 처음 공개되었다.

수능 어법

2 윗글의 (A), (B), (C)의 각 네모 안에서 어법에 맞는 표현으로 가장 적절한 것은?

	(A)		(B)		(C)
①	found	......	was	......	using
②	found	......	were	......	to use
③	found	......	were	......	using
④	finding	......	was	......	to use
⑤	finding	......	were	......	using

3 윗글의 흐름으로 보아, 주어진 문장이 들어가기에 가장 적절한 곳은?

They tried to think of a new use for the structure.

서술형

4 주어진 질문에 대한 답을 할 때, 빈칸에 알맞은 말을 본문에서 찾아 쓰시오. (2단어)

What inspired Robert Hammond to change the abandoned structure into a park?

→ ____________________ on the structure inspired him.

서울로7017 프로젝트

서울역 고가도로는 1970년에 서울 시내의 교통 문제 해결을 위해 지어진 후, 급속한 경제 발전 시기의 근대화를 상징하는 존재였다. 그러나 1990년대 말부터 노후화로 인한 안전 문제가 제기되어 왔고, 2006년에 서울시는 철거를 검토하게 되었다. 2014년에 서울시는 고가를 철거하는 대신 보행자를 위한 공간으로 재탄생시키기로 결정하였다. 2017년 완공된 서울로7017은 공중 정원과 각종 문화 체험 공간, 놀이터, 기념품점과 기타 편의 시설을 갖추어 시민과 관광객들이 즐겨 찾는 장소로 자리매김하였다.

sports field 운동장 **running track** 달리기 트랙 **rather** 오히려, 차라리 **onto** …(위)로 **structure** 구조; *구조물 **abandoned** 버려진, 유기된 **tear down** 파괴하다, 해체하다 **local** 지역의, 현지의 **organization** 단체, 조직 **oppose** 반대하다 **beneficial** 유익한, 이로운 **section** 구획 **imagination** 상상(력)

04

202 words 3'30"

Date:

Time Taken:

English Only

A Unique Way of Demonstrating

"Tree-sitting" is one form of demonstration that people use to stop loggers from cutting down forests. Perhaps the best known of these tree-sitting efforts took place in a wooded area of Northern California. Here a young woman named Julia "Butterfly" Hill showed incredible determination and strength by sitting in a tall *redwood for 738 days. Her efforts saved the tree and brought worldwide attention to the need to protect our forests from loggers. Julia holds the record for the longest tree-sitting effort by one person.

You may think it is just sitting down, but there is a lot more to tree-sitting than that. It is a dangerous activity that requires lots of strength and courage. ___(A)___, tree-sitters are often confronted by government officials and angry loggers. The weather gives them a hard time, too. ___(B)___ some days are filled with pleasant sunshine, others are filled with high winds and heavy rains, so endurance is a key quality of any tree-sitter. And there is always the danger of falling from the tree. Several tree-sitters have died this way in recent years. Clearly, tree-sitters deserve our appreciation for their efforts because they are helping to save our forests, which we can't live without.

*redwood 삼나무

유럽의 독특한 시위

인권과 환경 문제에 관한 시위 역사가 긴 유럽은 그만큼 다양하고 독특한 시위 문화가 존재한다. 일례로 스페인의 동물 권리 운동가들은, 한 축제에서 열리는 투우 경기에 반대하기 위해 몸을 붉게 물들이고 축제가 이루어지는 거리에 드러누웠다. 또한, 프랑스에서 테러 위험이 있다는 이유로 대규모 시위가 금지되자, 환경 운동가들은 파리에서 열린 UN 기후 정상 회의를 지지하고 환경에 관한 관심을 촉구하기 위해 광장에 자신들의 신발 수천 켤레를 전시하기도 했다.

정답 및 해설 p.59

1 **Which of the following is NOT true about tree-sitting?**

① It is a type of demonstration against cutting down forests.
② Julia Hill has the record for the longest tree-sitting effort by one person.
③ It is supported by governments and some loggers.
④ Tree-sitters stay in the trees even when the weather is bad.
⑤ Some people have died while tree-sitting.

2 **Choose the appropriate word for the blanks (A) and (B).**

	(A)		(B)
①	For example	……	Though
②	For example	……	After
③	As a result	……	Though
④	As a result	……	Because
⑤	On the other hand	……	After

3 **Which word best describes Julia Hill?**

① picky ② generous ③ dependent
④ emotional ⑤ strong-willed

서술형

4 **Write what the underlined "they" refers to using a word from the passage.**

demonstrate 시위하다 ※**demonstration** 시위, 데모 **logger** 벌목꾼 **cut down** 베어 넘어뜨리다 **take place** (일이) 일어나다, 발생하다 **incredible** 믿을 수 없는, 믿기 힘든 **determination** 투지 **bring attention to** …에 관심을 가져오다 **hold a record** 기록을 보유하다 **confront** (위험한 상황 등에) 부딪치다, 마주치다 **official** 공무상의, 공식적인; *공무원, 관리 **endurance** 인내, 참을성 **quality** 질, *(사람의) 자질 **deserve** …을 받을 만하다, …해야 마땅하다 **appreciation** 감탄, 감상; *감사 문제 **picky** 까다로운 **strong-willed** 의지가 강한

Review Test

· VOCA ·

A

다음 단어의 영영풀이를 바르게 연결하시오.

1 numerous · · ⓐ new and original
2 compassion · · ⓑ feeling or expressing thanks
3 innovative · · ⓒ existing in large numbers
4 grateful · · ⓓ a feeling of sympathy
5 endurance · · ⓔ the ability to do something difficult for a long time

B

괄호 안에서 적절한 단어를 고르시오.

1 (Tiny / Huge) fans were used to create strong winds in the factory.
2 He (deserves / observes) the Nobel Peace Prize because he has worked hard for world peace.
3 The sound of her alarm clock woke her up (instantly / distantly).
4 Most villagers (imposed / opposed) the building of atomic power plants because of its possible bad effect on their towns.

C

문맥상 다음 빈칸에 들어갈 가장 알맞은 단어를 고르시오.

1 Having felt tired for days, Julie decided to get a(n) __________ check-up.
① frigid ② latest ③ former ④ medical ⑤ official

2 Whenever she passes by the __________ house, she gets chills.
① nonprofit ② virtual ③ available ④ artificial ⑤ abandoned

3 Some experts say the trade agreement is __________ to both countries.
① freezing ② local ③ estimated ④ beneficial ⑤ adaptable

4 I think she is willing to __________ her fears about making changes now.
① plan ② donate ③ confront ④ include ⑤ distribute

정답 및 해설 p.60

• SENTENCE •

D

다음 문장을 밑줄 친 부분에 유의하여 우리말로 해석하시오.

1 There are numerous organizations that work to help the homeless.

▸ ______________________________

2 That's why AI plays many important roles, especially in the field of healthcare.

▸ ______________________________

3 All of these details can be stored in a database and recalled instantly.

▸ ______________________________

4 After deciding to take action, Lichtman started knocking on doors in her dormitory.

▸ ______________________________

E

우리말에 맞게 주어진 단어들을 바르게 배열하여 문장을 완성하시오.

1 그는 그것 위에 올라가서, 그것이 아름다운 야생화들로 뒤덮여 있는 것을 보았다.

He (saw / and / climbed onto / that / it) it was covered in beautiful wildflowers.

▸ He ______________________________ it was covered in beautiful wildflowers.

2 사람들은 벌목꾼들이 숲의 나무들을 베는 것을 막기 위해서 '트리 시팅'을 사용한다.

People use "Tree-sitting" (loggers / forests / to / cutting down / stop / from).

▸ People use "Tree-sitting" ______________________________.

3 많은 사람들이 그곳에서 지나가는 기차에 치이는 바람에, 그것은 '죽음의 거리'로 알려졌다.

It was known as "Death Avenue" because (by / people / were / a number of / hit) passing trains there.

▸ It was known as "Death Avenue" because ______________________________ passing trains there.

CAMPAIGN IN THE WORLD

• 환경 •

NATIONAL SWEATER DAY

난방 대신 스웨터 입기

2010년, WWF 캐나다(World Wildlife Fund Canada, 세계자연기금 캐나다 지부)는, 매년 2월 첫 번째 목요일을 '전국 스웨터의 날'로 지정했다. 겨울이 길고 추운 캐나다에서는 가정에서 소비하는 에너지의 80%가 난방에 집중되어 있다. 이 캠페인은 캐나다 국민들이 실내 온도를 2도 낮추면 온실 가스 배출량을 4메가톤이나 낮출 수 있다는 데 착안하여, 재생 가능 에너지 사용과 에너지 소비 습관 재고를 촉구하기 위해 시작되었다. 2010년 이래로 100만여 명에 달하는 캐나다 국민들이 캠페인에 참여해 왔으며, WWF 캐나다에서는 학교나 단체의 참여도 적극 권장하고 있다.

MEATLESS MONDAY

고기 없는 월요일

육류 생산을 위해 사육되는 소가 배출하는 메탄 가스는 전 세계 온실 가스 배출량의 13.5%를 차지하며, 사료 재배와 분뇨 처리로 발생하는 환경 오염 문제도 심각하다. 미국인 시드 러너(Sid Lerner)가 2003년 시작한 'Meatless Monday(고기 없는 월요일)' 캠페인은 이 문제를 더 건강하고 맛있는 방식으로 해결하고자 한다. 캠페인의 메시지는 간결하다. '지구와 개인의 건강을 위해, 월요일 하루 동안 고기 대신 다른 음식을 섭취하자'라는 것이다. 홈페이지(http://www.meatlessmonday.com/)에서는 캠페인 참가 방법과 고기 없는 식사를 제공하는 식당 리스트를 제공하고 있으며, 캠페인 참가자들은 SNS에서 #MeatlessMonday라는 해쉬태그를 달고 맛있는 채식 요리 레시피나 그렇게 만들어진 요리 사진을 활발하게 공유한다.

SECTION 09

과학 · 우주

01

끈 떨어진 우주 비행사

149 words 2'30"

Date:

Time Taken:

In the film *Gravity*, two astronauts accidentally drift off into space. The rope that attaches their spacesuits to their spacecraft breaks while they are on a spacewalk. Among astronauts, this situation is called "going overboard."

If this really happened, the astronauts would float away helplessly. Since they would be completely weightless, kicking and waving wouldn't help them change direction. They wouldn't be able to go back to their spacecraft and might end up falling toward Earth, eventually burning up in the atmosphere.

For this reason, NASA makes all astronauts wear a special emergency *jetpack called SAFER. First, the jetpack stops the astronauts from spinning around and around. Then it <u>provides</u> them with the ability to move through space. The jetpack has three pounds of fuel, and astronauts carry enough oxygen to breathe for seven and a half hours. Using both of these, they can return safely to the spacecraft!

*jetpack 제트팩 (등에 메는 개인용 분사 추진기)

정답 및 해설 p.61

1 윗글의 내용과 일치하지 않는 것은?

① 우주 유영 시 우주 비행사는 우주선과 줄로 연결된다.
② 무중력 상태에서는 방향을 바꾸는 것이 쉽지 않다.
③ 오버보드에 처하면 우주선으로 돌아가지 못할 수도 있다.
④ SAFER는 응급 상황을 위한 추진기이다.
⑤ SAFER에는 산소와 물이 들어 있어 우주 비행사의 생존을 돕는다.

VOCA

2 윗글의 밑줄 친 provides와 바꿔 쓸 수 있는 말로 가장 적절한 것은?

① allows ② supplies ③ requires
④ divides ⑤ proceeds

서술형

3 윗글의 내용과 일치하도록 빈칸에 알맞은 말을 본문에서 찾아 쓰시오.

It is called "going overboard" when ______________ lose their connection to the spacecraft while on a(n) ______________.

영화 그래비티 2013년에 개봉한 할리우드 영화로, 허블 망원경을 수리하기 위해 우주에 간 우주 비행사들이 우주선과의 연결이 끊기면서 광활한 우주에서 조난당하며 벌어지는 이야기를 다루고 있다. 영화를 본 관객들이 실제 우주에 간 듯한 느낌을 받는 등 3D 영화의 새로운 지평을 열었다는 찬사를 받았다. 제 86회 아카데미 시상식에서 시각효과상, 편집상, 음악상, 음향상, 음향편집상, 촬영상, 감독상 등 총 7개 부분을 수상했다.

astronaut 우주 비행사 **accidentally** 뜻하지 않게 **drift** 떠가다, 표류하다 **attach A to B** A를 B에 부착하다 **spacesuit** 우주복 **spacecraft** 우주선 **spacewalk** 우주 유영 **overboard** 선체 밖으로 **float** 떠가다, 떠돌다 **helplessly** 어찌해 볼 수도 없이 **weightless** 무게가 없는; *무중력의 **atmosphere** 대기 **fuel** 연료

02

추운 것도 싫은데…

Polar expeditions have contributed greatly to our understanding of science. For instance, we now know a lot more about ________ ________________________________.

184 words 2'50"

Date:

Time Taken:

In the early days, explorers often suffered from some sort of mental illness. One cause of the mental illness was later discovered. When people aren't used to living in extremely cold conditions, their bodies use up a lot of energy to keep warm, which gets rid of all the vitamins in the body. Deprived of vitamins, the brain can't work normally, and this can cause depression, sleep disorder, or rage.

The time spent in total darkness also (people's minds, on, effect, a, has, damaging). Winter in polar regions is characterized by permanent night and lasts several months. It is not natural for human beings to spend long periods of time in the dark. In northern *latitudes, many people get depressed during the dark winter months. That is because serotonin, a chemical that is believed to make people happy, cannot be released in the body without sunlight. This type of depression is known as SAD (Seasonal Affective Disorder).

*latitudes (위도상으로 본) 지방, 지대

정답 및 해설 p.63

1 윗글의 빈칸에 들어갈 말로 가장 적절한 것은?

① the importance of taking vitamins
② the way to overcome extreme cold
③ climate changes in the polar regions
④ the effects a polar climate has on people
⑤ the safest way for people to tour polar regions

서술형

2 윗글의 괄호 안에 주어진 단어들을 다음 우리말에 맞게 배열하시오.

사람들의 정신에 해로운 영향을 끼친다

→ ____________________

3 윗글의 내용을 다음과 같이 요약할 때, 빈칸 (A)와 (B)에 들어갈 말로 가장 적절한 것은?

> People in polar regions experience mental disorder or depression due to the lack of ___(A)___ in their bodies and long-lasting ___(B)___.

	(A)		(B)
①	water	……	cold
②	vitamins	……	darkness
③	protein	……	sunlight
④	blood	……	pain
⑤	oxygen	……	illness

계절성 정서 장애 SAD

일조량이 줄어드는 겨울철이 되면 계절성 정서 장애가 나타나는데, 북유럽이나 알래스카 등 북부 지방에 사는 사람들에게서 흔하게 관찰된다. 인간의 신체는 햇볕을 받으면 세로토닌이라는 신경 전달 물질의 생성이 증가되어 컨디션이 향상된다. 반면, 햇볕이 줄어 세로토닌 생성량이 감소하면 쉽게 우울해지고 피로를 느끼게 된다.

polar 북극[남극]의, 극지의 **expedition** 탐험 **contribute** 기여하다 **explorer** 탐사자 **use up** …을 다 써버리다 **get rid of** …을 없애다 **deprive of** …을 빼앗다 **depression** 우울증 ※**depressed** 우울한 **disorder** 엉망; *장애[이상] **rage** 분노 **region** 지방, 지역 **characterize** (…의) 특징이 되다 **permanent** 영구[영속]적인 **chemical** *화학물질; 화학의 **affective** 정서적인

03

소똥의 향기로운 변신

221 words 3'10"

Date:

Time Taken:

Do you like the smell of vanilla? How about vanilla ice cream? What would you think if I ⓐ(tell) you that the sweet smell of vanilla could be created by using cow dung? It may sound strange, but it's true!

Researchers working with a chemical company in Japan have found a way to produce the chemical *vanillin from cow dung. Vanillin is the main (A) [component / compromise] that's taken from vanilla beans. But it can also be found in the dung of animals that eat grass. The process of (B) [extracting / interacting] it from cow dung is a lot cheaper. In fact, the cost of making vanillin from cow dung is less than half the cost of making it from vanilla beans. This process is also an (C) [affective / effective] way of recycling cow dung. After the vanillin is obtained, the remaining dung can be used as fertilizer for the soil.

Researchers hope to eventually create a machine that will be able to process several tons of cow dung a day. The vanillin these machines produce will smell just like the real thing and could be used in such products as shampoos and candles, though probably not in food. Even though it's the same as the vanillin that comes from vanilla beans, consumers wouldn't be very interested in an ice cream that gets its flavor from cow dung.

*vanillin 바닐린 (바닐라로 만든 향료)

정답 및 해설 p.64

1 **윗글의 내용과 일치하지 않는 것은?**

① 초식동물의 똥에서 바닐린이 발견되기도 한다.
② 소똥에서 바닐린을 추출하는 것은 비용이 적게 드는 편이다.
③ 바닐린이 추출되고 남은 소똥은 비료로 재활용할 수 있다.
④ 하루에 대량의 소똥을 처리하는 기계가 이미 사용되고 있다.
⑤ 사람들은 소똥에서 추출된 바닐린을 식용화하는 것을 좋아하지 않을 것이다.

서술형

2 **윗글의 ⓐ에 주어진 동사를 어법에 알맞은 형태로 쓰시오.**

VOCA

3 **윗글의 (A), (B), (C)의 각 네모 안에서 문맥에 맞는 낱말로 가장 적절한 것은?**

	(A)		(B)		(C)
①	component	……	extracting	……	affective
②	component	……	interacting	……	effective
③	component	……	extracting	……	effective
④	compromise	……	interacting	……	effective
⑤	compromise	……	extracting	……	affective

미래의 식량, 곤충

세계 식량난 해결을 위해 과학자들은 GMO(유전자 조작) 식품부터 인공 고기에 이르기까지 다양한 식재료를 연구하고 있다. 그중에는 곤충을 원료로 하는 음식도 있다. 이를 연구하는 과학자들에 따르면 곤충은 양질의 단백질 공급원으로 소나 돼지를 키우는 데 비해 비용이 덜 들고 이산화탄소도 덜 배출하는 친환경적인 식품이다. 또한, 본래의 형체를 알아볼 수 없도록 '곤충 밀가루'를 만들어 3D 프린터 기술로 가공하면 곤충을 섭취하는 데 따르는 거부감도 해소할 수 있다고 한다. 일부 나라에서는 식용 곤충을 식재료로 활용하는 식당들이 영업 중이며, 앞으로 더 늘어날 전망이다.

dung 똥 **component** 구성, 요소 **compromise** 타협, 절충 **process** 과정; 처리하다 **extract** 추출하다 **interact** 소통하다 **recycle** 재활용하다 **remaining** 남아 있는 **fertilizer** 비료 **soil** 토양 **consumer** 소비자 **flavor** 풍미, 맛

04

236 words 3'40"

Date:

Time Taken:

English Only

How Hot Is It?

Anyone who enjoys hot food knows that some peppers are hotter than others. So, is there any way to measure their hotness? The answer is: yes, with the Scoville Heat Unit Scale.

Commonly known as the Scoville Scale, it measures the amount of the chemical *capsaicin present in each pepper. It then represents this number in Scoville heat units (SHU). The scale was first introduced in 1912 by a chemist named Wilbur Scoville. Here's the test: peppers are ground up and mixed with sugar water. Testers then sip the solution, which is gradually diluted until it no longer burns their tongues. Based on how much sugar water is required to dilute each pepper to this level, an SHU number is assigned.

These numbers are given in multiples of 100 SHU, and the scores range from zero for *sweet bell peppers to over one million SHU for an extremely spicy pepper known as Naga Jolokia. Scoville's system can give a good idea of how hot a pepper is. _____(A)_____, the problem with it is that it relies on the perceptions of individual tasters.

These days, when people want to measure levels of hotness more accurately, they use something known as High Performance Liquid *Chromatography. Like the Scoville Scale, it measures capsaicin levels, but it <u>does so</u> in a more scientific manner. _____(B)_____, in honor of Wilbur Scoville's work, it also uses "Scovilles" as its unit of measurement.

*capsaicin 캡사이신 (고추에서 추출되는 화합물) *sweet bell pepper 피망
*chromatography 크로마토그래피 (유기 혼합물의 분리 분석법)

정답 및 해설 p.65

1 Which of the following is NOT true about the Scoville Scale?

① It indicates peppers' level of hotness.

② A chemist first developed it by doing a test.

③ Sweet bell peppers score a zero on the scale.

④ It uses individual tasters to measure hotness.

⑤ It is the most accurate method of measuring hotness.

2 Which of the following best fits in both (A) and (B)?

① Likewise ② However ③ Moreover

④ Meanwhile ⑤ Nevertheless

서술형

3 Write what the underlined "does so" refers to using words from the passage. (3 words)

세계에서 가장 매운 고추

최근 미국의 사우스 캐롤라이나에 위치한 고추 농장에서 재배된 '캐롤라이나 리퍼(Carolina Reaper)'라는 고추가 세계에서 가장 매운 고추에 선정되었다. 이 고추는 스코빌 지수가 평균 156만 9300에 달하며, 가장 매운 개체의 경우 220만 스코빌에 육박한다. 참고로 청양고추의 매운맛은 최대 1만 2000 스코빌이라고 한다.

measure 측정하다 ※**measurement** 측정 **scale** 규모; *등급, 척도 **represent** 대표하다; *표현하다 **grind up** 갈아 부수다 **sip** 홀짝이다 **solution** 해법; *용액 **dilute** 희석하다 **assign** 맡기다; *부여하다 **multiple** 많은, 다수의; *배수 **range from A to B** (범위가) A에서 B까지 걸치다 **rely on** …에 의존하다 **perception** 지각, 자각 **accurately** 정확하게 **manner** (일의) 방식 **in honor of** …에게 경의를 표하여

Review Test

· VOCA ·

A

다음 중 단어의 뜻풀이가 잘못된 것을 고르시오.

① permanent: lasting forever

② rage: an extreme feeling of happiness

③ drift: to move slowly on water or in the air

④ expedition: a long journey for a scientific purpose

⑤ consumer: a person who buys goods or services

B

괄호 안에서 적절한 단어를 고르시오.

1 My sister loves the (flavor / flame) of strawberry ice cream.

2 My father (ensured / measured) the size of our dining table.

3 Even pets can get (depressed / impressed) if they are left home alone all day.

4 Andrew will scan some photos and (attach / detach) them to an email.

C

문맥상 다음 빈칸에 들어갈 가장 알맞은 단어를 고르시오.

1 I put a leaf in the river and watched it __________ away.

① hang ② settle ③ swallow ④ float ⑤ drown

2 This oil was __________ from olives.

① melted ② extracted ③ proved ④ damaged ⑤ brewed

3 Since the coffee tasted too strong, I __________ it by adding some ice.

① allowed ② contributed ③ limited ④ diluted ⑤ offered

4 The old lady __________ on a wheelchair because she can't walk.

① characterizes ② relies ③ borrows ④ interacts ⑤ deprives

정답 및 해설 p.67

· SENTENCE ·

D 다음 문장을 밑줄 친 부분에 유의하여 우리말로 해석하시오.

1 Scoville's system can give a good idea of how hot a pepper is.
▸ ______________________________

2 It is not natural for human beings to spend long periods of time in the dark.
▸ ______________________________

3 If this really happened, the astronauts would float away helplessly.
▸ ______________________________

4 The time spent in total darkness has a damaging effect on people's minds.
▸ ______________________________

E 우리말에 맞게 주어진 단어들을 바르게 배열하여 문장을 완성하시오.

1 그들은 무중력일 것이기 때문에, 발을 차고 팔다리를 흔드는 것은 그들이 방향을 바꾸는 데 도움이 되지 않을 것이다.
(they / weightless / since / be / would), kicking and waving wouldn't help them change direction.
▸ ______________________, kicking and waving wouldn't help them change direction.

2 극도로 추운 상태에서, 그들의 신체는 몸을 따뜻하게 유지하기 위해 많은 에너지를 쓴다.
In extremely cold conditions, their bodies (a lot of / keep / to / use up / warm / energy).
▸ In extremely cold conditions, their bodies ______________________.

3 연구원들은 소똥으로 화학물질 바닐린을 만들어내는 방법을 알아냈다.
Researchers (a way / to / produce / have found) the chemical vanillin from cow dung.
▸ Researchers ______________________ the chemical vanillin from cow dung.

표현의 유래

5

WET BLANKET

이 표현은 19세기 신문이나 잡지 등의 매체에서 '(젖은 담요로 불을 꺼버리듯) 열정적이고 흥미진진한 분위기에 찬물을 끼얹는 것'을 비유하는 말로 쓰이면서 하나의 관용 표현으로 자리잡았다. 오늘날에도 wet blanket이라고 하면 '흥을 깨는 사람이나 일'을 의미한다.

제인은 우리랑 전혀 어울리고 싶어 하지 않아. /
응, 완전 흥을 깨는 애야.

SECTION 10

생활

01

173 words 2'30"

Date:

Time Taken:

Work with Us!

Job Title : ________________

Employer : Houston Museum of Natural Science

Location : Houston, Texas

Job Type : Full Time, Temporary (Summer)

Job Description :

This summer the Houston Museum of Natural Science will be hosting one of the biggest prehistoric fossil exhibitions ever held in North America. This event will take place all summer, from July 1 to September 15. We are looking for (our, to, team, enthusiastic and talented, join, individuals) and run this event. Your duty will be to circulate throughout the exhibition hall and interact with visitors. You will be responsible for answering any questions they may have and giving tours in both English and Spanish. The pay is $12.00/hr.

Requirements :

- You must be outgoing and responsible.
- You must possess excellent interpersonal skills and be able to work well in a crowded and noisy environment with visitors of all backgrounds and ages.
- Having a natural history background is an advantage.

To Apply :

Send your résumé by e-mail to *mcohen@houstonmuseum.com*. Only candidates selected for interviews will be contacted.

Contact: Mark Cohen, Personnel Director

정답 및 해설 p.68

1 윗글의 빈칸에 들어갈 말로 가장 적절한 것은?

① Curator ② Translator
③ Security Guard ④ Exhibit Hall Staff
⑤ Natural History Specialist

서술형

2 윗글의 괄호 안에 주어진 단어들을 다음 우리말에 맞게 배열하시오.

저희 팀에 합류할 열의 있고 재능 있는 분들

→ ____________________

3 위 구인 정보의 내용과 일치하지 않는 것은?

① 전일 근무하는 임시직이다.
② 지원자는 영어와 스페인어를 할 줄 알아야 한다.
③ 급여는 시간당 12달러이다.
④ 지원자는 자연사에 관한 지식을 갖춰야 한다.
⑤ 이력서는 이메일로 접수한다.

휴스턴 자연 과학 박물관
Houston Museum of Natural Science

1909년에 설립된 박물관으로 북미의 자연과 역사를 소개하고 있으며, 30만 점에 이르는 조개류 전시로 유명하다. Burke Baker 천문관에서는 별들의 쇼를 하고, Wortham Giant Screen 극장에서는 대형 스크린을 통해 영화도 감상할 수 있다. Cockrell Butterfly Center에서는 열대우림 세트를 만들어 놓고 세상에서 가장 크고 색이 화려한, 살아 있는 나비들을 60여 종 넘게 전시하고 있다.

temporary 임시의, 일시적인 **description** 서술, 기술 **prehistoric** 선사 시대의 **fossil** 화석(의) **exhibition** 전시회, 전람회 **take place** 일어나다; *개최되다 **enthusiastic** 열성적인 **circulate** 순환하다; *돌아다니다 **be responsible for** …에 책임이 있다 **requirement** 필요; *요건 **outgoing** 외향적인 **interpersonal** 대인 관계의 **background** 배경; 기초지식 **advantage** 이점, 강점 **résumé** 이력서 **candidate** 후보자 **select** 선발하다 **contact** 연락하다 **personnel director** 인사 관리자

02 티켓을 예매하려면

173 words 2'40"

Date:

Time Taken:

★ Ticketing Information

Welcome all art lovers visiting the homepage of the London AllArt Center. We provide useful ticketing information on arts programs, performances, and exhibitions in the London area. You can ⓐ book tickets by phone or online (www.allarttickets.com). For more details, contact us at 20-7800-1400.

1. Reservation by Telephone

	Booking Office	Phone Number	Service Hours
Members	Service Plaza (On the 2nd floor of the Opera Center)	20-5800-1700 20-5800-4444	9 a.m.~6 p.m. (Except holidays and Sundays)
Non-Members	AllArt ticket office	20-6402-1577 20-6402-1515	10 a.m.~6 p.m. (Weekdays) 10 a.m.~5 p.m. (Saturdays)

2. Ticket Changes

- ▶ At least one day before the performance: You can change dates or times (only for the same performance).
- ▶ The day of the performance: ⓑ No changes are allowed unless there are tickets still available. There is an additional penalty fee of 10% for each ticket changed.

3. Refunds

- ▶ At least one day before the performance (by 5 p.m.): 90% refund (10% commission fee)
- ▶ At least one hour before the performance: 70% refund
- ▶ Less than one hour prior to the performance: No refund

정답 및 해설 p.70

VOCA

1 윗글의 밑줄 친 ⓐ book의 의미로 가장 적절한 것은?

① loan ② seize ③ reserve
④ function ⑤ preview

2 윗글에 따르면, 다음 중 올아트 센터 회원이 전화 예약을 할 수 있는 경우는?

① Call 20-5800-1700 on Tuesday, 7 p.m.
② Call 20-5800-1700 on Sunday, 10 a.m.
③ Call 20-5800-4444 on Friday, 11 a.m.
④ Call 20-6402-1515 on Monday, 8 a.m.
⑤ Call 20-6402-1577 on Thursday, 9 a.m.

서술형

3 윗글의 밑줄 친 ⓑ와 같은 뜻이 되도록 빈칸에 알맞은 말을 쓰시오.

Changes are allowed only __________ there __________ tickets still available.

4 티켓 변경 및 환불 조건으로, 윗글의 내용과 일치하지 않는 것은?

① 같은 공연에 한해 공연 하루 전날까지 날짜와 시간 변경이 가능하다.
② 공연 당일에는 변경이 불가능하며, 환불 시 10% 수수료가 부과된다.
③ 공연 전날 오후 5시 이전까지 티켓 요금의 90%를 환불받을 수 있다.
④ 공연 시작 1시간 전까지 티켓 요금의 70%를 환불받을 수 있다.
⑤ 공연 시작까지 1시간 미만이 남았을 경우 환불이 불가능하다.

provide 제공하다 **detail** 세부 사항 **reservation** 예약 **available** 이용 가능한 **additional** 추가의 **penalty** 벌금, 위약금 **fee** 요금, 수수료 **refund** 환불(금) **commission** 수수료 **prior to** …전[앞]에 문제 **loan** 빌려주다 **seize** 잡다

03

단추에 그런 의미가?

208 words 3'00"

Date:

Time Taken:

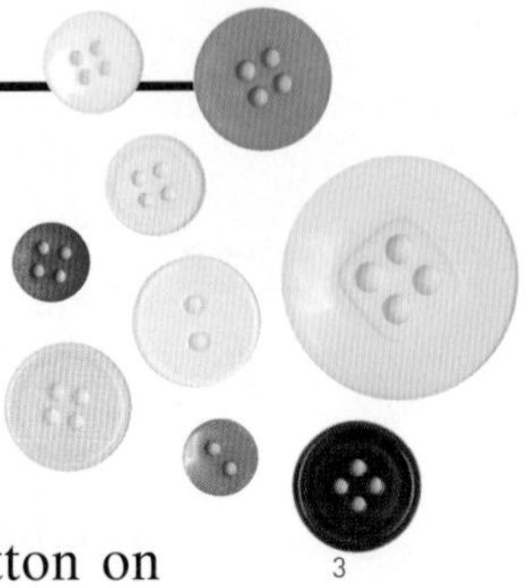

Unless you work as a clothing designer, you've probably never noticed that women's and men's shirts button from opposite sides. Men's shirts button on the right and women's button on the left. If most women were left handed and most men were right handed, this would seem logical. ______________________ So why are men's and women's buttons on opposite sides?

It's because of the history of fashion. A few hundred years ago, both women and men in Europe wore a lot more clothes than they do today. Men wore shirts, vests, pants, and coats. But women had far more complicated outfits, which included *petticoats, *bloomers, gowns, corsets, and *bustles.

In middle and upper-class homes, men usually dressed themselves, since it was relatively easy for them to put on their clothing. But for women, things were not that simple; they needed to be dressed by their maids. Tailors soon realized that designing women's clothes with buttons on the left side made this process faster and easier. Thus, a custom was created in clothes-making.

Most of us are not being dressed by maids today. However, the clothing industry continues to follow this tradition. Since few people notice or complain, no one has bothered to change it.

*petticoat 페티코트 (속치마)
*bloomer 블루머 (여성 · 아동용 짧은 바지)
*bustle (스커트 뒷자락을 부풀게 하는) 허리받이

정답 및 해설 p.71

1 윗글의 주제로 가장 적절한 것은?

① who invented buttons first
② when buttons are put on the left
③ how complicated clothing was in the past
④ why women needed to be dressed by maids
⑤ why men's and women's clothes button on different sides

2 윗글의 빈칸에 들어갈 말로 가장 적절한 것은?

① But most people are right handed.
② So, everyone should use both hands.
③ And some people use their right hand.
④ Also, they no longer use only one hand.
⑤ However, there are more right handed tailors.

서술형

3 빈칸에 들어갈 알맞은 말을 본문에서 찾아 쓰시오.

Since women in middle and upper-class homes were _________ by their maids, _________ were put on the left side to make the work easier.

버슬 Bustle 버슬 스타일은 19세기 후반에 유행했던 서양 여성의 복식 양식 중 하나이다. 버슬은 드레스의 뒷부분을 둥글게 부풀리기 위해 만들어진 버팀대를 말한다. 초기에는 고래수염이나 철사를 넣은 딱딱한 천을 스커트 뒤쪽 허리 부분에 넣어 부풀게 하였으나, 후기에는 철사를 얽어서 틀 모양을 한 것, 천으로 주름을 잡아서 만든 것 등 전용 용구가 만들어졌다.

button 단추를 잠그다; 단추가 채워지다; 단추 **logical** 논리적인 **complicated** 복잡한 **outfit** 옷(복장) **upper-class** 상류 계급의 **relatively** 비교적 **maid** 하녀, 가정부 **tailor** 재단사 **custom** 관습, 풍습 **bother** 귀찮게 하다; *신경 쓰다, 애를 쓰다

04

236 words 3'30"

Date:

Time Taken:

English Only

Can You Make Carbonara?

Spaghetti alla carbonara can easily be found in Italian restaurants around the world. When people outside of Italy order this dish, they expect a plate of pasta ① covered in cream sauce with mushrooms and pieces of ham. However, the original Italian recipe is a bit different. There is no cream or mushrooms, and its flavor is lighter. This authentic version of *spaghetti alla carbonara* is quick and easy ② to make, and it requires only a few ingredients.

Ingredients

500 g of spaghetti, 150 g of chopped Italian bacon, 120 g of grated Romano cheese, 5 eggs, olive oil, pepper

1. Mix the eggs in a bowl. Then slowly add the cheese while ③ stirring quickly. Also, add a little freshly ground pepper.
2. Meanwhile, start ④ cooking the pasta. In a saucepan, heat a small amount of olive oil, and cook the bacon in it. Then about one minute before the pasta is cooked *al dente*, pour a couple of tablespoons of the water from the pasta into the egg mixture.
3. After the pasta is cooked *al dente*, drain the water from it, and toss it straight into the pan ⑤ what you cooked the bacon.
4. Pour the egg mixture into the pan with the pasta and bacon, and stir it. The pasta is very hot now, so it will cook the raw eggs.
5. Finish off your *spaghetti alla carbonara* with pepper and some grated cheese!

*al dente (파스타가) 적당히 씹히는 맛이 있는

1 According to the recipe, which of the following is NOT true?

① You need just a few ingredients.

② You should cook bacon in olive oil.

③ You should stir the pasta with fresh cream.

④ The heat of pasta will cook the eggs.

⑤ For the last step, you can use some pepper and grated cheese.

수능어법

2 Which is grammatically incorrect among ①~⑤?

서술형

3 What ingredients are included in the egg mixture?

파스타의 유래 파스타의 유래에 대해서는 여러 가지 이야기가 존재한다. 먼저 1295년경 마르코 폴로에 의해 중국에서 이탈리아로 파스타가 들어왔다는 설이 있다. 동방견문록에 마르코 폴로가 원나라의 쿠빌라이 칸의 궁에서 파스타를 먹었다는 기록에 근거해 그가 이탈리아로 돌아올 때 파스타를 들여왔다는 것이다. 하지만 이를 부정하는 의견들도 있다. 1279년 제노바에서 마카로니가 들어 있는 나무 상자를 유산으로 남긴 사람이 있다는 기록이 있으며, 기원전 4세기의 이탈리아 에투르스칸족의 무덤에서 파스타를 만들었던 기구와 조각이 발굴되기도 했다.

order 주문하다 **recipe** 조리[요리]법 **flavor** 풍미, 맛 **authentic** 진짜인 **require** 필요로 하다 **ingredient** (요리) 재료 **chopped** 잘게 썬, 다진 **grated** (강판에) 간 **pepper** 후추 **stir** 젓다 **ground** 빻은, 가루로 만든 **meanwhile** 그동안에 **saucepan** 냄비 **heat** 뜨겁게 하다 **pour** 붓다 **mixture** 혼합물, 혼합재료 **drain** 물을 빼내다 **toss** (가볍게) 던지다 **raw** 익히지 않은, 날것의

Review Test

• VOCA •

A

다음 단어의 영영풀이를 바르게 연결하시오.

1 maid • • ⓐ not cooked

2 raw • • ⓑ liking to meet and talk to other people

3 refund • • ⓒ a female servant in a house or hotel

4 drain • • ⓓ money that is returned to a customer

5 outgoing • • ⓔ to remove liquid by making it flow away

B

괄호 안에서 적절한 단어를 고르시오.

1 Suitable (candidates / estimates) for the job will be chosen for interviews.

2 This website has a (temporary / permanent) problem, but it will be fixed soon.

3 I lost my credit card, so I (conducted / contacted) the credit card company.

4 Did you (collect / select) any place to spend your summer vacation?

C

문맥상 다음 빈칸에 들어갈 가장 알맞은 단어를 고르시오.

1 Exchanging presents is a Christmas __________.

① recipe ② custom ③ holiday ④ description ⑤ background

2 You can enjoy __________ Italian food at this restaurant because the chef is from Italy.

① relative ② private ③ authentic ④ responsible ⑤ detailed

3 The problem was so __________ that I couldn't explain how to solve it.

① easy ② logical ③ available ④ additional ⑤ complicated

4 An aging population will __________ more spending on health care.

① seize ② grow ③ provide ④ require ⑤ produce

정답 및 해설 p.75

· SENTENCE ·

D

다음 문장을 밑줄 친 부분에 유의하여 우리말로 해석하시오.

1 No changes are allowed unless there are tickets still available.

▸ ______________________________

2 This event will take place all summer, from July 1 to September 15.

▸ ______________________________

3 Since few people notice or complain, no one has bothered to change it.

▸ ______________________________

4 Toss the pasta straight into the pan where you cooked the bacon.

▸ ______________________________

E

우리말에 맞게 주어진 단어들을 바르게 배열하여 문장을 완성하시오.

1 당신의 업무는 전시장을 돌면서 관람객들과 교류하는 것이다.

(is / your duty / to / circulate) throughout the exhibition hall and interact with visitors.

▸ ______________________________ throughout the exhibition hall and interact with visitors.

2 유럽의 여성들과 남성들 모두 그들이 오늘날 그러는 것보다 훨씬 더 많은 옷을 입었다.

Both women and men in Europe wore (clothes / than / do / more / they / a lot) today.

▸ Both women and men in Europe wore ______________________________ today.

3 만약 당신이 의상 디자이너로 일하는 것이 아니라면, 그것을 아마 알아채지 못했을 것이다.

(a clothing designer / you / as / unless / work), you've probably never noticed that.

▸ ______________________________, you've probably never noticed that.

CAMPAIGN IN THE WORLD

• 노숙자 •

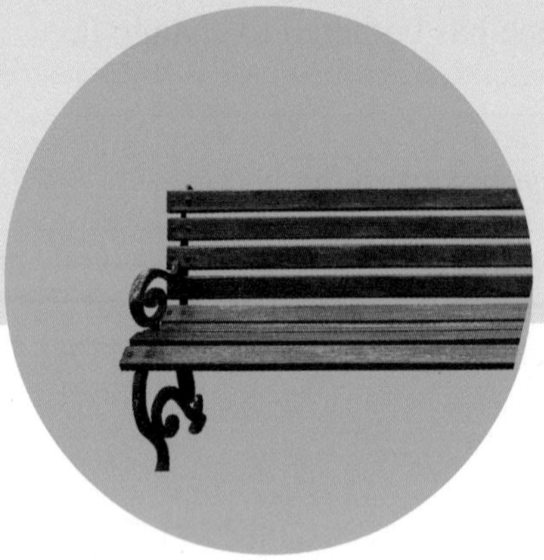

FAKTUM HOTEL

어떤 호텔에서 묵으실 건가요?

스웨덴의 Faktum Hotel 홈페이지에서는 폐허, 다리 밑, 공원 화장실, 길거리의 벤치 등 10개의 장소 중 하나를 골라 예약할 수 있다. 이 장소들은 스웨덴의 노숙자들이 실제 생활하는 공간으로, 호텔에서 방을 선택하듯이 이 장소들 중 한 곳을 예약하면 100크로나(스웨덴 통화)가 결제되고 이 금액은 노숙자를 위해 사용된다. Faktum Hotel은 실제로 노숙자들이 사용하고 있는 장소를 가감 없이 보여 주고 이를 통해 사람들의 관심을 환기시키고 기부를 유도한다.

THE WARMING HANGER

따뜻한 겨울나기

노숙자들에게 겨울은 더 춥다. 추운 겨울 밤을 보낼 수 있는 수용 시설은 노숙자 전체 수에 비해 턱없이 부족해 겨울마다 많은 노숙자들이 길 위에서 죽고 만다. 루마니아의 samusocial이라는 단체는 이런 문제를 해결하기 위해 The Warming Hanger라는 캠페인을 진행했다. 이 단체는 국내 드라이클리닝 업체와 제휴해 옷걸이에 입지 않는 헌옷을 기부해달라는 메시지를 붙였다. 이를 본 사람들은 다음에 세탁소에 옷을 맡길 때 헌옷을 가져와 기부했다. 이 캠페인은 사람들이 자신에게 필요하지 않은 것을 나누게 함으로써 경제가 어려운 상황에서도 큰 호응을 얻을 수 있었다.

SECTION 11

생물 · 동물

1 낙타가 이주를?
2 해파리는 몇 살?
3 코끼리가 동굴로 가는 까닭은…
4 The Amazing Sardine Run

01

175 words 2'30"

Date:

Time Taken:

October 5, 2018

Did Camels Migrate?

Can you imagine camels walking across a snowy field? It sounds strange, but this was probably a normal sight millions of years ago. Scientists recently discovered the bones of ancient camels in the Arctic region of Canada. Apparently, this is where they lived long, long ago.

Interestingly, similar camel bones have been found about 1,200 kilometers to the south. This shows that the species migrated south. About seven or eight million years ago, they crossed from North America to Asia. At that time, the two continents were ⓐ connected, so they could simply walk across. After a long journey, they eventually made their way to desert regions.

The fact that the camel migrated suggests that its evolution may have been influenced more by the Arctic than by the desert. Its hump would have allowed it to store food during the dark, frozen winter months. And its broad feet would have made it easier to walk across the snow without sinking in. Of course, ⓑ these features were extremely useful when the camel switched to a desert habitat.

대륙이동설 대륙이동설은 독일의 지구물리학자 알프레트 베게너가 주장한 것으로, 원래는 하나였던 큰 대륙이 갈라지고 이동하면서 현재의 대륙들이 자리 잡았다는 이론이다. 남아메리카의 동쪽 해안선과 아프리카 서쪽 해안선이 들어맞는다는 점, 멀리 떨어진 여러 대륙에서 같은 고생물 화석이 발견된 점 등이 증거로 제시되었다. 처음에 이 학설은 제대로 인정받지 못했지만, 후대의 과학자들에 의해 맨틀의 대류, 판구조론 등으로 계속 연구되고 있다.

정답 및 해설 p.76

1 윗글의 내용과 일치하지 않는 것은?

① Camels probably walked across snowy fields millions of years ago.
② The bones of ancient camels were found in the Arctic region.
③ Some camel bones show that the species migrated south.
④ North America and Asia were connected millions of years ago.
⑤ The evolution of camels was most influenced by the desert.

VOCA

2 윗글의 밑줄 친 ⓐ connected와 의미가 반대인 것은?

① joined ② linked ③ separated
④ united ⑤ attached

서술형

3 윗글의 밑줄 친 ⓑ these features가 가리키는 것을 본문에서 찾아 쓰시오.

The camel's __________ and __________ __________

migrate 이주하다, 이동하다 **sight** 시력; *광경, 모습 **ancient** 고대의 **arctic** 북극의 **apparently** 분명히 **species** 종(種) **continent** 대륙 **journey** 여행, 여정 **make one's way to** …로 나아가다, 가다 **evolution** 진화 **hump** 툭 솟아 오른 곳; *혹 **store** 저장하다 **frozen** 얼어붙은 **sink** 가라앉다, 빠지다 **feature** 특징, 특성 **switch** 바뀌다; *바꾸다 **habitat** 서식지

02

157 words 2'10"

Date:

Time Taken:

해파리는 몇 살?

Some trees live for thousands of years, while some insects live for only a few hours. But every living organism will eventually ______(A)______, right? Well, a discovery in the Caribbean Sea has made scientists rethink the issue of mortality. A rare jellyfish species ① known as *turritopsis nutricula might be able to ______(B)______ forever!

When ordinary jellyfish finish ② reproducing, they begin to die. But turritopsis nutricula does something different after mating. It has an unusual process whereby its cells don't decay. Instead, they change back to their original form, ③ becoming similar to ④ what are known as "stem cells." These cells join together to form a *polyp, which is exactly ⑤ that forms when a male jellyfish's sperm fuses with a female jellyfish's egg. In this sense, the jellyfish is literally born again; it turns itself back into a baby instead of dying. Amazingly, this cycle can repeat indefinitely, making this jellyfish one of the most unique organisms on earth.

*turritopsis nutricula 투리토프시스 누트리쿨라 (작은보호탑해파리)
*polyp 폴립(히드라 · 산호류 같은 원통형 해양 고착 생물)

정답 및 해설 p.77

1 윗글의 주제로 가장 적절한 것은?

① how jellyfish mate
② the life and death of insects
③ the life cycle of ordinary jellyfish
④ how certain jellyfish can live forever
⑤ the role of stem cells in reproduction

수능어법

2 윗글의 밑줄 친 ①~⑤ 중, 어법상 틀린 것은?

서술형

3 윗글의 빈칸 (A)와 (B)에 들어갈 알맞은 말을 본문에서 찾아 쓰시오.

(A) ________________ (B) ________________

해파리의 이동 방법

해파리는 이동 시 근육을 수축하여 아래로 물을 밀어내면서 그 반작용으로 움직이는데, 이러한 반작용의 힘만으로는 해파리가 이동하기에 부족하다. 따라서 해파리는 조류의 흐름에 의존해 주로 이동한다. 독이 있는 자세포를 가진 해파리는 이러한 수동적인 움직임으로 인해 더욱 더 위험한 존재가 된다. 조류와 파도의 흐름에 따라 움직일 수밖에 없으므로, 앞에 장애물이 나타나도 자의로 피하지 못하고 본능적으로 독이 있는 자포를 쏠 수밖에 없기 때문이다.

organism 유기체; *생물 **rethink** 다시 생각하다, 재고하다 **mortality** 죽음을 피할 수 없음 **jellyfish** 해파리 **reproduce** 복사[복제]하다; *번식하다 ※ **reproduction** 생식, 번식 **mate** 짝짓기를 하다 **whereby** (그것에 의하여) …하는 **decay** 부패하다, 썩다 **stem cell** 줄기세포 **sperm** 정자; 정액 **fuse** 녹이다, 녹다; *융합[결합]하다 **egg** 알; *난자 **literally** 문자[말] 그대로 **indefinitely** 무기한으로

03

코끼리가 동굴로 가는 까닭은…

276 words 3'40"

Date:

Time Taken:

The caves at the base of Mount Elgon, which is on the border of Uganda and Kenya, are some of the most interesting caves in the world. Inside, there are long furrows with holes that look as if they have been made by picks. The first explorers of the site assumed these to be the sign of ancient Egyptians' mining activity. But wildlife specialists observing the caves discovered that (humans, not, made, it, who, was, these marks) but elephants, which still visit the caves to this day!

While most elephants live on the plains of Africa, the herds near Mount Elgon live in the rainforest. Because of the wet climate, there is plenty of food for them. ______(A)______, the problem is that the heavy rainfall washes away the salt from the plants and the soil. As a result, the elephants do not get as much salt as they need in their diet. Thus, they go to the caves of Mount Elgon, where they can find salt-rich rocks.

The elephants travel there in family groups, sometimes going as far as 150 meters into the dark caves to find salt in the rocks. They use their tusks to chip off rough bits of the cave wall, which they then eat.

The elephants' journey is especially unusual because it is very dangerous. The elephants risk being attacked by predators like hyenas and leopards on the way to the caves. ______(B)______, the caves have big cracks and holes that the elephants could fall into since it is very dark inside. In spite of all the danger, they continue to wander deep into the caves to enjoy the tasty rewards!

1 윗글에서 코끼리들이 엘곤 산에 가는 이유로 가장 적절한 것은?

① to get salt
② to store food
③ to avoid predators
④ to sharpen their tusks
⑤ to take shelter from rain

서술형

2 윗글의 괄호 안에 주어진 단어들을 다음 우리말에 맞게 배열하시오.

이 표시들을 만든 것은 인간들이 아니었다

→ ____________________

3 윗글의 빈칸 (A)와 (B)에 들어갈 말로 가장 적절한 것은?

	(A)		(B)
①	Rather	……	In fact
②	Therefore	……	In short
③	Likewise	……	As a result
④	However	……	In addition
⑤	Moreover	……	Nevertheless

MEEM 팀
Mount Elgon Elephant Monitoring Team

엘곤 산 코끼리의 개체 수를 모니터링하고 그들의 행동을 연구하며, 코끼리의 대략적인 나이, 성별 등을 알아내는 활동들을 한다. 이 팀은 현지 주민으로 이루어진 수색자들과 엘곤 산 국립공원 관리원들로 이루어져 있다.

cave 동굴 **base** 기슭, 맨 아래 부분 **border** 국경, 경계 **furrow** 고랑, 골 **pick** 고르기, 선택; *곡괭이 **assume** 추정하다 **mining** 채굴; 광업 **observe** 관찰하다 **plain** 평원, 평지 **herd** 무리, 떼 **rainforest** 우림 **rainfall** 강우 **wash away** …을 유실되게 하다, 쓸어가다 **tusk** (코끼리의) 상아 **chip off** 떨어져 나가게 하다 **rough** 고르지 않은 **risk** …의 위험을 무릅쓰다 **predator** 포식 동물 **crack** (갈라져 생긴) 금 **in spite of** …에도 불구하고 **wander** 돌아다니다, 헤매다 **reward** 보상 문제 **sharpen** 날카롭게 하다 **take shelter** 대피하다

04

247 words 3'50"

Date:

Time Taken:

English Only

The Amazing Sardine Run

Every summer millions of little sardines swim along the coast of South Africa in a giant group. This amazing migration is kind of a mystery, but it certainly gets all the animals nearby excited.

After ⓐ <u>laying</u> their eggs in the Agulhas Bank off the southern coast, the sardines swim to the eastern coast of South Africa. They travel in an ⓑ <u>insignificant</u> group that can be miles in length, up to a mile in width, and over thirty meters deep. Planes flying ⓒ <u>low</u> over the ocean can even see this gigantic group of tiny fish. Tens of thousands of animals hungry for sardines ⓓ <u>hurry</u> to the area, including dolphins, whales, *gannets, *sailfish, and many kinds of sharks, as well as *orcas and seals — making it earth's biggest event for ⓔ <u>predators</u>.

(①) The dolphins have an incredible hunting strategy. (②) Once the sardines are rounded up, it is easy for the dolphins to snatch them. (③) And when the dolphins push the sardines to the top of the water, flocks of birds waiting to catch them can take advantage of the sudden opportunity. (④) Thousands of birds soar and dive into the water, creating another spectacle. (⑤)

Many people come to watch the Sardine Run from boats. Some bring snorkeling equipment to swim under the waves among all the excited fish. People enjoy the event and they all agree it's one of the most amazing sights they've ever seen.

*gannet 부비새류 *sailfish 돛새치 *orca 범고래

공격을 위해 무리를 이루는 어류

필리핀, 말레이시아 해역에서 서식하는 어류인 바라쿠다는 먹잇감을 발견하면 무리를 이루어 빙글빙글 돌며 먹잇감을 에워싼다. 그다음 당황한 먹잇감 물고기들을 동시에 공격해 먹는다. 고래 또한 무리를 이루어 사냥한다. 고래는 먹잇감을 발견하면 둥글게 원을 형성하면서 잠수한 뒤 분수공으로 공기를 내보내 공기방울 기둥을 만든다. 원을 그리며 만들어진 이 기둥들은 그물 역할을 하게 되고, 고래들은 자신들이 정한 순서에 따라 공기방울 기둥에 갇힌 먹잇감들을 순서대로 공격해 먹는다.

1 What is NOT mentioned in the passage?

① why sardines travel in a group
② the size of the sardine group
③ various predators of sardines
④ how dolphins hunt sardines
⑤ how people enjoy the Sardine Run

VOCA

2 Which is NOT appropriate among ⓐ~ⓔ?

① ⓐ ② ⓑ ③ ⓒ ④ ⓓ ⑤ ⓔ

3 Where would the given sentence best fit among ①~⑤?

They team up to collect the sardines into a round group, called a "bait ball."

서술형

4 Fill in the blanks using the appropriate words from the box.

birds	hungry	hunt	dive	enormous	migration

When the __________ of sardines starts, the __________ sea animals get excited. When dolphins __________ sardines, they push them to the top of the water, where waiting __________ can catch them, too.

sardine 정어리 **coast** 해안 **lay** (알을) 낳다(laid-laid) **gigantic** 거대한 **seal** 바다표범, 물개 **incredible** 믿을 수 없는 **snatch** 와락 붙잡다, 잡아채다 **take advantage of** …을 이용하다 **soar** (허공으로) 솟구치다 **spectacle** (굉장히 인상적인) 광경 **equipment** 장비
문제 **team up** 협력하다 **bait** 미끼

Review Test

· VOCA ·

A

다음 중 단어의 뜻풀이가 잘못된 것을 고르시오.

① decay: to break down through a natural process
② feature: an important or typical part of something
③ plain: an area of very wet land with wild plants
④ border: an official line dividing two countries
⑤ equipment: tools you need for a particular activity

B

괄호 안에서 적절한 단어를 고르시오.

1 Asia is the largest (conflict / continent) in the world.
2 A lot of animals are in danger of losing their natural (habits / habitats).
3 Fruit flies (reduce / reproduce) rapidly, laying about 500 eggs at a time.
4 The microscope enables us to (reserve / observe) tiny living things.

C

문맥상 다음 빈칸에 들어갈 가장 알맞은 단어를 고르시오.

1 Salmon __________ from oceans to fresh water to lay eggs.
① escape ② migrate ③ produce ④ maintain ⑤ store

2 I __________ around the park while waiting for my friend to arrive.
① fell ② switched ③ wandered ④ snatched ⑤ appeared

3 Sharks are the top __________ of the ocean, mainly eating small fish and squid.
① preys ② rivals ③ rewards ④ predators ⑤ ecosystems

4 The Earth was once ruled by __________ dinosaurs.
① sharp ② frozen ③ rare ④ apparent ⑤ gigantic

정답 및 해설 p.83

· SENTENCE ·

D

다음 문장을 밑줄 친 부분에 유의하여 우리말로 해석하시오.

1 The camel's broad feet would have <u>made it easier to walk across</u> the snow <u>without sinking in</u>.

▸ ______________________________

2 The jellyfish <u>turns itself back into a baby</u> instead of dying.

▸ ______________________________

3 They use their tusks to chip off rough bits of the cave wall, <u>which they then eat</u>.

▸ ______________________________

4 Flocks of birds <u>waiting to catch them</u> can take advantage of the sudden opportunity.

▸ ______________________________

E

우리말에 맞게 주어진 단어들을 바르게 배열하여 문장을 완성하시오.

1 코끼리들은 그들이 먹이에서 필요로 하는 만큼의 많은 소금을 얻지 못한다.

The elephants do not get (they / as / need / much / salt / as) in their diet.

▸ The elephants do not get ______________________ in their diet.

2 그것들은 원래의 형태로 되돌아가서, '줄기세포'로 알려진 것과 비슷해진다.

They change back to their original form, (similar / becoming / to / what / are) known as "stem cells."

▸ They change back to their original form, ______________________ known as "stem cells."

3 바다 위에 낮게 날아가는 비행기들은 아주 작은 물고기들의 이 무리를 볼 수도 있다.

(over / planes / the ocean / low / flying) can see this group of tiny fish.

▸ ______________________ can see this group of tiny fish.

6

STICK TO YOUR GUNS

서부 영화를 보면 서로 적대 관계에 있는 카우보이들이 우연히 마주치는 장면이 등장한다. 서로를 발견한 바로 그 순간, 조금이라도 주저한다면 어떻게 될까? 아마 망설이지 않고 판단을 내린 상대 카우보이의 총에 죽음을 맞게 될 것이다. 여기서 '주저하지 말고 소신 있게 행동하라'를 의미하는 표현 stick to your guns가 유래되었다.

어떻게 해야 하지? 모니카가 내가 잘못된 선택을 하는 거래! /
제발! 줏대 있게 행동해.

SECTION 12

연예 · 스포츠

01

184 words 2'40"

Date:
Time Taken:

내가 모델이 된다고?

A stylish woman poses on the street, and a man takes a picture of her. You might think she is a model or celebrity, but she is not. She is just an ordinary, but fashionable woman in her own clothes. The photographer is Scott Schuman, one of the world's most-famous fashion photographers.

After quitting his fashion sales job in 2005, Schuman went to the streets with his digital camera. He spent four to five hours a day (A) photographing / to photograph people's street wear. His target was anyone dressed attractively. It didn't matter (B) that / if they were wearing trendy clothes or expensive brands. Then he posted the photos to his blog, *The Sartorialist*.

The blog gained international attention because people found his pictures different from typical fashion photos. Millions of people of all backgrounds started visiting his blog (C) getting / to get style inspiration. Soon famous brands began collaborating with him on advertising campaigns, and magazines started running his pictures.

Schuman believes individuality is the most important thing in fashion. To him, a well-dressed person is one who displays a personal style, rather than a manufactured look created by stylists.

정답 및 해설 p.84

1 윗글의 주제로 가장 적절한 것은?

① the daily life of a young model
② how to be a successful blogger
③ the secret of fashionable people
④ a photographer who shoots street style
⑤ the relationship between fashion and photography

수능어법

2 윗글의 (A), (B), (C)의 각 네모 안에서 어법에 맞는 표현으로 가장 적절한 것은?

	(A)		(B)		(C)
①	photographing	……	that	……	getting
②	photographing	……	if	……	getting
③	photographing	……	if	……	to get
④	to photograph	……	if	……	to get
⑤	to photograph	……	that	……	getting

서술형

3 주어진 질문에 대한 답을 할 때, 빈칸에 알맞은 말을 본문에서 찾아 쓰시오. (1단어)

What does Scott Schuman think the most important thing in fashion is?
→ He believes ____________________ is the most important thing.

스콧 슈만 스콧 슈만은 자신의 블로그에 두 딸의 사진을 올리기 시작하면서 15년간 패션 업계에 종사한 이력을 뒤로하고 사진작가로서의 새로운 삶을 시작했다. 그의 블로그인 *The Sartorialist*(www.thesartorialist.com)은 패션에 민감한 세계 각지의 도시에서 촬영한 감각적인 패션 스타일링을 소개하며 패션 트렌드의 교과서로 자리 잡고 있다. 슈만은 『보그』, 『GQ』, 『엘르』 등 세계적인 잡지에 사진을 싣고 있으며 그의 블로그는 광고주들과 패션 피플의 주목을 받고 있다. 그는 또한 『타임』지가 뽑은 '디자인 부문 가장 영향력 있는 100인'에 선정되었다.

stylish 멋진 **pose** 포즈[자세]를 취하다 **celebrity** 유명 인사 **street wear** 길거리 패션 **target** 목표; *(목표로 하는) 대상 **matter** 중요하다, 문제되다 **trendy** 최신 유행의 **gain attention** 주목을 받다 **typical** 전형적인 **inspiration** 영감 **collaborate** 협력하다; 공동으로 작업하다 **individuality** 개성, 특성 **display** 보여 주다, 드러내다 **manufactured** 제작된 문제 **shoot** (총을) 쏘다; *(사진을) 촬영하다

02

최고의 운동 친구

221 words 3'10"

Date:

Time Taken:

Are you trying ⓐ(get) fit by jogging? Well, jogging can become lonely, boring, and repetitive, so most people wind up quitting after just a few weeks. But now there's new technology that can help you stay interested and motivated.

A new smartphone application called "Running Mate" will allow you to map your runs and check your progress as you go. Using the smartphone's GPS and *accelerometer technology, you're able to record the pace, the distance, and the route of your run. While jogging, you can hear voice feedback on how you're doing, tap the map to check your location, and see whether you're on track to beat your record time. If that doesn't ____________ you to keep going, try listening to fun motivational messages from famous athletes, or play your favorite music to lift your mood.

With Running Mate, you'll never be lonely again when out jogging. You can send the details of your runs to a community website in order ⓑ(boast) about your fastest time, set goals and challenges, and stay in touch with friends. The application is also compatible with Facebook and Twitter, so you can broadcast your achievements to the world.

This application will help turn jogging from a chore into a treat. You'll get fitter and faster, and you'll have a lot of fun, too!

*accelerometer 가속도계

정답 및 해설 p.85

1 윗글에서 Running Mate의 기능으로 언급되지 않은 것은?

① checking one's progress
② listening to the radio
③ logging running distance
④ checking location
⑤ posting on social websites

2 윗글의 빈칸에 들어갈 말로 적절하지 않은 것은?

① force ② inspire ③ motivate
④ stimulate ⑤ encourage

서술형

3 윗글의 ⓐ와 ⓑ 안에 주어진 동사를 어법에 알맞은 형태로 쓰시오.

ⓐ ________________ ⓑ ________________

러너스 하이 Runners' High

중간 강도의 운동을 30분 이상 계속할 때 느끼는 행복감을 러너스 하이라 부른다. 러너스 하이가 발생하는 메커니즘은 아직 확실히 밝혀지지 않았지만, 중추신경계에서 환각 성분의 화학적 구조와 기능이 비슷한 오피오이드 펩타이드라는 물질이 많이 분비되기 때문이라는 주장이 있다. 마라톤을 비롯해 수영, 자전거, 축구, 스키, 서핑 등 장시간 지속하는 운동을 할 때 러너스 하이를 느낄 수 있다.

fit (운동으로 몸이) 건강한, 탄탄한 **repetitive** 반복적인 **wind up v-ing** …하게 되다 **motivated** 자극받은, 동기가 부여된 **application** 지원; 적용; *응용 프로그램 **progress** 진전 **pace** 속도 **tap** (가볍게) 톡톡 두드리다[치다] **be on track** 착착 나아가다[진행 중이다] **beat** 이기다; *능가하다 **lift** 들어 올리다; *(기분 · 사기 등을) 좋아지게 하다, 북돋우다 **boast** 뽐내다, 자랑하다 **compatible** 호환이 되는 **broadcast** 방송하다; *널리 알리다 **achievement** 업적, 성취한 것 문제 **log** 일지에 기록하다 **stimulate** 자극[격려]하다

03

스타들의 숨겨진 과거

249 words 3'20"

Date:

Time Taken:

At times, it seems like celebrities have no difficulties, doesn't it? They're beautiful and charismatic. But they sometimes face obstacles, too. You may be surprised to know that many celebrities have learning disabilities. The following is a list of inspirational stars that have learned to live with disabilities.

Bruce Willis is a skilled actor, but he wasn't always natural on camera. Until he reached the age of twenty, he had a stuttering problem. In an interview, he explained that acting helped him beat his stutter and work on his sense of humor. By being funny, Willis kept people's attention off his disability and on his acting skills. In doing so, he gained confidence.

American swimmer Michael Phelps is fast and alert in the pool. But Phelps' focus wasn't always strong, as he had *ADHD. In school, Phelps sometimes (still, got, for, not, in trouble, sitting) in class. When he turned his attention to swimming, however, he was able to develop his concentration. After years of training, his hard work led to several Olympic gold medals.

When Keira Knightley was young, her classmates teased her because she could not read. It turned out she had dyslexia, which causes people to read incorrectly. To help her defeat her disability, Knightley's parents made a deal with her. They agreed to find her an acting agent if she learned to read. Well, you can probably imagine <u>how it turned out</u>, because Keira is now one of the most famous actresses in the world.

*ADHD 주의력 결핍 및 과잉행동 장애 (Attention Deficit Hyperactivity Disorder)

정답 및 해설 p.87

1

스타들의 어린 시절에 관한 윗글의 내용과 일치하지 않는 것은?

① 브루스 윌리스는 어렸을 때 말을 더듬었다.
② 브루스 윌리스는 연기를 통해 자신감을 길렀다.
③ 마이클 펠프스는 수영 훈련을 위해 학업을 포기했다.
④ 마이클 펠프스는 ADHD 판정을 받았다.
⑤ 키이라 나이틀리는 학교에서 놀림을 받았다.

서술형

2

윗글의 괄호 안에 주어진 단어들을 다음 우리말에 맞게 배열하시오.

가만히 앉아 있지 못하여 곤란에 처했다

→ ____________________

3

윗글의 밑줄 친 부분이 의미하는 것은?

① Keira Knightley was cast in a movie.
② Keira Knightley was a talented actress.
③ Keira Knightley overcame her disability.
④ Keira Knightley is still suffering from dyslexia.
⑤ Keira Knightley stopped acting due to her disability.

주의력 결핍 및 과잉행동 장애 ADHD

ADHD는 지속적으로 주의력이 부족하고 과잉행동, 충동성을 보이는 상태를 가리키며 아동기에 많이 나타난다. ADHD 아동들은 한곳에 오래 집중하지 못하고, 허락 없이 자리에서 일어나 뛰어다니거나 팔과 다리를 끊임없이 움직이기도 한다. 억제나 집중 등의 행동을 지시하는 뇌 전두엽이 제대로 기능하지 않거나 미성숙할 때 발생하는 것으로 알려져 있다. 약물치료, 교육, 학습 및 놀이치료를 통해 충분히 호전될 수 있다.

at times 가끔은, 때때로 **charismatic** 카리스마가 있는 **obstacle** 장애물 **learning disability** 학습 장애 **skilled** 숙련된 **stuttering** 말을 더듬는 ※ **stutter** 말을 더듬다; *말더듬증 **alert** 기민한 **still** 가만히 있는 **concentration** 집중력 **tease** 놀리다 **turn out** …인 것으로 드러나다[밝혀지다] **dyslexia** 난독증 **defeat** 물리치다, 이기다 **make a deal** 거래[타협]하다

04

237 words 3'50"

Date:

Time Taken:

English Only

Why Runners Run Counterclockwise

Everyone enjoys watching the track and field events at the Olympics. Understandably, the focus is only on how fast the athletes are running. But there's something else most people probably don't notice. In all the events, the athletes run in a counterclockwise direction. Why is that?

Firstly, it is related to the structure of the human body. Specifically, the position of the heart, which is the body's most vital organ, is slightly to the left of the center. (A) On a left-hand turn, *centrifugal force pushes to the right and helps the heart to pump blood more easily to the other organs in the body. (B) When a runner turns to the left in a counterclockwise direction, he or she encounters centrifugal force. (C) This increase in blood circulation means the runner does not tire too quickly. Turning to the right has the opposite effect, as blood is pushed to the left and away from the other organs.

The other key point is that turning to the left is more natural for most people. The act of turning to the left requires pushing harder with the right foot. Just as most people are right-handed, most also have a stronger right foot. Thus, turning left is an easier motion.

Next time you visit an athletics track, try running around it in a clockwise direction. You'll feel how much more difficult it is, and understand why we normally run the other way!

*centrifugal force 원심력

원심력과 구심력 기차에 타고 있을 때 기차가 선로를 따라 커브를 돌면 커브 바깥쪽으로 몸이 기우는 느낌을 받게 된다. 이는 우리 몸은 관성에 의해 원래 향하던 방향으로 가고자 하는 반면, 우리가 탄 기차는 커브를 틀어 방향을 돌렸기 때문이다. 이처럼 원 운동을 하는 물체가 관성에 의해 원의 중심으로부터 멀어지려고 하는 힘이 원심력이다. 반대로, 물체가 원 운동을 할 수 있도록 중심으로 끌어당기는 힘은 구심력이다. 물체가 원의 궤도에 따라 일정한 속력으로 운동을 계속하려면, 원의 궤도를 따라 물체가 방향을 바꾸도록 하는 힘이 필요한데, 이것이 바로 구심력이다.

정답 및 해설 p.88

1 Mark the following statements T (True) or F (False).

	T	F
(1) When you're taking a left-hand turn, blood is pushed to the right.	□	□
(2) You may feel tired quickly when running in a clockwise direction.	□	□
(3) Turning to the right is more natural for most people.	□	□

VOCA

2 Which is the closest in meaning to the underlined word "vital"?

① stiff ② fatal ③ sensitive ④ essential ⑤ independent

3 Choose the right order of (A), (B), and (C) according to the context.

① (A) – (B) – (C) ② (A) – (C) – (B)

③ (B) – (A) – (C) ④ (B) – (C) – (A)

⑤ (C) – (A) – (B)

서술형

4 Why do runners run counterclockwise? Fill in the blanks using appropriate words from the passage.

→ It is because centrifugal force helps the heart to pump __________ more easily, and most people have a stronger __________ foot.

counterclockwise 시계 반대 방향으로; 시계 반대 방향의 **track and field** 육상경기 **understandably** 당연히 **specifically** 분명히, *구체적으로 **vital** 필수적인 **organ** 장기[기관] **slightly** 약간, 조금 **encounter** 맞닥뜨리다, 부딪히다 **blood circulation** 혈액순환 **motion** 운동, 움직임 **athletics** 육상경기 **clockwise** 시계 방향의 문제 **stiff** 뻣뻣한 **fatal** 죽음을 초래하는, 치명적인

Review Test

• VOCA •

A 다음 단어의 영영풀이를 바르게 연결하시오.

1 tease •   • ⓐ not moving

2 still •   • ⓑ very important or essential

3 vital •   • ⓒ involving the same thing occurring many times

4 organ •   • ⓓ to laugh at or make fun of someone

5 repetitive •   • ⓔ a part of the body such as the liver or the heart

B 괄호 안에서 적절한 단어를 고르시오.

1 The marathoner kept a fast (pace / face) throughout the race.

2 It doesn't (matter / manage) whether you believe the news or not.

3 The whole team (complained / collaborated) to achieve a common goal.

4 The (process / progress) of scientific technology has changed our lives in many ways.

C 문맥상 다음 빈칸에 들어갈 가장 알맞은 단어를 고르시오.

1 Readers of this book will learn how to overcome life's __________.

① benefits ② solutions ③ obstacles ④ compliments ⑤ achievements

2 In the finals, Maria __________ her rival and became the champion.

① played ② served ③ defeated ④ dropped ⑤ posed

3 My nephew has __________ a great talent for basketball since he was young.

① guided ② displayed ③ operated ④ analyzed ⑤ supported

4 The civil war in Pakistan gained __________ from all over the world.

① weight ② access ③ strength ④ attention ⑤ confidence

· SENTENCE ·

D

다음 문장을 밑줄 친 부분에 유의하여 우리말로 해석하시오.

1 People found Schuman's pictures different from typical fashion photos.

▸ ______________________________

2 While jogging, you can hear voice feedback on how you're doing.

▸ ______________________________

3 You may be surprised to know that many celebrities have learning disabilities.

▸ ______________________________

4 There's something else most people probably don't notice.

▸ ______________________________

E

우리말에 맞게 주어진 단어들을 바르게 배열하여 문장을 완성하시오.

1 만약 그것이 당신이 계속하도록 격려하지 않는다면, 좋아하는 음악을 틀어라.

If that doesn't (you / keep / inspire / to / going), play your favorite music.

▸ If that doesn't ______________________________, play your favorite music.

2 다음에 당신이 육상 트랙을 방문하면, 시계 방향으로 달리는 것을 시도해 보라.

(you / an athletics track / next time / visit), try running in a clockwise direction.

▸ ______________________________, try running in a clockwise direction.

3 요점은 왼쪽으로 도는 것이 대부분의 사람들에게 더 자연스럽다는 것이다.

The key point is that (the left / is / natural / turning / more / to) for most people.

▸ The key point is that ______________________________ for most people.

지은이

NE능률 영어교육연구소

NE능률 영어교육연구소는 혁신적이며 효율적인 영어 교재를 개발하고
영어 학습의 질을 한 단계 높이고자 노력하는 NE능률의 연구조직입니다.

리딩튜터 〈실력〉

펴 낸 이 주민홍
펴 낸 곳 서울특별시 마포구 월드컵북로 396(상암동) 누리꿈스퀘어 비즈니스타워 10층
㈜NE능률 (우편번호 03925)
펴 낸 날 2018년 8월 5일 개정판 제1쇄 발행
2023년 12월 15일 제14쇄
전 화 02 2014 7114
팩 스 02 3142 0356
홈페이지 www.neungyule.com
등록번호 제1-68호
I S B N 979-11-253-2388-4 53740
정 가 13,000원

고객센터

교재 내용 문의 : contact.nebooks.co.kr (별도의 가입 절차 없이 작성 가능)
제품 구매, 교환, 불량, 반품 문의 : 02-2014-7114
☎ 전화문의는 본사 업무시간 중에만 가능합니다.

MEMO

NE능률 교재 MAP

독해

아래 교재 MAP을 참고하여 본인의 현재 혹은 목표 수준에 따라 교재를 선택하세요.
NE능률 교재들과 함께 영어실력을 쑥쑥~ 올려보세요!
MP3 등 교재 부가 학습 서비스 및 자세한 교재 정보는 www.nebooks.co.kr 에서 확인하세요.

초1-2
- 초등영어 리딩이 된다 Start 1
- 초등영어 리딩이 된다 Start 2
- 초등영어 리딩이 된다 Start 3
- 초등영어 리딩이 된다 Start 4

초3
- 리딩버디 1

초3-4
- 리딩버디 2
- 초등영어 리딩이 된다 Basic 1
- 초등영어 리딩이 된다 Basic 2
- 초등영어 리딩이 된다 Basic 3
- 초등영어 리딩이 된다 Basic 4

초4-5
- 리딩버디 3
- 주니어 리딩튜터 스타터 1

초5-6
- 초등영어 리딩이 된다 Jump 1
- 초등영어 리딩이 된다 Jump 2
- 초등영어 리딩이 된다 Jump 3
- 초등영어 리딩이 된다 Jump 4
- 주니어 리딩튜터 스타터 2

초6-예비중
- 주니어 리딩튜터 1
- Junior Reading Expert 1
- Reading Forward Basic 1

중1
- 1316 Reading 1
- 주니어 리딩튜터 2
- Junior Reading Expert 2
- Reading Forward Basic 2
- 열중 16강 독해+문법 1
- Reading Inside Starter

중1-2
- 1316 Reading 2
- 주니어 리딩튜터 3
- 정말 기특한 구문독해 입문
- Junior Reading Expert 3
- Reading Forward Intermediate 1
- 열중 16강 독해+문법 2
- Reading Inside 1

중2-3
- 1316 Reading 3
- 주니어 리딩튜터 4
- 정말 기특한 구문독해 기본
- Junior Reading Expert 4
- Reading Forward Intermediate 2
- Reading Inside 2

중3
- 리딩튜터 입문
- 정말 기특한 구문독해 완성
- Reading Forward Advanced 1
- 열중 16강 독해+문법 3
- Reading Inside 3

중3-예비고
- Reading Expert 1
- 리딩튜터 기본
- Reading Forward Advanced 2

고1
- 빠바 기초세우기
- 리딩튜터 실력
- Reading Expert 2
- TEPS BY STEP G+R Basic

고1-2
- 빠바 구문독해
- 리딩튜터 수능 PLUS
- Reading Expert 3

고2-3, 수능 실전
- 빠바 유형독해
- 빠바 종합실전편
- Reading Expert 4
- TEPS BY STEP G+R 1

고3 이상, 수능 고난도
- Reading Expert 5
- 능률 고급영문독해

수능 이상/ 토플 80-89 · 텝스 600-699점
- ADVANCED Reading Expert 1
- TEPS BY STEP G+R 2
- RADIX TOEFL Blue Label Reading 1,2

수능 이상/ 토플 90-99 · 텝스 700-799점
- ADVANCED Reading Expert 2
- RADIX TOEFL Black Label Reading 1

수능 이상/ 토플 100 · 텝스 800점 이상
- RADIX TOEFL Black Label Reading 2
- TEPS BY STEP G+R 3

READING TUTOR

고등 독해의
절대 자신감

리딩튜터 실력
정답 및 해설

NE 능률

READING TUTOR

고등 독해의 절대 자신감

리딩튜터 실력

정답 및 해설

SECTION 01

세계의 문화

01 **1** ① **2** ⑤ **3** turn your hand so that your palm is facing towards you

02 **1** ⑤ **2** Do you think why → Why do you think **3** ④ **4** (1) F (2) T (3) F

03 **1** ⑤ **2** ③ **3** have restaurants serving traditional food from many countries

04 **1** ④ **2** ④ **3** whose → that[which] **4** ①

01 손을 들어 모두, 샤카! P. 10

정답 1 ① 2 ⑤ 3 turn your hand so that your palm is facing towards you

문제해설

1 ① 은행가, 사업가에서 서퍼들까지 하와이의 모든 이들이 널리 사용하는 제스처라고 했다. (③번 문장)
② (→ ④번 문장) ③ (→ ⑤번 문장) ④ (→ ⑥번 문장) ⑤ (→ ⑩, ⑪번 문장)

2 주어진 문장의 then은 리피 에스핀다가 방송에서 샤카를 사용한 때를 의미하므로, ⑤에 들어가는 것이 가장 적절하다.

3 '…이 당신 쪽을 향하다'라는 의미로 is facing towards you를 쓸 수 있으며, '…하도록'은 「so that+S+V」의 형태로 배열한다.

본문

① If you ever visit Hawaii, / the locals will probably greet you / with an unusual hand gesture / and the words "shaka brah." ② This warm welcome, / known as the *shaka*, / is popular throughout the islands. ③ From bankers and businessmen to surfers, / everyone uses this friendly gesture. ④ It helps / to promote peace and harmony / among the wide range of ethnic groups / living there.

⑤ No one is sure / where the *shaka* first originated, / but the most common theory is / that it stems from beach culture. ⑥ The term *shaka* itself / is probably a variation / on the common expression "shark eye," / a compliment / paid to show respect. ⑦ The *shaka* gesture / became popular in the 1960s / thanks to local celebrity Lippy Espinda, / who used it / in television advertisements. ⑧ From then on, / everyone began using the *shaka* / as a friendly show of goodwill.

⑨ Here's how to make a *shaka* sign. ⑩ The first step is / to make a fist. ⑪ Then extend your thumb and pinky, / but be sure / not to uncurl your middle fingers. ⑫ Then, turn your hand / so that your palm is facing towards you. ⑬ Finally, move it / as if writing the letter "J." ⑭ That's it. ⑮ Now / you are ready to greet people / the Hawaiian way!

해석

① 당신이 언젠가 하와이를 방문한다면, 현지인들은 아마도 독특한 손짓과 '샤카 브라'라는 말로 당신을 맞이할 것이다. ② '샤카'라고 알려진 이 따뜻한 환영은, 하와이 제도 전체에 걸쳐 인기가 있다. ③ 은행가와 사업가에서부터 서퍼들에 이르기까지, 모든 사람들이 이 다정한 제스처를 사용한다. ④ 이것은 그곳에 살고 있는 폭넓은 민족들 사이에서 평화와 조화를 증진하도록 돕는다.

⑤ 누구도 '샤카'가 처음에 어디에서 유래했는지 확신하지 못하지만, 가장 일반적인 이론은 그것이 해변 문화에서 비

롯한다는 것이다. ⑥ '샤카'라는 용어 자체는 아마도 존경심을 나타내기 위해 바쳐지는 찬사인 '상어의 눈'이라는 흔한 표현의 변형일 것이다. ⑦ 샤카 제스처는 1960년대에 지역 유명 인사인 리피 에스핀다 덕분에 인기를 얻게 되었는데, 그는 이것을 텔레비전 광고에서 사용했다. ⑧ 그때부터 모든 사람들이 '샤카'를 다정한 호의의 표시로 사용하기 시작했다.

⑨ 여기 샤카 표시를 만드는 방법이 있다. ⑩ 첫 번째 단계는 주먹을 쥐는 것이다. ⑪ 그리고 당신의 엄지손가락과 새끼손가락을 펼치되, 중간의 손가락들은 펴지 않도록 명심하라. ⑫ 그러고 나서 당신의 손바닥이 당신 쪽을 향하도록 손을 돌려라. ⑬ 마지막으로 마치 문자 'J'를 쓰는 것처럼 손을 움직여라. ⑭ 그것이 전부이다. ⑮ 이제 당신은 사람들을 하와이 식으로 맞을 준비가 된 것이다!

구문해설

⑤ ..., but the most common theory is [**that** it stems from beach culture].
→ that은 보어로 쓰인 명사절을 이끄는 접속사

⑪ ..., but **be sure** ***not to uncurl*** your middle fingers.
→ be sure to-v: 꼭[반드시] …해라
→ to부정사의 부정은 not을 to 앞에 붙임.

⑬ Finally, move it **as if** (you were) writing the letter "J."
→ as if 다음에 「주어+be동사」인 you were가 생략됨.

02 보기만 해도 아찔해요! P. 12

정답

1 ⑤ **2** Do you think why → Why do you think **3** ④ **4** (1) F (2) T (3) F

문제해설

1 ⑤ 나무 기둥에 의지한 채 절벽에 매달려 있는 듯한 독특한 외관을 지닌 절인 중국의 현공사에 대한 글이다.
① 중국에서 가장 오래된 절 ② 현공사의 역사 ③ 내면의 평화를 찾는 방법
④ 중국의 세 가지 전통 종교 ⑤ 현공사: 절벽에 지어진 절

2 간접의문문은 「의문사+주어+동사」의 어순이 되지만, 주절의 동사가 think, believe, suppose, guess 등일 때는 반드시 의문사를 맨 앞에 두므로 Why do you think가 되어야 한다.

3 절이 높은 절벽에 매달려 있으면 홍수로부터 안전할 것이므로 '위태롭게 만들다'라는 뜻의 ④ endangers는 '보호하다'라는 뜻의 protects가 되는 것이 적절하다.

4 (1) 현공사는 절벽 위 75m 높이에 건축되었다. → 현공사는 절벽 위로 75m 높이가 아닌 땅 위로 75m 이상 떨어진 절벽에 지어졌다. (⑤번 문장)
(2) 세 개의 다른 종교가 이 절과 관련되어 있다. → 현공사는 불교, 도교, 유교 모두를 위한 장소라고 하였다. (⑭번 문장)
(3) 절의 위치 때문에 이 절을 찾는 관광객이 거의 없다. → 접근하기 어려운 위치에도 불구하고, 현공사는 관광객으로 붐빈다고 하였다. (㉑번 문장)

본문

① Your legs tremble / and your palms sweat / as you walk. ② Where are you? ③ You are climbing to Xuan Kong Si, / also called the Hanging Temple, / in China.

④ The temple is famous / for its location. ⑤ It is built into a cliff, / more than 75 meters / above the ground. ⑥ It looks very fragile. ⑦ But surprisingly, / the Hanging Temple has been "hanging" there / for about 1,500 years!

⑧ The secret is / in its unique building design. ⑨ Its long, thin wooden poles / were built into the rock / as the foundation. ⑩ They seem to support the structure. ⑪ But it was actually constructed in a way / that lets the rock in back / carry most of the weight.

⑫ The temple is not only special outside. ⑬ The inside is also unique. ⑭ It is a place / for three different traditional religions: / Buddhism, Taoism, and Confucianism. ⑮ The temple includes forty chambers / connected by narrow stairs and bridges. ⑯ There are eighty-seven statues / from all three religions inside / as well.

⑰ Why / do you think / the temple was built like this? ⑱ One reason is / that the location protects the temple / from the nearby river's floods. ⑲ The other reason is spiritual. ⑳ The quiet location is ideal / for meditating / and searching for inner peace. ㉑ Ironically, the temple is now / a busy tourist attraction. ㉒ Would you like to go?

해석

① 당신이 걸어갈 때, 다리는 떨리고 손바닥에는 땀이 난다. ② 당신은 어디에 있는 걸까? ③ 당신은 '매달려 있는 절(Hanging Temple)'이라고도 불리는, 중국의 현공사로 올라가고 있다.

④ 이 절은 절이 위치한 장소로 유명하다. ⑤ 그것은 땅에서 75미터 넘게 떨어진 절벽에 지어져 있다. ⑥ 절은 매우 약해 보인다. ⑦ 하지만 놀랍게도, 현공사는 그곳에 약 1500년 동안 '매달려' 있었다!

⑧ 비밀은 그 절의 독특한 건물 설계에 있다. ⑨ 절의 길고 가느다란 나무 기둥들이 건물의 토대가 되어 바위 속에 꽂혀 있다. ⑩ 그 기둥들이 건축물을 떠받치고 있는 것처럼 보인다. ⑪ 그러나 그 절은 실제로는 뒤에 있는 바위가 대부분의 하중을 견디게 하는 방식으로 지어졌다.

⑫ 그 절은 단지 외관만 특별한 것은 아니다. ⑬ 내부 역시 독특하다. ⑭ 이 절은 불교, 도교, 유교라는 세 가지 각기 다른 전통적인 종교를 위한 공간이다. ⑮ 절에는 좁은 계단과 다리들로 연결된 40개의 방이 있다. ⑯ 내부에는 또한 세 종교의 인물상 87개도 있다.

⑰ 이 절이 왜 이렇게 지어졌다고 생각하는가? ⑱ 한 가지 이유는 그 위치가 절을 근처 강의 범람으로부터 보호해준다는 것이다. ⑲ 다른 이유는 영적인 것이다. ⑳ 절의 조용한 위치는 명상을 하고 내면의 평화를 찾는 데 이상적이다. ㉑ 얄궂게도, 이 절은 현재 붐비는 관광 명소이다. ㉒ 당신이라면 가보고 싶겠는가?

구문해설

③ You are climbing to Xuan Kong Si, [also called the Hanging Temple], in China.
→ [ ]는 삽입어구로 쓰인 과거분사구로 Xuan Kong Si를 부연 설명함.

⑪ But it was actually constructed in a way [**that** *lets* the rock in back *carry* most of the weight].
(that: S, lets: V, the rock in back: O, carry: OC)
→ that은 a way를 선행사로 하는 주격 관계대명사
→ let(사역동사) + 목적어 + 동사원형: (목적어)가 …하게 하다

⑮ The temple includes forty chambers [connected by narrow stairs and bridges].
→ [ ]는 forty chambers를 뒤에서 수식하는 과거분사구

⑱ One reason is [**that** the location protects the temple from the nearby river's floods].
→ that은 보어로 쓰인 명사절을 이끄는 접속사

⑳ The quiet location is ideal for **meditating** and **searching** for inner peace.
→ 전치사 for의 목적어로 동명사 meditating과 searching이 and로 연결된 병렬구조

03 니스 카니발로의 초대장 P. 14

정답 1 ⑤ 2 ③ 3 have restaurants serving traditional food from many countries

문제해설 1 ⑤ 퍼레이드 티켓 가격은 10~25유로 사이로 다양하다. (⑯번 문장)
① (→ ②번 문장) ② (→ ⑩번 문장) ③ (→ ⑫번 문장) ④ (→ ⑮번 문장)

2 (A) 수식하는 앞의 명사 city와 의미상 수동의 관계이므로, 과거분사 crowded가 적절하다.
(B) 분사구문으로, 동시동작의 의미를 가진 현재분사 enjoying이 적절하다.
(C) 수식하는 앞의 명사 floats와 의미상 수동의 관계이므로, 과거분사 covered가 적절하다.

3 serving이 이끄는 현재분사구가 restaurants를 뒤에서 수식하는 문장으로 배열한다.

본문

① In February, / Nice, in France, / is transformed into an exciting city / crowded with people / looking for fun. ② That's because / February is the month / of the city's biggest annual event, / the Nice Carnival. ③ Everyone gets into the party spirit / during this month, / enjoying the parades, fireworks and other delightful activities / during the day and at night. ④ You can also enjoy this amazing experience. ⑤ Here's some travel information / that will help you.

⑥ **Things to Do**

⑦ Attending the parades / is a must-do activity. ⑧ The most incredible are the Flower Parades, / where you can see 20 floats / covered in flowers / parade along the *Promenade des Anglais*. ⑨ These show off / all of the French Riviera's most beautiful flowers. ⑩ At the same time, / men and women in costume / walk alongside the floats / and toss 100,000 flowers / into the audience. ⑪ The other great event / is the Grand Parade / at the end of the festival. ⑫ It finishes with an amazing fireworks display, / which is well worth seeing.

⑬ **Getting Tickets**

⑭ Many of the events are free, / though there is a charge / for the Parades. ⑮ It is a good idea / to buy tickets early / so that you can reserve a seat / with a good view. ⑯ The fee ranges / from 10 to 25 euros, / depending on whether you want to stand or sit.

⑰ **Dining**

⑱ Nice is home / to a wide variety of fabulous restaurants. ⑲ The main streets have restaurants / serving traditional food from many countries, / such as France, Italy, Turkey, and China.

해석 ① 2월에 프랑스의 니스는 즐거움을 찾는 사람들로 북적거리는 신나는 도시로 바뀝니다. ② 그것은 2월이 그 도시의 가장 큰 연례 행사인 니스 카니발의 달이기 때문입니다. ③ 모든 사람들은 이달 동안 파티 기분에 젖어 퍼레이드, 불꽃놀이, 그리고 다른 즐거운 활동들을 밤낮으로 즐깁니다. ④ 여러분도 이 놀라운 경험을 즐길 수 있습니다. ⑤ 여기

여러분을 도와줄 여행 정보가 있습니다.

⑥ **할 것들**

⑦ 퍼레이드에 참여하는 것은 꼭 해야 하는 활동입니다. ⑧ 가장 놀라운 것은 플라워 퍼레이드인데, 여기서 여러분은 꽃으로 덮인 스무 대의 장식 차량이 '영국인의 산책로'를 따라 행진하는 것을 볼 수 있습니다. ⑨ 이것들은 프랑스 리비에라 지방의 가장 아름다운 꽃들 전부를 뽐냅니다. ⑩ 동시에, 의상을 입은 남녀들이 장식 차량과 나란히 걸으며 십만 송이의 꽃들을 관중들에게 던집니다. ⑪ 또 다른 대단한 행사는 축제의 마지막에 열리는 그랜드 퍼레이드입니다. ⑫ 그것은 놀라운 불꽃놀이로 끝이 나는데 그것은 아주 볼 만한 가치가 있습니다.

⑬ **티켓 구하기**

⑭ 대다수의 행사들이 무료이지만, 퍼레이드에는 요금이 있습니다. ⑮ 전망이 좋은 자리를 예약할 수 있도록 티켓을 일찍 구매하는 것이 좋습니다. ⑯ 요금은 서고 싶은지 앉고 싶은지에 따라 10유로에서 25유로까지 다양합니다.

⑰ **식사**

⑱ 니스는 매우 다양한 멋진 식당들의 본거지입니다. ⑲ 중심가에는 프랑스, 이탈리아, 터키, 그리고 중국 같은 많은 나라들의 전통 음식을 제공하는 식당들이 있습니다.

구문해설 ① ..., Nice, in France, is transformed into an exciting city [crowded with people {looking for fun}].

→ [ ]는 an exciting city를 수식하는 과거분사구

→ { }는 people을 수식하는 현재분사구

⑧ ... the Flower Parades, [where you can **see** 20 floats covered in flowers **parade** along ...].

→ [ ]는 선행사 the Flower Parades를 부연 설명하는 계속적 용법의 관계부사절

→ 「지각동사(see) + 목적어(20 ... flowers) + 목적격보어(parade)」 구문으로, 목적격보어로 동사원형을 사용함.

⑫ It finishes with an amazing fireworks display, **which** *is* well *worth seeing*.

→ which는 선행사 an amazing fireworks display를 부연 설명하는 계속적 용법의 주격 관계대명사

→ be worth v-ing: …할 가치가 있다

⑮ **It** is a good idea [**to buy** tickets early *so that* you *can* reserve a seat with a good view].

→ It은 가주어, [ ]가 진주어

→ so that ... can ~: …가 ~할 수 있도록

04 Let's Enjoy the Night of the Radishes in Mexico! P. 16

정답 1 ④ 2 ④ 3 whose → that[which] 4 ①

문제해설 1 ④ 조각된 무가 어떻게 생겼는지에 대한 언급은 없다.

[문제] 윗글에서 언급되지 않은 것은?

① 와하카의 조각 전통이 언제 시작되었는지 (⑦번 문장)

② 사람들이 왜 무를 조각하기 시작했는지 (⑧번 문장)

③ 요즘 누가 조각가로서 축제에 참가하는지 (⑫번 문장)

④ 조각된 무가 어떻게 생겼는지

⑤ 최고의 무 조각가는 상으로 무엇을 받는지 (⑯번 문장)

2 주어진 문장의 They는 사람들을 가리키며, 사람들이 조각된 무를 사서 크리스마스 저녁 식탁에 놓았다는 내용은 사람들이 그것들을 정말 좋아했다는 내용 뒤인 ④에 오는 것이 적절하다.

[문제] ①~⑤ 중 주어진 문장이 들어가기에 가장 적절한 곳은?

3 선행사는 special radishes, 그 이하는 선행사를 수식하는 주격 관계대명사절로 선행사가 사물일 때 주격 관계대명사는 which 또는 that을 쓰므로, whose를 which 또는 that으로 고쳐야 한다.

[문제] 밑줄 친 문장 ⓐ에서 어법상 틀린 부분을 찾아 바르게 고쳐 쓰시오.

4 '전시하다'라는 의미의 exhibit과 의미가 가장 가까운 것은 displaying이다.

[문제] 밑줄 친 단어 exhibiting과 의미가 가장 가까운 것은?

① 전시하기 ② 판매하기 ③ 위장하기 ④ 운반하기 ⑤ 홍보하기

본문

① On Halloween, / people in the United States / carve scary faces into pumpkins. ② These jack-o-lanterns are / a beloved Halloween tradition. ③ But south of the border, / in Oaxaca, Mexico, / there is a different carving tradition. ④ It happens around Christmas / instead of Halloween. ⑤ And rather than pumpkins, / people carve radishes!

⑥ The celebration is called Noche de Rabanos, / or Night of the Radishes, / and it takes place on December 23. ⑦ It was started / more than 100 years ago / by merchants at the town plaza. ⑧ Hoping to attract Christmas shoppers, / they would carve designs / into the bright red skin of radishes. ⑨ People loved them! ⑩ They bought the carved radishes / and placed them / in the center of the table / at Christmas dinner. ⑪ In 1897, / Noche de Rabanos became an official holiday / in Oaxaca.

⑫ Today, the carvings are made / by local artists and amateurs. ⑬ They use special radishes / that[which] are larger than normal / and not used for food. ⑭ These radishes, / which can weigh as much as three kilograms, / are harvested / on December 18. ⑮ This gives the carvers a few days / to work on their creations / before exhibiting them / in the town plaza. ⑯ The person who carves the best radish / wins a grand prize of 15,000 pesos.

⑰ If you're ever in Mexico / during the holiday season, / you should head to Oaxaca / and check out these wonderful Christmas radishes!

해석

① 핼러윈에, 미국인들은 호박에 무서운 얼굴을 새긴다. ② 이 호박등은 사랑받는 핼러윈 전통이다. ③ 하지만 국경 남쪽, 멕시코의 와하카에는, 다른 조각 전통이 있다. ④ 그것은 핼러윈 대신에 크리스마스 무렵에 벌어진다. ⑤ 그리고 호박보다는, 사람들은 무를 조각한다!

⑥ 이 축하 행사는 Noche de Rabanos, 즉 '무의 밤'이라고 불리고, 12월 23일에 개최된다. ⑦ 그것은 100년도 더 전에 마을 광장에서 상인들에 의해 시작되었다. ⑧ 크리스마스 쇼핑객들을 끌어모으기를 바라며, 그들은 무의 밝은 붉은색 껍질에 무늬를 새겨 넣곤 했다. ⑨ 사람들은 그것들을 정말 좋아했다! ⑩ 그들은 조각된 무를 사서 그것들을 크리스마스 저녁 식탁 가운데에 놓았다. ⑪ 1897년에, Noche de Rabanos는 와하카의 공휴일이 되었다.

⑫ 오늘날, 조각품은 지역 예술가와 아마추어들에 의해 만들어진다. ⑬ 그들은 보통 무보다 더 크고 식용이 아닌 특별한 무를 사용한다. ⑭ 무게가 무려 3kg나 되기도 하는 이 무는 12월 18일에 수확된다. ⑮ 이것은 조각가들이 마을

광장에서 그것들을 전시하기 전에 그들의 작품에 공을 들일 며칠을 준다. ⑯ 최고의 무를 조각하는 사람은 15,000 페소의 상금을 받는다.

⑰ 여러분이 크리스마스 시즌에 멕시코에 있게 된다면, 여러분은 와하카로 가서 이 멋진 크리스마스 무를 확인해야 한다!

구문해설 ⑧ [Hoping to attract Christmas shoppers], they **would** carve designs into the bright red skin of radishes.

→ [ ]는 접속사와 주어가 생략된 분사구문 (=Because they hoped ....)

→ would는 과거의 불규칙한 습관을 나타내는 조동사로 쓰임.

⑭ These radishes (S), [which can weigh **as much as** three kilograms], are harvested (V) ....

→ [ ]는 선행사 These radishes를 부연 설명하는 계속적 용법의 관계대명사절

→ as much as: …만큼, …정도

⑮ This gives the carvers a few days **to work on** their creations ....

→ to work on은 a few days를 수식하는 형용사적 용법의 to부정사

⑯ The person (S) [who carves the best radish] wins (V) a grand prize of 15,000 pesos.

→ [ ]는 선행사 The person을 수식하는 주격 관계대명사절

Review Test P. 18

A ⑤ B **1** fragile **2** costume **3** compliment **4** endanger C **1** ③ **2** ⑤ **3** ① **4** ④ D **1** 그것은 놀라운 불꽃놀이로 끝이 나는데 그것은 아주 볼 만한 가치가 있습니다. **2** 하지만 놀랍게도, 현공사는 그곳에 약 1500년 동안 매달려 있었다! **3** '샤카'라고 알려진 이 따뜻한 환영은, 제도 전체에 걸쳐 인기가 있다. **4** 이것은 조각가들이 마을 광장에서 그것들을 전시하기 전에 그들의 작품에 공을 들일 며칠을 준다. E **1** chambers connected by narrow stairs and bridges **2** than 100 years ago by merchants **3** so that you can reserve a seat

해석 **A**

① 유명 인사: 유명한 사람

② 끌어들이다: 남의 관심을 얻다

③ 촉진하다: 어떤 일이 일어나도록 하기 위해 노력하다

④ 떨다: 춥거나 무서워서 (몸이) 떨리다

⑤ 건설하다: 길이나 다리 같은 것을 파괴하다

B

1 이 꽃병들은 약합니다. 그것들을 특별히 주의해서 다루어 주세요.

2 그 오페라 가수는 무대에서 공주 의상을 입고 공연하였다.

3 우리 반의 반장은 그의 탁월한 리더십으로 칭찬을 받았다.

4 드론은 여객기의 항로를 침범하여 수백 명의 생명을 위험에 빠뜨릴 수도 있다.

C

1 몇몇 지역 주민들이 주민 협회를 만들기 위해 모였다.

① 수직의 ② 매년의 ③ 지역의 ④ 비싼 ⑤ 나무로 된

2 그 아이디어는 단순한 관찰에서 비롯되었다.

① 보호했다 ② 지지했다 ③ 위험에 빠뜨렸다 ④ 격려했다 ⑤ 비롯되었다

3 농작물을 수확하기 위해, 그들은 적절한 장비와 저장 시설이 필요하다.

① 수확하다 ② 예약하다 ③ 짓다 ④ 참석하다 ⑤ 환영하다

4 우리 가족은 아이들이 자기 생일 케이크를 직접 장식하게 하는 전통이 있다.

① 용어 ② 가두 행진 ③ 이론 ④ 전통 ⑤ 전시

SECTION 02

역사 속 인물

01 **1** ④ **2** ② **3** ② **4** horizontally, different

02 **1** ② **2** ⑤ **3** ③ **4** weren't → wasn't

03 **1** ⑤ **2** ⑤ **3** he could have reduced the number of victims

04 **1** ⑤ **2** ① **3** ③ **4** The story she wrote about her experience

01 그에 관한 진실 P. 22

정답 **1** ④ **2** ② **3** ② **4** horizontally, different

문제해설 **1** ④ 나폴레옹이 키가 작았다는 것이 오해라 밝히며, 그 이유가 무엇인지 설명하고 있는 글이다.

① 나폴레옹의 마지막 나날들 ② 나폴레옹 모자의 유래 ③ 나폴레옹과 그의 근위대

④ 나폴레옹은 정말 키가 작은 사람이었을까? ⑤ 나폴레옹 초상화의 비밀

2 삼각형 모자는 세로로 쓰면 키가 더 커 보이는데 나폴레옹은 가로로 써서 작아 보였고, 사망 조사를 한 의사가 기록한 나폴레옹의 키에서 오해가 비롯되었다는 내용이 각각 연결되고 있으므로 ② However가 가장 적절하다.

3 (A) the fact의 내용을 설명해 주는 내용이 이어지고 있으므로 명사절을 이끄는 동격의 접속사 that이 적절하다.

(B) 뒤에 명사구가 나오므로 명사(구)를 취하는 전치사 due to가 적절하다. because 뒤에는 절이 나온다.

(C) '결국 …이 되다'는 end up v-ing로 나타낸다.

4 나폴레옹이 키가 작다는 오해를 사게 된 이유는 모자를 가로로 써서 세로로 쓴 다른 병사들에 비해 작아 보였고 (④번 문장), 영국과 프랑스의 '피트' 단위가 달랐기 때문(⑦번 문장)이다.

나폴레옹은 두 가지 이유 때문에 키가 작은 남자로 여겨졌는데, 그가 모자를 가로로 썼고 프랑스와 영국의 피트 단위가 달랐기 때문이다.

본문

① Everyone thinks / that Napoleon Bonaparte was a very short man. ② Actually, / the triangular hat / he loved to wear / played a role / in making him look so short. ③ The hats / used by Napoleon's Imperial Guards / were worn vertically, / making the towering men / look even taller. ④ However, / Napoleon liked to wear his hat horizontally, / making him look short / in comparison.

⑤ Another crucial reason / why Napoleon has become the symbol of the short man / is that the doctor / who examined him upon his death / recorded his height as 5 feet 2 inches, / or 158 cm. ⑥ However, / Napoleon was actually 169 cm, / about the average height / for European men / at the time. ⑦ The 11 cm difference resulted from the fact / that the French unit of "feet" / and the British unit of "feet" / were different. ⑧ Due to this error, / the French emperor Napoleon Bonaparte, / whose name commanded respect and fear / throughout all of Europe, / lost 11 cm of his height / and ended up becoming a hero / for short men everywhere.

해석

① 모든 사람들은 나폴레옹 보나파르트가 키가 아주 작은 사람이었다고 생각한다. ② 실은, 그가 즐겨 쓰던 삼각형 모자가 그를 그렇게 작아 보이도록 만드는 데 한몫을 했다. ③ 나폴레옹의 근위대가 사용하던 모자는 세로로 쓰게 되어 있어 키가 큰 남자들을 훨씬 더 커 보이게 했다. ④ 그러나 나폴레옹은 그의 모자를 가로로 쓰는 것을 좋아해서, 그것이 비교해 볼 때 그를 작아 보이게 했다.

⑤ 나폴레옹이 키 작은 남자의 상징이 된 또 다른 결정적인 이유는 그의 사망을 조사한 의사가 그의 키를 5피트 2인치, 즉 158센티미터로 기록했기 때문이다. ⑥ 그러나 나폴레옹은 사실 그 당시 유럽 남성의 평균 신장인 169센티미터였다. ⑦ 그 11센티미터의 차이는 프랑스의 '피트' 단위와 영국의 '피트' 단위가 달랐기 때문에 생겨났다. ⑧ 이 착오 때문에, 그 이름만으로 유럽 전역에서 존경과 두려움을 일으켰던 프랑스 황제 나폴레옹 보나파르트는 그의 키 11센티미터를 잃어버렸고, 결국 전 세계 키 작은 사람들의 영웅이 되었다.

구문해설

② ..., the triangular hat [(that[which]) he loved to wear] **played a role in** making him look so short.
S / V

→ [ ]는 선행사 the triangular hat을 수식하는 관계대명사절로, 목적격 관계대명사 that[which]가 생략됨.

→ play a role in: …에(서) 역할을 하다

⑤ Another crucial reason [why Napoleon has become the symbol of the short man] is that the doctor [who examined him upon his death] recorded his height ....

→ 첫 번째 [ ]는 선행사 Another crucial reason을 수식하는 관계부사절

→ 두 번째 [ ]는 선행사 the doctor를 수식하는 주격 관계대명사절

⑧ ... Napoleon Bonaparte, [whose name commanded respect and fear ... Europe], **lost** ... his height and ***ended up*** *becoming* a hero ....

→ [ ]는 선행사 Napoleon Bonaparte를 부연 설명하는 계속적 용법의 관계대명사절

→ lost와 ended up은 둘 다 문장의 동사로 병렬 연결됨.

→ end up v-ing: 결국 …이 되다

02 크림 전쟁의 숨은 영웅 P. 24

정답 1 ② 2 ⑤ 3 ③ 4 weren't→ wasn't

문제해설 1 ② 간호사로 잘 알려진 나이팅게일이 통계학자로서 병원 환경 개선에 기여했다는 내용이다.
① 숫자와 도표 사용의 효과
② 통계학자로서의 나이팅게일의 기여
③ 19세기 병원의 열악한 환경
④ 영국 공중 위생의 역사
⑤ 크림 전쟁에서의 군인 사망의 실제 원인

2 빈칸 뒤에 부상병들이 사망하는 원인에 대한 내용이 나오므로 빈칸에는 ⑤가 적절하다.
① 심각한 질병을 예측하고 예방하다
② 병원이 간호사들을 효과적으로 훈련시키는 것을 돕다
③ 전쟁 동안 고통받은 군인들을 후원하다
④ 군대에 충분한 의료 보급품을 제공하다
⑤ 전쟁 중 병원 내 사망의 원인을 분석하다

3 ③ 나이팅게일은 부상병 사망의 실제 원인이 비위생적인 환경이라는 것을 알아냈다. (⑩번 문장)
① (→ ①번 문장) ② (→ ⑥번 문장) ④ (→ ⑪번 문장) ⑤ (→ ⑭번 문장)

4 that절의 주어가 동명사구 simply reading a list of numbers이므로 that절의 동사는 단수 동사 wasn't 이 되어야 한다.

본문

① Although Florence Nightingale is best known / as the founder of modern nursing, / she was also a skilled statistician. ② Nightingale used statistics / to figure out / why so many people died in the Crimean War. ③ She then used this information effectively / to change public opinion.
④ Nightingale was sent / to a British hospital in Turkey in 1854 / in order to improve its conditions. ⑤ Many injured soldiers were dying / in the hospital, / which suffered from shortages of food and medicine, / an overworked staff, / and unclean conditions. ⑥ By the time the war ended in 1856, / Nightingale and her team had successfully improved the hospital, / significantly lowering the death rates of wounded soldiers.
⑦ Despite this success, / Nightingale worried / that similar situations would occur in the future. ⑧ So she used her abilities as a statistician / to analyze the cause of hospital deaths during the war. ⑨ It was commonly believed / that most of the deaths were / due to shortages of food and medicine. ⑩ However, Nightingale found / that the real cause was unsanitary conditions. ⑪ Nightingale was asked / to present this information / to the queen and her council. ⑫ She knew / that simply reading a list of numbers / wasn't enough. ⑬ So she arranged the numbers into charts / to make them clearer.
⑭ Charts weren't commonly used in those days, / but they had a powerful impact. ⑮ They convinced many people / that something had to be done. ⑯ Thanks to Florence Nightingale's statistical skills, / public sanitation and the British hospital system were improved, / saving countless lives.

해석 ① 플로렌스 나이팅게일은 근대 간호학의 창시자로 가장 잘 알려져 있지만, 그녀는 또한 숙련된 통계학자이기도 했다. ② 나이팅게일은 왜 그렇게 많은 사람들이 크림 전쟁에서 죽었는지 알아내기 위해 통계학을 활용했다. ③ 그러고 나서 그녀는 이 정보를 효과적으로 활용해서 여론을 바꾸었다.

④ 나이팅게일은 1854년에 터키에 있는 한 영국군 병원의 환경을 개선하기 위해 그곳으로 파견되었다. ⑤ 많은 부상병들이 그 병원에서 죽어가고 있었는데, 그곳은 식량과 약품 부족, 직원들의 업무 과다, 그리고 불결한 환경에 시달렸다. ⑥ 1856년 전쟁이 끝날 때에는, 나이팅게일과 그녀의 팀이 그 병원을 성공적으로 개선해서, 부상병들의 사망률을 상당히 낮추었다.

⑦ 이러한 성공에도 불구하고, 나이팅게일은 비슷한 상황이 앞으로도 발생할 것을 우려했다. ⑧ 그래서 그녀는 통계학자로서의 자신의 능력을 이용해서 전쟁 중 병원 내 사망의 원인을 분석했다. ⑨ 대부분의 사망은 식량과 약품 부족 때문이라고 흔히 여겨졌다. ⑩ 그러나, 나이팅게일은 실제 원인은 비위생적인 환경이라는 것을 알아냈다. ⑪ 나이팅게일은 이러한 정보를 여왕과 의회에 제시하라는 요청을 받았다. ⑫ 그녀는 그저 나열된 숫자를 읽는 것만으로는 충분하지 않다는 것을 알았다. ⑬ 그래서 그녀는 그것들을 더 분명하게 만들기 위해 숫자들을 도표로 작성했다.

⑭ 도표는 그 당시에 흔히 사용되지 않았지만, 영향력은 강력했다.⑮ 도표는 많은 사람들에게 무언가 행해져야 한다는 것을 확신시켰다. ⑯ 플로렌스 나이팅게일의 통계학 기술 덕분에 공중 위생과 영국 병원 시스템은 개선되었고, 이는 수많은 생명들을 살렸다.

구문해설 ② Nightingale used statistics **to figure out** [why so many people died in the Crimean War].

→ to figure out은 〈목적〉을 나타내는 부사적 용법의 to부정사

→ [ ]는 figure out의 목적어가 되는 간접의문문으로 「의문사+주어+동사」의 어순

⑤ Many injured soldiers were dying in the hospital, **which** suffered from shortages of food and medicine, an overworked staff, and unclean conditions.

→ which는 the hospital을 부연 설명하는 계속적 용법의 관계대명사(=and it)

⑯ **Thanks to** Florence Nightingale's statistical skills, public sanitation and the British hospital system were improved, *saving* countless lives.

→ thanks to: … 덕분에

→ saving 이하는 〈연속동작〉을 나타내는 분사구문 (=and they saved ....)

03 전쟁 속의 또 다른 비극 P. 26

정답 1 ⑤ 2 ⑤ 3 he could have reduced the number of victims

문제해설 1 ⑤ 처칠은 인도인들에게 식량을 공급하지 않고 굶어 죽게 했다. (⑨, ⑪번 문장)

① 전 세계가 처칠에게 존경심을 보였다. → 모든 사람이 그를 훌륭한 사람으로 생각한 것은 아니라고 했다. (③번 문장)

② 벵골 지역은 대영제국의 지배를 받지 않았다. → 1943년 당시 지배를 받았다고 했다. (⑤번 문장)

③ 인도에서는 쌀이 재배되지 않고 있었다. → 많은 양의 쌀이 재배되고 있었다고 했다. (⑥번 문장)

④ 벵골의 사람들은 미국으로부터 식량 원조를 받았다. → 미국이 제안했으나 처칠이 거절했다고 했다. (⑦번 문장)

⑤ 처칠은 굶주리는 인도인들을 굶어 죽게 놔두었다.

2 기근으로 고통받고 있는 벵골에 쌀을 보내지 않았을 뿐만 아니라 다른 국가로부터의 원조도 거절한 결과 벵골 사람들이 아사하였으므로 '살아남다'라는 의미의 ⑤ survive는 적절하지 않고 문맥상 '죽다', '굶어 죽다'의 의미로 die 또는 starve to death가 되어야 한다.

3 '희생자 수를 줄일 수도 있었지만 그렇게 하지 않았다'라는 뜻이므로 「조동사+have+p.p.」를 이용해 could have reduced로 나타낸다.

본문

① Many people view Winston Churchill / as one of the greatest leaders / of World War II. ② As the Prime Minister of the United Kingdom, / he held his country together / during difficult times / and helped to lead the Allied Forces / to victory.
③ But not everyone / saw Churchill as a great man, / especially not those living in areas / colonized by the British Empire. ④ In fact, / he is considered / to be partially responsible for / millions of deaths in Bengal, / a region in northeastern India. ⑤ In 1943, / Bengal was ruled by Britain / and was suffering from / a serious famine. ⑥ There was plenty of rice / being grown in other parts of India, / but most of it was being exported / to feed British soldiers. ⑦ Not only did Churchill refuse / to send some of this rice / to Bengal, / but he also turned down offers / from the United States and Canada / to provide food. ⑧ His reason was / that he feared enemy soldiers / who were near Bengal / would take the food. ⑨ In the end, / approximately 3 million people / starved to death / in Bengal. ⑩ Although Churchill had no way / of preventing the famine, / he could have reduced / the number of victims. ⑪ Instead, / he turned his back on the people of Bengal / and let them die. ⑫ Because he coldly decided / to put his country before human lives, / some people view him / as a heartless and cruel man.

해석

① 많은 사람들이 윈스턴 처칠을 2차 세계대전의 가장 위대한 지도자 중 한 명으로 여긴다. ② 영국의 수상으로서, 처칠은 어려운 시기에 자신의 나라를 하나로 단결시키고 연합군을 승리로 이끄는 것을 도왔다.
③ 그러나 모두가 처칠을 위대한 사람으로 여기는 것은 아니었는데 특히 대영제국에 의해 식민화된 지역에 사는 사람들이 그러했다. ④ 사실, 그는 인도 북동부에 있는 지역인 벵골에서 있었던 수백만 명의 사망에 부분적으로 책임이 있다고 여겨진다. ⑤ 1943년, 벵골은 영국의 지배를 받고 있었고, 심각한 기근으로 고통받고 있었다. ⑥ 인도의 다른 지방에서는 많은 양의 쌀이 재배되고 있었지만, 그 대부분은 영국 병사들을 먹이기 위해 수출되고 있었다. ⑦ 처칠은 이 쌀의 일부를 벵골에 보내는 것을 거부했을 뿐만 아니라 식량을 제공하겠다는 미국과 캐나다의 제의 역시 거절했다. ⑧ 그 이유는 벵골 근처에 있는 적군이 그 식량을 빼앗을 것을 처칠이 두려워했기 때문이다. ⑨ 결국, 거의 3백만 명에 달하는 사람들이 벵골에서 굶어 죽었다.
⑩ 비록 처칠에게 기근을 예방할 수 있는 방법이 있던 것은 아니었지만, 그는 희생자의 수를 줄일 수도 있었다. ⑪ 대신, 그는 벵골 사람들에게 등을 돌리고 그들이 죽게 내버려 두었다. ⑫ 그가 자신의 나라를 사람의 생명보다 우선시하기로 냉정하게 결정했기 때문에 어떤 사람들은 그를 무정하고 잔인한 사람으로 여긴다.

구문해설

③ But **not everyone** saw Churchill as a great man, especially not those [living in areas {colonized by the British Empire}].
→ not everyone은 부분 부정으로 '모두가 …인 것은 아니다'라는 의미

→ [ ]는 those를 수식하는 현재분사구
→ { }는 areas를 수식하는 과거분사구

⑥ There was plenty of rice [being grown in other parts of India], but most of it was being exported **to feed** British soldiers.
→ [ ]는 plenty of rice를 수식하는 현재분사구
→ to feed는 〈목적〉을 나타내는 부사적 용법의 to부정사

⑦ **Not only did Churchill refuse** to send some of this rice to Bengal, **but** he **also** turned down offers from the United States and Canada *to provide* food.
→ not only A but also B(A뿐만 아니라 B도)의 not only가 문두로 나오면서 「부정어+do[did]+주어+동사」 어순으로 도치가 일어남.
→ to provide는 offers를 수식하는 형용사적 용법의 to부정사

04 Do You Know of Nellie Bly? P. 28

정답 **1** ⑤ **2** ① **3** ③ **4** The story she wrote about her experience

문제해설 **1** ⑤ 정신 병원에 직접 입원해서 병원 실태를 조사하여 폭로하고 세계 일주 기록을 세운 후 책을 쓴 언론인 넬리 블라이를 소개하는 글이다.
[문제] 윗글의 제목으로 가장 적절한 것은?
① 탐사 보도란 무엇인가?
② 『뉴욕 월드』에서 일자리 얻기
③ 정신 병원의 한 가짜 환자
④ 미국의 굉장한 여행 작가들
⑤ 넬리 블라이: 여성 언론 개척자

2 ① 블라이가 기자가 되도록 격려한 사람에 대해서는 언급되지 않았다.
[문제] 윗글에서 블라이에 관해 언급되지 않은 것은?
① 누가 그녀에게 기자가 되도록 격려했는지
② 그녀가 『뉴욕 월드』에서 일하고 싶어 한 이유 (③번 문장)
③ 그녀가 정신 병원에 들어가기 위해 한 일 (⑥번 문장)
④ 정신병원에 관한 그녀의 이야기가 끼친 영향들이 무엇이었는지 (⑦, ⑧번 문장)
⑤ 그녀가 72일간의 세계 일주를 간 이유 (⑨번 문장)

3 편집장이 블라이에게 정신병원에 실제로 입원해서 실태 조사를 하라고 한 것이므로 빈칸에는 '과제' 또는 '도전'을 의미하는 ③이 적절하다.
[문제] 다음 중 빈칸에 들어갈 말로 가장 적절한 것은?
① 인상 ② 승진 ③ 도전, 과제 ④ 칭찬 ⑤ 합의

4 밑줄 친 It은 바로 앞 문장에서 언급된 '그녀가 자신의 경험에 대해 쓴 기사'를 가리킨다.
[문제] 밑줄 친 It이 가리키는 것을 본문에서 찾아 쓰시오.

본문

① In 1887, / 23-year-old Nellie Bly / already had a career as a journalist / in the small city of Pittsburgh. ② However, / most of the stories / she was asked to write / were directed only at women. ③ Bly dreamed of writing important stories / for all readers, / so she moved to New York / and tried to find work / at the *New York World*, / which was one of the nation's leading newspapers at that time.

④ The editor of the newspaper offered her a challenge. ⑤ He asked her to investigate a local mental hospital / with a bad reputation / for treating patients poorly. ⑥ In order to get inside, / Bly pretended to be mentally ill for 10 days. ⑦ The story / she wrote about her experience / was published as a six-part series, / and it made her / one of America's most famous journalists. ⑧ It also helped start a new style of reporting / called investigative journalism.

⑨ Later, / after reading the famous book *Around the World in 80 Days*, / Bly decided to break the world record / for the fastest trip around the world. ⑩ Completing the trip in just 72 days, / she set the record / and then wrote a book about the experience.⑪ Today, / Bly is remembered as / both an important journalist and a brave woman.

해석

① 1887년에, 23살의 넬리 블라이는 소도시 피츠버그에서 이미 기자로서의 경력이 있었다. ② 그러나, 그녀가 작성하도록 요청받은 기사 대부분은 여성들만을 겨냥하고 있었다. ③ 블라이는 모든 독자들에게 중요한 기사를 쓰는 것을 꿈꿔서, 뉴욕으로 이주해서 『뉴욕 월드』에서 일자리를 구하려고 했는데, 이곳은 당시에 그 나라의 대표 신문사 중 하나였다.

④ 그 신문사의 편집장은 그녀에게 과제를 제시했다. ⑤ 그는 그녀에게 환자들을 형편없이 대하는 것으로 악명 높은 지역 정신병원을 조사해달라고 요청했다. ⑥ 병원에 잠입하기 위해, 블라이는 10일 동안 정신병이 있는 척했다. ⑦ 그녀가 자신의 경험에 대해 쓴 기사는 여섯 부분으로 나누어진 시리즈로 출간되었고, 그것은 그녀를 미국의 가장 유명한 기자 중 한 명으로 만들었다. ⑧ 그것은 또한 탐사 보도라고 하는 새로운 형태의 보도를 시작하는 데도 일조했다.

⑨ 이후에, 『80일간의 세계 일주』라는 유명한 책을 읽은 후에, 블라이는 가장 빠른 세계 일주 기록을 깨기로 결심했다. ⑩ 단지 72일 만에 여행을 끝낸 후에, 그녀는 기록을 세우고 나서 그 경험에 대해 책 한 권을 썼다. ⑪ 오늘날, 블라이는 영향력이 큰 기자이자 용감한 여성으로 기억된다.

구문해설

② However, most of the stories [(that[which]) she **was asked to write**] were directed only at women.
S — V

→ [ ]는 선행사 the stories를 수식하는 목적격 관계대명사절

→ be asked to-v: …하도록 요청을 받다

③ ..., so she moved to New York and **tried to find** work at the *New York World*, *which* was one of the nation's leading newspapers at that time.

→ try to-v: …하려고 노력하다

→ which는 *New York World*를 부연 설명하는 계속적 용법의 관계대명사(=and it)

⑩ [Completing the trip in just 72 days], she set the record and then wrote a book about the experience.

→ [ ]는 〈시간〉을 나타내는 분사구문 (=After she completed ....)

Review Test

P. 30

A 1 ⓑ 2 ⓐ 3 ⓔ 4 ⓒ 5 ⓓ B 1 vertically 2 refused 3 comparison 4 shortage C 1 ③ 2 ⑤ 3 ④ 4 ② D 1 그녀가 작성하도록 요청받은 기사 대부분은 여성들만을 겨냥하고 있었다. 2 이러한 성공에도 불구하고, 나이팅게일은 비슷한 상황이 앞으로도 발생할 것을 우려했다. 3 그가 즐겨 쓰던 삼각형 모자가 그를 그렇게 작아 보이도록 만드는 데 한몫을 했다. 4 모두가 처칠을 위대한 사람으로 여기는 것은 아니었는데 특히 대영제국에 의해 식민화된 지역에 사는 사람들이 그러했다. E 1 to figure out why so many people died 2 both an important journalist and a brave woman 3 enemy soldiers who were near Bengal would take the food

해석 A

1 …인 척하다: ⓑ 사실이 아닌 방식으로 행동하다
2 통치하다: ⓐ 한 나라에 대한 권력을 가지다
3 (존경 등을) 모으다, 일으키다: ⓔ 주목을 받다
4 수출하다: ⓒ 판매를 위해 상품을 다른 나라로 보내다
5 고통받다: ⓓ 고통을 느끼다

B

1 그는 줄무늬를 벽에 천장에서 바닥까지 수직으로 페인트칠 했다.
2 그는 경찰관의 질문에 대답하기를 거절했다.
3 두 상품의 비교는 한 개가 다른 것보다 훨씬 더 낫다는 것을 보여주었다.
4 물 부족으로 인해 그 지역의 농작물 수확량이 형편없었다.

C

1 스티븐은 그 문제를 다루는 데 있어서 중요한 역할을 했다.
① 기본적인 ② 정치적인 ③ 중요한 ④ 약한 ⑤ 끊임없는

2 나는 그들의 제안을 받아들여야 된다는 결론에 이르렀다.
① 갈등 ② 변화 ③ 증거 ④ 지식 ⑤ 제안

3 의사는 내 혈압을 낮추기 위해 내 식단을 바꿀 것을 권장했다.
① 올리다 ② 늘이다 ③ 대하다 ④ 줄이다 ⑤ 향상시키다

4 그 교수는 생명공학 분야의 선도적인 인물이다.
① 키가 큰 ② 최고의 ③ 마지막의 ④ 책임지고 있는 ⑤ 중요하지 않은

SECTION 03

심리

01 1 ③ 2 ④ 3 ⓐ thinking, ⓑ to wash 4 (1) F (2) F
02 1 ③ 2 ② 3 ⑤ 4 a catfish
03 1 ③ 2 do we realize that we are dreaming 3 ④
04 1 ② 2 ⑤ 3 replacing 4 ②

01 손을 씻으면 사라져요 P. 34

정답 1 ③ 2 ④ 3 ⓐ thinking, ⓑ to wash 4 (1) F (2) F

문제해설

1 ③ 맥베스 부인 효과의 정의와 그것의 부정적인 면에 대한 내용이다.
① 『맥베스』에 대한 다른 견해들
② 맥베스 부인 효과의 기원
③ 맥베스 부인 효과: 그것이 무엇인지와 그것의 어두운 면
④ 씻기의 신체적 · 정신적 이점들
⑤ 죄책감이 없는 사람들의 특징

2 손을 씻으면 나쁜 행동에 대한 죄책감을 덜 느끼게 되고 자원봉사 활동도 나중에 덜 하게 된다고 했으므로 ④가 적절하다.
① 다른 사람들에 대한 신뢰
② 개인의 위생 관념
③ 질병 가능성
④ 도덕성과 관련된 감정
⑤ 청결에 대한 개인의 선호

3 ⓐ 의미를 분명히 하기 위해 접속사를 생략하지 않은 분사구문으로, 주절의 주어(people)와 능동 관계에 있으므로 현재분사 thinking이 되어야 한다.
ⓑ 「allow+목적어+to-v」의 수동태 문장으로, allow의 목적격보어인 to wash는 수동태에서 동사 뒤에 그대로 쓰이므로, to wash가 되어야 한다.

4 (1) 셰익스피어의 『맥베스』에서, 맥베스 부인은 왕을 죽인다. → 맥베스 부인은 자신의 남편에게 왕을 죽이도록 부추기고 실제로 왕을 죽인 것은 그녀의 남편이다. (①번 문장)
(2) 자기 과거에 대해 죄책감을 느끼지 않는 사람들은 죄책감을 느끼는 사람들보다 자주 손을 씻을 가능성이 더 높다. → 자신들의 나쁜 행동에 대해 생각한 후에 사람들은 비누나 물티슈 같은 세정 용품을 선택할 가능성이 높다고 했다. (⑧번 문장)

본문

① In the famous Shakespeare play *Macbeth*, / Lady Macbeth encourages her husband to kill the king / but begins to feel terrible guilt / after he actually does. ② She imagines / there is blood on her hands / and tries to wash it off. ③ Although this is just fiction, / some psychologists believe / it really is possible to wash away guilt / through physical washing.

④ They call it the "Lady Macbeth Effect," / and, unfortunately, / it's not always a good thing. ⑤ In a study, / the psychologists asked certain participants / to think about times / they had behaved unethically in the past. ⑥ They then thanked everyone for participating / and allowed each person to choose a reward. ⑦ The rewards / they offered / were small, everyday items, / including pens, kitchen tools, and cleaning products. ⑧ After thinking about their bad behavior, / people were much more likely to choose a cleaning product, / such as soap or hand wipes, / than any of the other products.

⑨ Researchers in a similar study / also asked people / to think about bad things / they had done. ⑩ But this time / half of them were allowed / to wash their hands afterwards, / while the others were not. ⑪ The researchers found / that those who had washed their hands / felt less guilt / and were less likely to do volunteer work later. ⑫ This suggests that washing one's hands / can reduce bad feelings, / but it can also reduce emotions / related to morality.

해석

① 셰익스피어의 유명한 희곡 『맥베스』에서, 맥베스 부인은 그녀의 남편이 왕을 죽이도록 부추기지만 그가 실제로 그렇게 하자 심한 죄책감을 느끼기 시작한다. ② 그녀는 자신의 손에 피가 묻어 있다고 생각하고 그것을 씻어내려고 애쓴다. ③ 이것은 그저 허구이긴 하지만, 일부 심리학자들은 육체를 씻어내는 것을 통해 죄책감을 씻어내 버리는 것이 정말 가능하다고 생각한다. ④ 그들은 그것을 '맥베스 부인 효과'라고 부르고, 불행하게도, 그것이 항상 좋은 것만은 아니다.

⑤ 한 연구에서, 심리학자들은 어떤 참가자들에게 그들이 과거에 비윤리적으로 행동했던 때들에 대해 생각해 보라고 요청했다. ⑥ 그들은 그러고 나서 모든 사람들에게 참여해준 것에 대해 감사를 표했고 각각의 사람이 보상을 선택하게 해주었다. ⑦ 그들이 제공한 보상은 펜, 주방 도구와 세정 제품을 포함한, 작은 일상 용품들이었다. ⑧ 자신들의 나쁜 행동에 대해 생각한 후에, 사람들은 다른 어떤 제품들보다, 비누나 물티슈 같은 세정 제품을 선택할 가능성이 훨씬 더 높았다.

⑨ 비슷한 연구에서 연구원들은 또한 사람들에게 그들이 저지른 나쁜 일들에 대해 생각해 보라고 요청했다. ⑩ 하지만 이번에는 그들 중 절반이 나중에 그들의 손을 씻는 것이 허용된 반면에, 나머지 사람들은 허용되지 않았다. ⑪ 연구원들은 손을 씻은 사람들은 죄책감을 덜 느끼고 나중에 자원봉사를 할 가능성이 더 낮다는 것을 발견했다. ⑫ 이것은 손을 씻는 것은 나쁜 감정을 줄일 수 있지만, 그것은 또한 도덕성과 관련된 감정도 줄일 수 있다는 것을 시사한다.

구문해설

① In the famous Shakespeare play *Macbeth*, Lady Macbeth **encourages** her husband **to kill** the king but begins to feel terrible guilt after he actually does.
→ encourage+목적어+to-v: (목적어)가 …하도록 부추기다[조장하다]

⑥ They then thanked everyone for participating and **allowed** each person **to choose** a reward.
→ allow+목적어+to-v: (목적어)가 …하게 해주다

⑦ The rewards (S) [(that[which]) they offered] were (V) small, everyday items, including pens, kitchen tools and cleaning products.
→ [ ]는 선행사 The rewards를 수식하는 관계대명사절로, 앞에 목적격 관계대명사 that[which]이 생략됨.

⑪ The researchers found [that those {who had washed their hands} felt less guilt and **were** less **likely to do** volunteer work later].
→ [ ]는 found의 목적어로 쓰인 명사절

→ { }는 선행사 those를 수식하는 주격 관계대명사절
→ be likely to-v: …할 가능성이 있다

02 메기가 나타나면… P. 36

정답 1 ③ 2 ② 3 ⑤ 4 a catfish

문제해설 1 ③ 새로운 경쟁 상대의 출현이 어떤 사람이나 집단이 더 분발하도록 만든다는 '메기 효과'에 대해서 소개하는 글이다.
① 정어리의 천적 ② 위험한 상황을 피하는 방법 ③ 무엇이 최고의 능력을 이끌어 내는가
④ 물고기를 오랫동안 살아 있게 하는 방법 ⑤ 사업에서 경쟁의 의미

2 came up with는 '…을 찾아냈다', '생각해 냈다'라는 뜻이므로 ② thought of와 바꿔 쓸 수 있다.
① …을 켰다 ② …을 생각했다 ③ …을 지적했다 ④ …을 기대했다 ⑤ 합쳤다

3 (A) '계속해서 …하다'는 「keep+v-ing」이므로 swimming이 적절하다.
(B) avoid는 동명사를 목적어로 취하므로 losing이 적절하다.
(C) 사역동사 make는 목적격보어로 동사원형을 취하므로 work가 적절하다.

4 밑줄 친 '이 포식자'는 바로 앞 문장에 언급된 '메기(a catfish)'를 가리킨다.

본문

① Sardine fishermen were facing a problem. ② The fish would die quickly / after being caught in their nets. ③ But live sardines could be sold / at a higher price. ④ So one fisherman came up with a great idea. ⑤ He put a catfish / into each container of sardines. ⑥ To avoid this predator, / the sardines had to keep swimming / around and around. ⑦ This kept them alive longer.
⑧ This is called / the "catfish effect." ⑨ It can be applied to / situations in many fields. ⑩ In sports, / for example, / coaches know / that bringing a new, talented player onto a team / makes the other players better. ⑪ This is / because they start trying harder / to avoid losing their position / on the team. ⑫ Businesses can use this effect / to motivate their employees, too. ⑬ In economics, / it explains / how companies become creative and innovative. ⑭ When strong competitors enter the market, / other companies have to become more dynamic / to survive. ⑮ This makes the entire economy stronger. ⑯ In short, / pressure and stimulation from competitors / can make people and businesses / work harder.

해석 ① 정어리잡이 어부들이 어떤 문제에 직면하고 있었다. ② 정어리는 그물에 잡힌 후에 빨리 죽곤 했다. ③ 하지만 살아 있는 정어리가 더 높은 가격에 팔릴 수 있었다. ④ 그래서 한 어부가 아주 좋은 아이디어를 냈다. ⑤ 그는 정어리가 담긴 각 통에 메기를 한 마리씩 넣었다. ⑥ 이 포식자를 피하기 위해서, 정어리들은 계속해서 주위를 헤엄쳐야만 했다. ⑦ 이것은 정어리들이 더 오래 살아 있게 했다.
⑧ 이것은 '메기 효과'라고 불린다. ⑨ 이것은 많은 분야의 상황에 적용될 수 있다. ⑩ 예를 들어, 스포츠에서 감독들은 새로운 재능 있는 선수를 팀에 영입하는 것이 다른 선수들을 더 잘하게 만든다는 것을 알고 있다. ⑪ 이는 그들이 팀에서 자신의 자리를 잃지 않기 위해서 더 열심히 노력하기 시작하기 때문이다. ⑫ 기업들 역시 고용인들에게 동기

를 부여하기 위해 이 효과를 사용할 수 있다. ⑬ 경제학에서는, 이것이 회사들이 창조적이고 획기적이 되는 방법을 설명한다. ⑭ 강력한 경쟁 상대들이 시장에 진입하면, 다른 회사들은 살아남기 위해 더 역동적이 되어야 한다. ⑮ 이것은 전체 경제를 더 튼튼하게 만든다. ⑯ 간단히 말해서, 경쟁 상대로부터의 압력과 자극은 사람들과 기업들이 더 열심히 일하게 할 수 있다.

구문해설

② The fish would die quickly [after being caught in their nets].

→ [ ]는 의미를 명확히 하기 위해 접속사를 생략하지 않은 분사구문으로 〈시간〉을 나타냄. 또는 「전치사+동명사」 구문으로 볼 수도 있음.

⑥ **To avoid** this predator, the sardines had to keep swimming around and around.

→ To avoid는 〈목적〉을 나타내는 부사적 용법의 to부정사

⑩ In sports, for example, coaches know [**that** {bringing a new, talented player onto a team}(S) *makes*(V) the other players(O) better(OC)].

→ that은 know의 목적어가 되는 명사절을 이끄는 접속사

→ { }는 주어로 쓰인 동명사구이므로 동사는 3인칭 단수형(makes)을 사용함.

⑬ In economics, it explains **how** companies become creative and innovative.

→ how는 〈방법〉을 나타내는 관계부사로, how는 the way로 바꿔 쓸 수 있음. the way와 how가 함께 쓰일 수 없고 둘 중 하나만 쓰임.

03 꿈을 꾸고 있어요 P. 38

정답 1 ③ 2 do we realize that we are dreaming 3 ④

문제해설

1 ③ 일반 꿈은 짧은 기간 동안에만 기억할 수 있지만 자각몽은 깨고 난 오래 뒤에도 기억된다고 했다. (⑨~⑪번 문장)

① 우리는 자각몽을 꾸는 동안 꿈을 통제할 수 있다. (④, ⑤번 문장)

② 일반적인 꿈에서 우리는 무슨 일이 일어나고 있는지 의식할 수 없다. (⑥번 문장)

③ 일반적인 꿈보다 자각몽을 기억하는 것이 더 어렵다.

④ 자각몽을 꾸는 것은 우리를 매우 피곤하게 만들 수 있다. (⑬, ⑭번 문장)

⑤ 어떤 사람들은 자각몽을 재미있는 경험 이상이라고 생각한다. (⑯번 문장)

2 We not only realize that we are dreaming에서 not only가 문장 맨 앞에 오면 도치가 일어나면서 「not only do[does/did]+주어+동사」의 어순이 되어야 하므로 Not only do we realize that we are dreaming이 되어야 한다.

3 바로 뒤에 이어지는 내용에서 사람들이 자각몽을 이용해 자신감을 얻고 두려움을 극복할 수 있다고 했으므로, ④ '개인의 발전'이 가장 적절하다.

① 신체 건강 ② 우울증 ③ 행동 장애 ⑤ 더 나은 수면 패턴

본문

① Dreams can be / fun, exciting, or even scary. ② Most of the time / we can't control them at all. ③ But sometimes / we have special dreams. ④ Not only do we realize / that we are dreaming, / but we can also control / what happens! ⑤ These are called "lucid dreams."

⑥ Normally, / when we dream, / we are no longer self-aware. ⑦ But in a lucid dream, / it is as if the brain wakes up / while we are dreaming. ⑧ This allows us to move around / and explore our dream environment / as though we were completely awake. ⑨ What's more, / normal dreams usually fade / as soon as we wake up. ⑩ So we can only remember them / for a short time. ⑪ But lucid dreams can be remembered / long after we have woken up! ⑫ However, / there are some problems / with lucid dreams. ⑬ First of all, / they can be exhausting. ⑭ They interrupt normal sleep patterns, / preventing us from getting enough rest. ⑮ Also, they can be addictive.

⑯ But there are some people / who believe / that lucid dreams are more than / just an interesting experience. ⑰ They say / these dreams can lead / to personal development. ⑱ People can use them / to gain confidence / and overcome their fears. ⑲ If there's something / they're afraid to try / in real life, / they can experience it / in their dreams instead!

해석

① 꿈은 재미있거나, 신이 나거나, 심지어는 무서울 수도 있다. ② 대체로 우리는 꿈을 전혀 통제할 수 없다. ③ 그러나 가끔 우리는 특별한 꿈을 꾼다. ④ 우리가 꿈을 꾸는 중이라는 것을 깨달을 뿐만 아니라, (꿈속에서) 일어나고 있는 일을 통제할 수도 있다! ⑤ 이런 꿈들은 '자각몽'이라고 불린다.

⑥ 보통은, 우리는 꿈을 꿀 때 더 이상 자신을 인식하지 않는다. ⑦ 그러나 자각몽에서는, 꿈을 꾸는 동안 마치 두뇌가 깨어나는 것 같다. ⑧ 이것은 마치 우리가 완전히 깨어 있는 상태인 것처럼 꿈속 환경을 돌아다니고 탐험할 수 있게 해준다. ⑨ 게다가, 보통의 꿈은 잠에서 깨자마자 대개 서서히 사라진다. ⑩ 따라서 우리는 꿈을 잠시 동안만 기억할 수 있을 뿐이다. ⑪ 그러나 자각몽은 우리가 잠을 깬 한참 뒤에도 기억될 수 있다! ⑫ 그러나 자각몽에는 몇 가지 문제점들이 있다. ⑬ 우선, 자각몽은 우리를 기진맥진하게 만들 수 있다. ⑭ 자각몽은 정상적인 수면 패턴을 방해해 우리가 충분한 휴식을 취하는 것을 막는다. ⑮ 또한, 자각몽은 중독성이 있기도 하다.

⑯ 하지만 자각몽을 그저 흥미로운 경험 이상으로 여기는 사람들도 있다. ⑰ 그들은 자각몽이 개인의 발전으로 이어질 수 있다고 말한다. ⑱ 사람들은 자각몽을 자신감을 얻고 두려움을 극복하는 데에 이용할 수 있다. ⑲ 실제 삶에서 해 보기 두려워하는 무언가가 있다면, 대신 꿈속에서 그것을 경험할 수 있는 것이다!

구문해설

⑦ But in a lucid dream, it is **as if** the brain **wakes up** while we are dreaming.

→ as if 절에 일어날 가능성이 있는 일이나 확실하지 않은 상황이 언급되는 경우 as if 다음에 가정법이 아닌 직설법이 올 수 있음.

⑧ This **allows** us **to move** around and (**to**) **explore** our dream environment *as though* we *were* completely awake.

→ allow+목적어+to-v: (목적어)가 …하게 해주다

→ as though+가정법 과거: 마치 …인 것처럼 (실제로는 …가 아닌)

⑭ They interrupt normal sleep patterns, ***preventing*** *us from getting* enough rest.

→ preventing 이하는 연속동작을 나타내는 분사구문 (= and they prevent....)

→ prevent A from v-ing: A가 …하는 것을 막다

⑯ But there are some people [**who** believe {*that* lucid dreams are more than just an

interesting experience}].
→ who는 some people을 선행사로 하는 주격 관계대명사
→ that은 believe의 목적어가 되는 명사절을 이끄는 접속사

04 A Behavior Experiment with Monkeys P. 40

정답 1 ② 2 ⑤ 3 replacing 4 ②

문제해설 1 ② 새로 온 원숭이들은 방 안에 있던 원숭이들의 경고만으로 기둥 위에 오르는 것을 거부했으므로, (A)에는 '거부하다'라는 의미의 refused가, (B)에는 '위험한'을 의미하는 dangerous가 적절하다.
[문제] 다음 중, 빈칸 (A)와 (B)에 들어갈 말로 가장 적절한 것은?

실험에서, 새 원숭이들은 그것이 위험하다고 널리 여겨졌기 때문에 꼭대기에 있는 바나나를 얻는 것을 거부했다.

2 앞 문장에서 과학자들이 바나나를 기둥에 매단다는 내용이 나왔으므로 이어서 바나나 위쪽 천장에 샤워 꼭지를 숨겨둔다는 내용인 (C)가 나오고, 바나나를 잡으려는 원숭이에게 차가운 물을 뿌린다는 내용인 (B)가 나오고, 마지막으로 물에 젖은 원숭이가 소리지르며 뛰어내린다는 (A)로 이어지는 것이 가장 자연스럽다.
[문제] 글의 흐름에 맞게 (A), (B), (C)를 배열한 것을 고르시오.

3 〈연속동작〉을 나타내는 분사구문으로, 주절의 주어 they (=the scientists)와 replace는 능동 관계이므로 ⓐ는 현재분사 replacing이 되어야 한다.
[문제] ⓐ를 어법에 알맞은 형태로 쓰시오.

4 어떤 일이 벌어질지 모르면서 다른 원숭이들의 경고만으로 바나나 얻기를 포기한 원숭이들처럼, 사람들 역시 이유를 생각해 보지 않고 기존의 방식에 따라 자신의 목표를 포기한다는 것이 문맥상 자연스러우므로 빈칸에는 ② goals가 적절하다.
[문제] 다음 중 빈칸에 들어갈 말로 가장 적절한 것은?
① 실험 ② 목표 ③ 돈 ④ 연구 ⑤ 동기

본문

① Here's an interesting experiment. ② Some scientists place 12 monkeys / in a room. ③ The scientists tie a bunch of bananas / on the top of a tall pole / to attract the monkeys. ④ (C) Just above the bananas, / they conceal a showerhead / in the ceiling. ⑤ (B) Each time the monkeys try to get the bananas, / the scientists turn on the shower / and spray them with cold water. ⑥ (A) The wet monkeys scream and jump down, / refraining from attempting / to grab the bananas. ⑦ Next, / the scientists remove the showerhead. ⑧ They also take one of the monkeys / out of the room, / replacing it with another one.
⑨ When the new monkey attempts to climb the pole / to get the bananas, / the other monkeys pull it back, / screaming and pointing to the ceiling. ⑩ The scientists replace / all twelve of the original monkeys, / one by one, / in the room. ⑪ Although none of the new monkeys / have been sprayed / by the water, / they all refuse to climb the pole / to reach the bananas / at the top.

⑫ This experiment can teach us / an important lesson. ⑬ The new monkeys don't climb up / because no other monkeys do it. ⑭ Lots of people act similarly. ⑮ Without examining why, / they give up on their goals / and follow the way / that things have been done before.

해석 ① 여기 한 흥미로운 실험이 있다. ② 몇몇 과학자들이 원숭이 열두 마리를 한 방에 둔다. ③ 과학자들은 원숭이들을 유인하기 위해 바나나 한 다발을 높은 기둥 꼭대기에 매단다. ④ (C) 그들은 그 바나나 바로 위쪽 천장에 샤워 꼭지를 숨겨 둔다. ⑤ (B) 원숭이들이 바나나를 잡으려 할 때마다, 과학자들은 샤워기를 틀어 원숭이들에게 차가운 물을 뿌린다. ⑥ (A) 물에 젖은 원숭이들은 바나나를 잡으려는 시도를 그만두고 소리를 지르며 뛰어내린다. ⑦ 그 다음, 과학자들은 샤워 꼭지를 치운다. ⑧ 또한, 그들은 원숭이 중 한 마리를 방 밖으로 데리고 나가 다른 원숭이로 바꾼다.
⑨ 새로 온 원숭이가 바나나를 가지러 기둥을 오르려고 하자, 나머지 원숭이들이 소리를 지르고 천장을 가리키면서 그 원숭이를 잡아당긴다. ⑩ 과학자들은 방에 원래 있었던 원숭이 열두 마리 전부를 차례차례 (다른 원숭이로) 교체한다. ⑪ 새로 온 원숭이 중 아무도 물을 맞은 적이 없었음에도 불구하고, 그들은 모두 꼭대기에 있는 바나나를 가지러 기둥에 올라가려 하지 않는다.
⑫ 이 실험은 우리에게 중요한 교훈을 가르쳐 줄 수 있다. ⑬ 다른 원숭이들이 아무도 (기둥에) 오르지 않기 때문에 새로 온 원숭이들도 오르지 않는다. ⑭ 많은 사람들이 비슷하게 행동한다. ⑮ 이유는 생각해보지 않은 채, 사람들은 자신들의 목표를 포기해 버리고, 일들이 이전에 행해지던 방식을 따른다.

구문해설 ⑥ The wet monkeys scream and jump down, **refraining** from attempting to grab the bananas.
→ refraining 이하는 〈동시동작〉을 나타내는 분사구문 (= as they refrain ... the bananas)

⑪ Although none of the new monkeys **have** been sprayed by the water, they all refuse *to climb* the pole to reach the bananas at the top.
→ 「none of + 복수명사」가 주어일 때 동사는 복수명사의 수에 일치시키므로 have를 씀.
→ refuse는 목적어로 to부정사를 취함.
→ to reach는 〈목적〉을 나타내는 부사적 용법의 to부정사

⑫ This experiment can **teach us an important lesson**.
→ 「teach + 간접목적어(us) + 직접목적어(an important lesson)」의 어순임.

⑮ **Without examining** why, they give up on their goals and follow the way [*that* things have been done before].
→ without v-ing: …하지 않고
→ that은 the way를 선행사로 하는 관계부사

Review Test

P. 42

A 1 ① B 1 facing 2 concealed 3 reward 4 interrupted C 1 ① 2 ④ 3 ② 4 ⑤ D 1 게다가, 보통의 꿈은 잠에서 깨자마자 대개 서서히 사라진다. 2 이는 그들이 팀에서 자신의 자리를 잃지 않기 위해서 더 열심히 노력하기 시작하기 때문이다. 3 또한, 그들은 원숭이 중 한 마리를 방 밖으로 데리고 나가 다른 원숭이로 바꾼다. 4 비슷한 연구에서 연구원들은 또한 사람들이 그들이 저지른 나쁜 일들에 대해 생각해 보도록 했다. E 1 after being caught in the nets 2 as if the brain wakes up 3 were allowed to wash their hands

해석 A

① 서서히 사라지다: 갑자기 사라지다

② 기진맥진하게 만드는: 누군가를 매우 피곤하게 만드는

③ 획기적인: 어떤 것을 새롭고 더 나은 방식으로 하는

④ 활발한; 역동적인: 늘 활동적이거나 많은 에너지를 보여 주는

⑤ 포식자: 다른 동물들을 사냥하고 먹는 동물

B

1 너는 인생에서 많은 도전들을 직면함으로써 더 강해질 것이다.

2 경찰관은 테이블 아래 감추어진 마이크를 발견했다.

3 그 직원은 근로에 대한 보상으로 현금 보너스를 받았다.

4 그 사고로 철도 운행이 일시적으로 중단되었다.

C

1 나는 고양이의 발톱을 다듬어 주려고 시도했으나 실패했다.

① 시도했다 ② 그만두었다 ③ 피했다 ④ 적용했다 ⑤ 탐험했다

2 당신은 당신의 목표를 시각화함으로써 스스로 동기를 부여할 수 있다.

① 논쟁하다 ② 벌주다 ③ 불쾌하게 하다 ④ 동기를 부여하다 ⑤ 거절하다

3 연구는 설탕이 담배나 카페인보다 훨씬 더 중독성이 있다는 것을 알아냈다.

① 상대적인 ② 중독성이 있는 ③ 창의적인 ④ 지원하는 ⑤ 대체 가능한

4 낮잠을 자는 것은 육체의 피로를 푸는 데 도움을 줄 수 있다.

① 본래의 ② 비윤리적인 ③ 비슷한 ④ 무례한 ⑤ 육체의

SECTION 04

문화 · 예술

01 **1** ⑤ **2** ③ **3** contained **4** ⑤

02 **1** ④ **2** ③ **3** ① **4** earth, universe

03 **1** ④ **2** ⑤ **3** digital, brush, strokes

04 **1** ⑤ **2** ⑤ **3** generational, coffee

01 그림일까 글씨일까 P. 46

정답 **1** ⑤ **2** ③ **3** contained **4** ⑤

문제해설 **1** ⑤ 캘리그램의 정의와 변천사에 대한 내용이다.

① 과거 캘리그램의 인기

② 아폴리네르라는 프랑스 예술가의 삶
③ 자신만의 캘리그램을 만들고 공유하는 방법
④ 캘리그램과 시의 차이점
⑤ 캘리그램이 무엇이고 어떻게 변화했는지

2 주어진 문장은 'La Tour Eiffel'이나 'Cheval'이라는 작품이 각각 에펠탑과 말을 닮았다는 내용이며, 이것은 시가 제목과 일치하는 이미지를 형성한 사례이다. 따라서 주어진 문장은 ③에 들어가는 것이 적절하다.

3 문장의 주어는 All of the poems, 동사는 form이므로 주어와 동사 사이에 있는 구는 주어를 뒤에서 수식하는 분사구로 보아야 한다. the poems와 ⓐ는 수동 관계(시집에 '포함된' 시들)이므로 과거분사 contained가 되어야 한다.

4 캘리그램이 과거에는 손으로 만들어지고 보통 흑백이었다는 내용인 (C)에 이어 오늘날에는 컴퓨터 프로그램을 이용하고 색상도 다양하다는 내용인 (B)가 오는 것이 자연스럽고, 거기에 덧붙여 오늘날은 캘리그램을 공유하기도 더 쉽다는 내용인 (A)가 오는 것이 자연스럽다.

본문

① "A picture is worth a thousand words" / is a common proverb, / but calligrams are both words and pictures. ② They are created / by arranging letters, words, or phrases into an image. ③ Ideally, a calligram's image expresses the meaning of its words.
④ The most famous calligram artist was Guillaume Apollinaire, / who was born in Rome in 1880. ⑤ He published a volume of poems / called *Calligrammes* in 1918. ⑥ All of the poems / contained in the book / form images. ⑦ <u>For example, / "La Tour Eiffel" is shaped like the Eiffel Tower, / and "Cheval" resembles a horse.</u> ⑧ After the release of the book, / he, / as well as calligrams, / became popular around the world.
⑨ Calligrams are even more popular today. ⑩ (C) In the past, / they were created by hand, / which took a lot of time and labor, / and were usually black-and-white, / since people made them with ink and paper. ⑪ (B) But now they can be made using computer programs, / so they are easier to make / and can include a wide range of colors. ⑫ (A) It is also easier for people to share their calligrams today, / and they do so on blogs, Web sites, and online galleries. ⑬ Why don't you join in the fun / by creating a calligram yourself?

해석

① '그림 하나가 천 마디의 가치가 있다'는 흔한 격언이지만, 캘리그램은 말이면서 그림이기도 하다. ② 그것은 글자, 단어나 구를 이미지로 배열함으로써 만들어진다. ③ 이상적으로, 캘리그램의 이미지는 그 단어의 의미를 나타낸다.
④ 가장 유명한 캘리그램 예술가는 기욤 아폴리네르인데, 그는 1880년에 로마에서 태어났다. ⑤ 그는 1918년에 『칼리그람』이라는 시집 한 권을 발간했다. ⑥ 그 시집에 포함된 모든 시들은 이미지를 형성한다. ⑦ <u>예를 들어, 'La Tour Eiffel'은 에펠 탑처럼 생겼고, 'Cheval'은 말을 닮았다.</u> ⑧ 그 시집 발간 후에, 캘리그램뿐만 아니라 그도 전 세계적으로 인기를 얻었다.
⑨ 캘리그램은 오늘날 훨씬 더 인기 있다. ⑩ (C) 과거에, 그것들은 손으로 만들어졌는데, 여기에는 시간과 노력이 많이 필요했고, 보통 흑백이었는데, 왜냐하면 사람들은 그것들을 잉크와 종이로 만들었기 때문이다. ⑪ (B) 하지만 지금 그것들은 컴퓨터 프로그램을 이용하여 만들어질 수 있어서, 만들기가 더 쉽고 다양한 색상을 포함할 수 있다. ⑫ (A) 또한 오늘날 사람들이 자신들의 캘리그램을 공유하는 것이 더 쉽고, 그들은 블로그, 웹사이트, 온라인 미술관에서 그렇게 한다. ⑬ 캘리그램을 직접 만들어 봄으로써 재미를 함께하지 않겠는가?

구문해설

④ The most famous calligram artist was Guillaume Apollinaire, **who** was born in Rome in 1880.
→ who는 선행사 Guillaume Apollinaire를 부연 설명하는 계속적 용법의 관계대명사(=and he)

⑧ After the release of the book, he, **as well as** calligrams, became popular around the world.
→ B as well as A: A뿐만 아니라 B도(=not only A but also B)

⑩ In the past, they were created by hand, **which** took a lot of time and labor, and were usually black-and-white, *since* people made them with ink and paper.
→ which는 앞의 절을 부연 설명하는 계속적 용법의 관계대명사(=and it)
→ since는 〈이유〉를 나타내는 접속사

⑪ ..., so they are easier **to make** and can include a wide range of colors.
→ to make는 〈한정〉을 나타내는 부사적 용법의 to부정사

02 물방울무늬의 여왕 P. 48

정답

1 ④ 2 ③ 3 ① 4 earth, universe

문제해설

1 ④ 〈인피니티 룸〉은 회화 작품이 아니라 거울과 작은 전등으로 가득 찬 어두운 방이다. (⑨번 문장)
① (→ ②번 문장) ② (→ ③~⑥번 문장) ③ (→ ⑦번 문장) ⑤ (→ ⑩번 문장)

2 (A) 지각 동사 hear는 목적격보어로 동사원형이나 분사를 취하므로 현재분사 talking이 적절하다.
(B) allow는 목적격보어로 to부정사를 취하므로 to experience가 적절하다.
(C) the fact와 동격 관계인 명사절을 이끄는 접속사가 와야 하므로 that이 적절하다.

3 inspire는 '고무하다', '격려하다'라는 의미이므로 motivate와 바꿔 쓸 수 있다.
① 동기를 부여했다 ② 좌절시켰다 ③ 형성했다 ④ 생산했다 ⑤ 배열했다

4 야요이 쿠사마는 지구가 우주의 작은 점이라는 것을 상징하고, 자신의 작품을 나머지 우주와 연결하기 위해 작품을 점으로 뒤덮는다. (⑪, ⑫번 문장)
야요이 쿠사마는 왜 점으로 그녀의 작품을 채우는가?
그녀는 지구가 우리의 우주에서 그저 작은 하나의 점이고 그녀의 작품에서 점은 우주의 나머지에 대한 연결이라는 것을 보여주고 싶어하기 때문이다.

본문

① A Japanese artist / named Yayoi Kusama / is often called "the princess of polka dots." ② This is / because all of her artwork has one thing in common / — it is covered in dots.
③ It started with a strange experience in childhood / that had a powerful impact on her. ④ As she was standing / in the middle of a large field of flowers, / she imagined / she could hear the flowers talking to her. ⑤ Looking around, / it seemed as though she were standing / in a field of endless dots. ⑥ This inspired her to become an artist. ⑦ Later, / in the 1950s, / she moved to New York / and became part of the city's art scene, / meeting such famous artists / as Andy Warhol.

⑧ Yayoi is best known for her special *Infinity Rooms*, / which allow people to experience the same feeling / she had as a child / standing in the field of flowers. ⑨ When people enter one of these dark rooms / filled with mirrors and small flashing lights, / they feel as though / they were standing / in the middle of an endless space.
⑩ Besides these rooms, / Yayoi also creates paintings, drawings, clothes, and other objects, / all of which she covers in dots. ⑪ She does this / to symbolize the fact / that the earth is just one small dot / in our enormous universe. ⑫ By covering her artwork in dots, / she is connecting it / to the rest of the universe.

해석

① 야요이 쿠사마라는 한 일본인 예술가는 흔히 '물방울무늬의 여왕'이라고 불린다. ② 이는 그녀의 모든 미술품이 점으로 덮여 있다는 한 가지 공통점이 있기 때문이다.
③ 그것은 그녀에게 강렬한 영향을 미친, 어린 시절의 이상한 경험에서 시작되었다. ④ 그녀가 커다란 꽃밭 가운데 서 있었을 때, 그녀는 꽃들이 그녀에게 이야기하고 있는 것을 들을 수 있다고 상상했다. ⑤ 주위를 둘러봤을 때, 그녀는 마치 끝없는 점으로 이루어진 들판에 서 있는 것 같았다. ⑥ 이것은 그녀가 예술가가 되도록 고무했다. ⑦ 이후에, 1950년대에, 그녀는 뉴욕으로 이주했고 앤디 워홀과 같은 유명한 예술가들을 만나면서, 그 도시 예술계의 일부가 되었다.
⑧ 야요이는 그녀의 특별한 〈인피니티 룸〉으로 가장 잘 알려져 있는데, 이것은 사람들이 그녀가 어린 시절 꽃밭에 서 있던 때 느낀 것과 똑같은 감정을 경험하도록 해준다. ⑨ 사람들이 거울과 반짝이는 작은 등들로 가득 찬 이 어두운 방 중 한 곳에 들어가면 그들은 끝없는 공간 한가운데 서 있는 것처럼 느낀다.
⑩ 이 방 이외에, 야요이는 또한 회화, 소묘, 옷, 그리고 다른 물건들을 만드는데, 이 모든 것을 그녀는 점으로 뒤덮는다. ⑪ 그녀는 우리의 거대한 우주에서 지구는 그저 하나의 작은 점이라는 사실을 상징하기 위해 이렇게 한다. ⑫ 그녀는 자신의 예술 작품을 점으로 덮음으로써, 그것을 우주의 나머지와 연결하고 있다.

구문해설

③ It started with a strange experience in childhood [that had a powerful impact on her].
→ [ ]는 선행사 a strange experience를 수식하는 주격 관계대명사절

⑤ [**Looking** around], it seemed *as though she were standing* in a field of endless dots.
→ [ ]는 〈시간〉을 나타내는 분사구문(=When she looked around)
→ as though+가정법 과거: 마치 …인 것처럼(실제로는 …가 아님)

⑦ ..., she **moved** to New York and **became** part of the city's art scene, *meeting* such famous artists as Andy Warhol.
→ moved와 became은 둘 다 문장의 동사로 등위접속사 and로 병렬 연결됨.
→ meeting 이하는 〈동시동작〉을 나타내는 분사구문
→ such A as B: B 같은 A

⑧ Yayoi is best known for her special *Infinity Rooms*, **which** allow people to experience the same feeling [(that) she had as a child {standing in the field of flowers}].
→ which는 *Infinity Rooms*를 부연 설명하는 계속적 용법의 관계대명사(=and they)
→ [ ]는 선행사 the same feeling을 수식하는 관계대명사절로, 목적격 관계대명사 that이 생략됨.
→ { }는 〈시간〉을 나타내는 분사구문(=when she was standing ....)

03 쉽게 속일 수 없을걸? P. 50

정답 1 ④ 2 ⑤ 3 digital, brush, strokes

문제해설

1 ④ 위조된 작품을 진품과 구별해내는 새로운 기술에 대한 내용이다.
① 유명한 그림을 위조하는 방법
② 모조품을 발견하는 것의 어려움
③ 역사상 가장 많이 위조된 명작들
④ 위조 미술품을 찾기 위한 새로운 기술
⑤ 모조품이 많은 작품을 그린 유명 화가

2 시간이나 조건의 부사절에서는 미래의 일을 나타낼 때 현재시제를 써야 하므로 ⑤는 will try가 아니라 tries가 되어야 한다.

3 수학을 이용해 모조품을 가려내는 새로운 기술이 소개되었고, 그 기술은 디지털 이미지를 이용해 원본과 사본의 붓 자국을 비교한다고 했다. (⑦, ⑧, ⑨번 문장)
모조품의 디지털 이미지가 더 작은 이미지로 분해된 후, 그것의 붓 자국이 원본의 붓 자국과 비교된다.

본문

① Real or fake? ② In the world of art, / this is an important question. ③ Famous paintings / by well-known artists / can sell for millions of dollars. ④ So people often try to sell paintings / that are imitations of the real thing. ⑤ When the forgeries are done well, / spotting them can be a major challenge, / even for experts.
⑥ Now, / researchers say / they have found a new way / to tell the real from the fake / using mathematics. ⑦ They start with a digital image. ⑧ Then they use a mathematical technique / to break the image down / into a collection of smaller, more basic images. ⑨ This method is especially useful / for comparing brush strokes. ⑩ When an imitator tries to copy a master artist, / his or her brush strokes / will most surely be different.
⑪ A team of researchers used this new technique / to analyze eight drawings / by a 16th-century artist / named Pieter Brueghel the Elder. ⑫ They then compared the data / obtained from these drawings / with measurements from five imitations. ⑬ The team found / that the genuine Brueghel drawings / all had similar patterns. ⑭ By the same measure, / the fakes were different from each other / and from the original drawings.

해석

① 진짜냐 가짜냐? ② 예술계에서, 이것은 중요한 질문이다. ③ 잘 알려진 화가들에 의해 그려진 유명한 그림들은 수백만 달러에 팔릴 수 있다. ④ 그래서 종종 사람들은 진짜 그림의 모조품을 팔려고 한다. ⑤ 위조가 잘되면, 모조품을 찾아내는 것은 전문가들에게조차도 큰 난제가 될 수 있다.
⑥ 오늘날, 연구가들은 수학을 이용해 진짜와 가짜를 구별하는 새로운 방법을 찾았다고 말한다. ⑦ 그들은 디지털 이미지로 시작한다. ⑧ 그러고 나서 수학적 기법을 이용해 그 이미지를 더 작고 더 기본적인 이미지의 모음으로 분해한다. ⑨ 이 방법은 붓 자국을 비교해 보는 데 특히 유용하다. ⑩ 한 위조자가 거장 화가의 그림을 베끼려고 할 때, 그 혹은 그녀의 붓 자국은 확실히 매우 다를 것이다.
⑪ 연구원들 한 팀이 대(大) 피터르 브뤼헐이라는 16세기 화가가 그린 8개의 그림을 분석하기 위해 이 새로운 기술을

이용했다. ⑫ 그러고 나서 그들은 이 그림들로부터 얻어진 자료와 다섯 개의 모조품들에서 얻은 측정값을 비교했다. ⑬ 그 팀은 진짜 브뤼헐의 그림들은 모두 유사한 패턴을 가지고 있다는 것을 알아냈다. ⑭ 같은 방법으로 측정해 보니, 모조품들은 (패턴이) 서로서로 달랐고, 진짜 그림들과도 (패턴이) 달랐다.

구문해설 ⑥ Now, researchers say they have found a new way [to **tell** the real **from** the fake ...].

→ [ ]는 a new way를 수식하는 to부정사구(형용사적 용법)

→ tell A from B: A와 B를 구별하다

⑪ A team of researchers used this new technique **to analyze** eight drawings by a 16th-century artist [named Pieter Brueghel the Elder].

→ to analyze는 〈목적〉을 나타내는 부사적 용법의 to부정사

→ [ ]는 a 16th-century artist를 수식하는 과거분사구

⑫ They then **compared** the data [obtained from these drawings] **with** measurements ....

→ compare A with B: A와 B를 비교하다

→ [ ]는 the data를 수식하는 과거분사구

04 Let's Play Music for Coffee P. 52

정답 **1** ⑤ **2** ⑤ **3** generational, coffee

문제해설 **1** ⑤ 〈커피 칸타타〉가 독일인들의 커피에 대한 견해를 어떻게 바꾸었는지는 언급되지 않았다.

[문제] 이 글에서 언급되지 않은 것은?

① 왜 독일인들은 커피 마시는 것을 싫어했나 → 맥주에 대한 위협이라고 생각했다고 한다. (②번 문장)

② 독일인들은 커피 마시는 것을 자제시키기 위해 무엇을 하였나 → 법과 세금을 만들었다고 했다. (③번 문장)

③ 누가 〈커피 칸타타〉를 작곡했나 → 1732년에 요한 제바스티안 바흐가 작곡했다고 했다. (④번 문장)

④ 〈커피 칸타타〉는 처음에 어디에서 공연되었나 → 인기 있는 커피숍에서 공연되었다고 했다. (⑪번 문장)

⑤ 〈커피 칸타타〉가 커피에 대한 독일인들의 견해를 어떻게 바꾸었는가

2 주어진 문장의 she는 바흐의 〈커피 칸타타〉에 등장하는 딸을 가리키며, Therefore가 있으므로 그녀가 커피 마시기를 중단하는 데 동의하는 이유가 앞에 와야 한다. 따라서, 커피를 사랑하지만 결혼하지 않은 채 살기를 원하지는 않는다는 내용 뒤인 ⑤가 적절하다.

[문제] ①~⑤ 중, 주어진 문장이 들어가기에 가장 적절한 곳은?

3 〈커피 칸타타〉는 그 당시 커피에 대한 세대 차이를 보여 줬다고 했다. (⑤, ⑫번 문장)

[문제] 다음은 이 글의 요약문이다. 빈칸에 알맞은 말을 본문에서 찾아 쓰시오.

〈커피 칸타타〉는 커피 마시는 것에 대한 전통적인 아버지와 현대적인 딸의 세대 간 차이를 보여 준다.

본문

① Although most of Europe had embraced / the habit of drinking coffee / by the 17th century, / it wasn't until the second half of the 18th century / that it was accepted in Germany. ② Before that time, / many Germans, / who distrusted foreign influences / on their culture, / saw coffee as a threat / to their preferred local drink, beer. ③ As a result, / there were laws and taxes / designed to discourage coffee drinking.

④ In 1732, / the legendary composer Johann Sebastian Bach / became involved in these "coffee wars" / with his *Coffee Cantata*. ⑤ It was a comical operetta / about a traditional father / and his modern, coffee-drinking daughter. ⑥ He tries to break her habit / by telling her / that she has to choose / between getting married / and drinking coffee. ⑦ Despite this threat, / she sings / "Ah, how sweet coffee tastes — / lovelier than a thousand kisses, / far sweeter than muscatel." ⑧ But / as much as she loves coffee, / the daughter does not want to go through life unmarried. / ⑨ Therefore, / she agrees to stop drinking coffee. ⑩ However, / she secretly explains to the men / her father introduces / that she won't marry anyone / who tries to keep her away from coffee.

⑪ The *Coffee Cantata*, / which was originally performed / at a popular German coffee shop, / had a simple message / for its audiences: / there's nothing wrong / with drinking coffee. ⑫ By telling a tale / that pointed out the generational differences of the time / in a humorous way, / Bach's work amused and entertained / both coffee-loving and coffee-hating Germans.

해석

① 비록 대부분의 유럽에서 17세기 즈음에는 커피 마시는 습관을 받아들이게 되었지만, 그것이 독일에서 받아들여진 것은 18세기 후반이 되어서였다. ② 그 시대 이전에는 많은 독일 사람들이 그들의 문화에 대한 외국의 영향력을 불신하여, 커피를 그들이 선호하는 현지 음료인 맥주에 대한 위협으로 여겼다. ③ 결과적으로, 커피 마시는 것을 자제시키려 만들어진 법과 세금이 있었다.

④ 1732년, 전설적인 작곡가 요한 제바스티안 바흐는 그의 〈커피 칸타타〉로 이 '커피 전쟁'에 개입하게 되었다. ⑤ 그것은 전통적인 아버지와 커피를 마시는 현대적인 딸에 관한 재미있는 오페레타였다. ⑥ 그는 그녀에게 결혼하는 것과 커피를 마시는 것 중에서 선택을 해야 한다고 말함으로써 그녀의 습관을 없애려고 한다. ⑦ 이런 협박에도 불구하고 그녀는 "아, 커피가 얼마나 달콤한 맛인가, 천 번의 키스보다 더 사랑스럽고, 백포도주보다 훨씬 더 달콤하다네"라고 노래한다. ⑧ 하지만 그녀는 자신이 커피를 사랑하는 만큼이나, 결혼하지 않은 채로 살기를 원하지는 않는다. ⑨ 따라서 그녀는 커피를 마시는 것을 중단하는 데에 동의한다. ⑩ 하지만, 그녀는 자신의 아버지가 소개하는 남자들에게 자신을 커피에서 멀어지게 하려는 사람과는 결혼하지 않겠다고 몰래 설명한다.

⑪ 〈커피 칸타타〉는 원래 독일의 한 인기 있는 커피숍에서 공연되었는데, 관객들을 위한 간단한 메시지를 담고 있었다. 커피를 마시는 데에는 아무 문제가 없다는 것이다. ⑫ 그 시대의 세대 차이를 지적하는 이야기를 유머러스한 방식으로 함으로써, 바흐의 작품은 커피를 좋아하는 독일인들과 커피를 싫어하는 독일인들 모두를 재미있고 즐겁게 해주었다.

구문해설

① ..., **it was**n't until the second half of the 18th century **that** it was accepted in Germany.

→ 「it is[was] ... that ~」 강조 구문에 not until이 들어 있으며, '~은 …가 되어서이다[되어서였다]'라고 해석함.

③ ..., there were laws and taxes [designed to discourage coffee drinking].

→ [ ]는 laws and taxes를 뒤에서 수식하는 과거분사구

⑪ The *Coffee Cantata*, [which was originally performed at a popular German coffee shop], ... **there's nothing wrong with** drinking coffee.

→ [ ]는 선행사인 The *Coffee Cantata*를 부연 설명하는 계속적 용법의 관계대명사절

→ there's nothing wrong with: …에 아무런 이상[문제]이 없다

Review Test

P. 54

A **1** ⓓ **2** ⓒ **3** ⓔ **4** ⓑ **5** ⓐ B **1** inspire **2** difference **3** threat **4** obtained C **1** ② **2** ④ **3** ③ **4** ⑤ D **1** 그녀는 자신의 예술 작품을 점으로 덮음으로써, 그것을 우주의 나머지와 연결하고 있다. **2** 주위를 둘러봤을 때, 그녀는 마치 끝없는 점으로 된 들판에 서 있는 것 같았다. **3** 그 책 발간 후에, 캘리그램뿐만 아니라 그도 전 세계적으로 인기를 얻었다. **4** 캘리그램은 컴퓨터 프로그램을 이용하여 만들어질 수 있어서, 만들기가 더 쉽고 다양한 색상을 포함할 수 있다. E **1** has one thing in common **2** that are imitations of the real thing **3** designed to discourage coffee drinking

해석

A

1 인기 있는: ⓓ 많은 사람들이 좋아하고 즐기는

2 거대한, 막대한: ⓒ 양이나 크기가 매우 큰

3 전설적인: ⓔ 매우 유명하거나 잘 알려져 있는

4 강력한, 강한: ⓑ 힘이나 영향력이 큰

5 진짜의: ⓐ 실제의, 진짜의

B

1 그 가수는 자신의 음악이 아이들이 꿈을 갖도록 격려하기를 바란다.

2 건강한 식단은 당신의 일상 생활에 큰 차이를 만들 수 있다.

3 과학자들은 플라스틱 물질이 해양 환경에 심각한 위협이 된다고 경고한다.

4 멜라니는 그 사진가의 허락을 받아 자신의 책에 그의 사진들을 사용했다.

C

1 그는 정치에 관여되지 않는 것을 선호한다.

① …이 들어 있는 ② 관여하는 ③ 출판된 ④ 배열된 ⑤ 해방된, 공개된

2 내 친구와 나는 우리에게 긍정적인 영향을 미친 선생님들에 대해 이야기했다.

① 조언 ② 속담 ③ 끌림, 명소 ④ 영향(력) ⑤ 약함, 약점

3 앵무새는 사람의 말을 모방할 수 있는 유일한 동물이다.

① 이끌다 ② 보호하다 ③ 모방하다 ④ 상징하다 ⑤ 받아들이다

4 인터넷은 여러 면에서 우리 생활에 큰 영향을 미치는 것처럼 보인다.

① 용량 ② 무한성 ③ 이야기 ④ 결과 ⑤ 영향

SECTION 05

유머 · 감동

01 1 ③ 2 ① 3 worried 4 ①

02 1 ⑤ 2 was finding it extremely difficult to get ready 3 ② 4 (1) T (2) F

03 1 ② 2 ⑤ 3 ②

04 1 ⑤ 2 ② 3 pain, signals

01 딱 한 번만 팔았을 뿐인데… P. 58

정답 1 ③ 2 ① 3 worried 4 ①

문제해설 1 ③ 근무 첫날에 5만 달러의 매출을 올린 영업 사원이 어떻게 물건을 팔았는지에 관한 내용이다.

① 실패에서 얻은 소중한 교훈

② 화가 난 고객을 다루기

③ 놀라운 영업 사원이 일하는 법

④ 두통을 치료하는 가장 효과적인 방법

⑤ 하루 5만 달러의 이윤을 내는 관리자

2 ① 아스피린은 영업 사원이 권한 것이 아니라 고객이 원래 사려고 했던 물건이다. (⑬번 문장)

② (→ ⑧번 문장) ③ (→ ⑧번 문장) ④ (→ ⑨번 문장) ⑤ (→ ⑩번 문장)

3 he가 '걱정스러워 하는(걱정스러움을 느끼는)' 것이므로 과거분사 worried가 되어야 한다.

감정이나 기분을 나타내는 분사에서 '(…이) ~한 감정을 불러일으키다'를 표현할 때는 현재분사를, '(사람이) …한 감정을 느끼다'를 표현할 때는 과거분사를 쓴다.

4 '치료약'을 의미하는 remedy와 유사한 의미를 가진 단어는 ① cure이다.

① 치료제 ② 보살핌 ③ 부상 ④ 이유 ⑤ 결과

본문

① A confident new employee / at the region's largest department store / told his manager / at the beginning of his first shift, / "I'm the world's greatest salesperson." ② The manager laughed skeptically / and replied, "We shall see."

③ At closing time, / when the manager inquired / how many sales the man had made, / he replied / that he had made a single sale. ④ The manager turned red with rage / and shouted / that most of his coworkers had made dozens of sales / worth hundreds of dollars. ⑤ The man winked / and explained / that his one sale was worth $50,000.

⑥ "Fifty thousand dollars?" / gasped the astonished manager. ⑦ "How is that possible?"

⑧ "Well, first I sold the customer a fishing rod, / along with some expensive fishing gear. ⑨ Then, after I informed him / that the biggest fish are / in the middle of the lake, / I sold him a new speedboat. ⑩ And since he was worried / that his vehicle wasn't powerful enough / to tow the boat, / I sold him a new four-wheel-drive SUV."

⑪ "You're kidding! ⑫ A customer wanted to purchase a fishing rod, / and you sold him all that?" / asked the manager.
⑬ "Actually, / he came in to buy some aspirin, / and I convinced him that fishing is the best remedy for a headache," / answered the employee.

해석 ① 지역 최대의 백화점의 한 자신감 있는 신입 사원은 그의 첫 근무를 시작할 때 관리자에게 말했다. "저는 세계 최고의 영업 사원입니다." ② 관리자는 회의적으로 웃으며 대답했다. "두고 봅시다."
③ 문을 닫을 시간에, 관리자가 그 남자가 판매를 몇 건이나 성사시켰는지 물었을 때, 그는 한 건의 판매만 성사시켰다고 대답했다. ④ 관리자는 매우 화가 나서 얼굴이 붉어졌고 그의 동료 대부분이 수백 달러어치의 판매 수십 건을 성사시켰다고 큰 소리로 말했다. ⑤ 신입 사원은 윙크를 하고 자신이 성사시킨 단 한 건의 판매는 5만 달러의 값어치가 있다고 설명했다.
⑥ "5만 달러라고요?" 놀란 관리자가 숨을 헉 하고 쉬며 말했다. ⑦ "그게 어떻게 가능합니까?"
⑧ "음, 처음에 저는 고객에게 몇 가지 비싼 낚시 장비와 함께 낚싯대 하나를 팔았습니다. ⑨ 그러고 나서, 제가 그분에게 가장 큰 물고기가 호수 가운데에 있다고 알려 드린 후에, 저는 그분에게 새 고속 모터보트를 팔았습니다. ⑩ 그리고 그분이 자신의 차량이 그 보트를 끌 만큼 충분히 강력하지 않다고 걱정하셨기 때문에, 저는 그분에게 신형 사륜구동 SUV를 판매했습니다."
⑪ "설마요! ⑫ 한 고객이 낚싯대를 사고 싶어 했는데, 당신은 그분에게 그 모든 것을 판매했다고요?"라고 관리자가 물었다.
⑬ "사실은, 그분은 아스피린을 좀 사러 오셨고, 저는 그분에게 낚시가 두통의 최고 치료제라고 확신시켜드렸습니다."라고 그 사원이 대답했다.

구문해설 ③ At closing time, when the manager inquired [how many sales the man **had made**], he replied [that he **had made** a single sale].
→ 첫 번째 [ ]는 inquired의 목적어가 되는 간접의문문으로 「의문사+주어+동사」의 어순
→ 두 번째 [ ]는 replied의 목적어로 쓰인 명사절
→ had made는 주절보다 한 시제 앞선 과거를 나타내는 대과거

⑩ And **since** he was worried that his vehicle wasn't *powerful enough to tow* the boat, I sold him a new four-wheel-drive SUV."
→ since는 〈이유〉를 나타내는 접속사
→ 형용사[부사]+enough to-v: …할 정도로 충분히 ~한[하게]

02 공연하기 참 힘드네 P. 60

정답 1 ⑤ 2 was finding it extremely difficult to get ready 3 ② 4 (1) T (2) F

문제해설 1 빌리가 리허설에 한 번도 빠지지 않은 것을 높게 평가했는데, 정작 공연 당일에 빠질 예정이라는 말을 들었기 때문에 리더의 심경 변화는 ⑤가 가장 적절하다.
① 슬픈 → 행복한 ② 질투하는 → 속상한 ③ 화난 → 시기하는
④ 만족하는 → 동정심 있는 ⑤ 감사하는 → 실망한

2 동사 was finding 뒤에 가목적어 it을 먼저 쓴 후 목적격보어를 쓰고, 맨 뒤에 진목적어 to부정사구를 쓰는 어순으로 배열한다.

3 모든 리허설에 빠지지 않고 참여한 사람을 묘사하는 표현이므로, ② faithful이 가장 적절하다.
① 무례한 ② 충실한, 성실한 ③ 겸손한 ④ 오만한 ⑤ 완고한

4 (1) 밴드의 리더는 누가 리허설에 결석했는지 적어 두고 있었다. (③번 문장)
(2) 밴드의 드러머는 대부분의 리허설에 참여하지 않았다. → 밴드의 드러머는 모든 리허설에 참석한 유일한 사람이라고 했다. (⑥, ⑦번 문장)

본문

① The leader of a rock band / was finding it extremely difficult / to get ready for an important performance / because the members of the band / were never all present / at any of the rehearsals. ② Then the final rehearsal / before the show / came, / and again / one of the band members was not there. ③ At the end of the rehearsal, / the leader gathered / all the members of the band / who were present / and said, / "I have been making a note / of everyone who has been absent / from our rehearsals. ④ Here it is." ⑤ He took a piece of paper / out of his pocket / and looked at it carefully. ⑥ "I see / that there is only one member / who has been hard-working / and faithful enough / to be present at every rehearsal. ⑦ That person is Billy, / our drummer." ⑧ The drummer's face suddenly went very red. ⑨ He slowly stood up / and answered, / "Well, / I thought / it was the right thing to do... / since I won't be able / to come to the concert / tomorrow night."

해석

① 한 록 밴드의 리더는 밴드 멤버들이 어떤 리허설에도 전원 참석하는 법이 없었기 때문에, 중요한 공연을 위한 준비를 하는 것이 매우 어렵다는 것을 알았다. ② 그러다 공연 전 마지막 리허설이 왔고, 또다시 밴드 멤버들 중 한 명이 불참했다. ③ 리허설이 끝날 때에 그 리더는 참석한 밴드 멤버 모두를 모아 놓고 말했다. "나는 우리가 했던 리허설들에 불참했던 사람을 모두 적어 두고 있었어. ④ 그것이 여기 있어." ⑤ 그는 자신의 주머니에서 종이 한 장을 꺼내 주의 깊게 보았다. ⑥ "여기 보니 모든 리허설에 참석할 정도로 충분히 부지런하고 성실한 멤버가 단 한 명 보이는군. ⑦ 그 사람은 바로 우리의 드러머인 빌리야." ⑧ 그 드러머의 얼굴이 갑자기 아주 새빨개졌다. ⑨ 그는 천천히 일어나 "저기, 난 마땅히 해야 할 일을 했다고 생각해... 내일 밤 콘서트엔 올 수가 없거든."하고 대답했다.

구문해설

③ ..., the leader gathered all the members of the band [who were present] and said, "I **have been making** a note of everyone [who has been absent from our rehearsals].

→ 첫 번째 [ ]는 선행사 all the members of the band를 수식하는 주격 관계대명사절
→ 두 번째 [ ]는 선행사 everyone을 수식하는 주격 관계대명사절
→ have been making은 현재완료 진행형으로, 동작이 과거부터 현재까지 계속되고 있음을 강조함.

⑥ ... and **faithful enough to be** present at every rehearsal.
→ 형용사[부사] + enough to-v: …할 정도로 충분히 ~한(하게)

03 앙카라의 헌책 도서관

P. 62

정답 1 ② 2 ⑤ 3 ②

문제해설

1 ② 앙카라의 환경미화원들이 버려진 낡은 책들을 활용하여 도서관을 만들어서 운영하게 되었다는 내용이다.
① 터키에서 가장 오래된 도서관
② 환경미화원들이 쓰레기를 보물로 바꾸다
③ 쓰레기로 지어진 앙카라의 도서관 건물
④ 도시를 깨끗하게 만든 단 하나의 간단한 생각
⑤ 한 권을 읽고, 한 권을 기부하다: 새로운 기부 문화

2 ⑤ 쓰레기 트럭을 이동 도서관으로 개조할 계획이 있다. (⑭번 문장)
① (→ ④번 문장) ② (→ ⑥번 문장) ③ (→ ⑦번 문장) ④ (→ ⑨번 문장)

3 (A) 주어 they와 접속사가 생략된 분사구문으로, 주어와 분사가 능동 관계이므로 현재분사 Working이 적절하다.
(B) a lounge를 부연 설명하는 관계사가 와야 하는데, 뒤의 절이 완전한 절이고 선행사가 lounge라는 장소를 나타내므로 관계부사 where가 적절하다.
(C) 지각동사 see는 목적격보어로 동사원형이나 분사를 취하므로 동사원형 go가 적절하다.

본문

① What happens to old books / when their owners don't want them anymore? ② Sadly, / many of them are tossed into the trash. ③ Sanitation workers / in Ankara, Turkey, / noticed this, / so they began to rescue the books / and bring them back to the sanitation department's headquarters. ④ As their collection grew larger and larger, / these kind-hearted workers decided / to put the books to good use.
⑤ Working together, / they created their own library. ⑥ At first it was only used / by their friends and families, / but soon they opened it to the public. ⑦ The library is located in their headquarters, / and it includes more than 6,000 books. ⑧ There are textbooks, comic books, children's books, science fiction novels, / and more! ⑨ The library even includes a lounge, / where local people can drink tea, play chess, / or just sit back and enjoy a good book. ⑩ Today, the library continues to expand. ⑪ It has become an essential part / of the local community. ⑫ People now donate their unwanted books / directly to the library. ⑬ And thanks to the local government, / it now has a full-time librarian. ⑭ There are even plans / to convert an old garbage truck / into a mobile library, / which will be driven around the city / and to nearby villages, / bringing books to people / who need them.
⑮ All of this began with some sanitation workers / who didn't want to see books go to waste. ⑯ Together, they showed the world / that anyone can take action / and make their community a better place.

해석

① 그것들의 주인이 낡은 책들을 더 이상 원하지 않을 때 그 책들에게 무슨 일이 생기는가? ② 슬프게도, 그것들 중 많은 것들이 쓰레기통으로 던져진다. ③ 터키 앙카라의 환경미화원들은 이것을 알아차리고, 책을 구해내서 공중 위생

부 본부로 가져가기 시작했다. ④ 그들의 수집품이 점점 더 방대해짐에 따라, 이 마음씨 고운 환경미화원들은 그 책들을 뜻있게 사용하기로 결정했다.
⑤ 그들은 함께 일하면서, 그들만의 도서관을 만들었다. ⑥ 처음에 그곳은 단지 그들의 친구와 가족에 의해서만 사용되었지만, 곧 그들은 그곳을 대중에게 공개했다. ⑦ 도서관은 그들의 본부에 있고, 6,000권이 넘는 책을 소장하고 있다. ⑧ 교과서, 만화책, 아동 도서, 공상 과학 소설 등, 그 밖에도 많이 있다! ⑨ 도서관에는 심지어 휴게실도 있는데, 그곳에서 지역 사람들은 차를 마시고, 체스를 두거나, 그냥 뒤로 기대앉아 좋은 책을 즐길 수 있다.
⑩ 오늘날, 이 도서관은 계속해서 커지고 있다. ⑪ 그곳은 지역 사회의 필수적인 부분이 되었다. ⑫ 사람들은 이제 그들이 원하지 않는 책들을 도서관에 직접 기증한다. ⑬ 그리고 지역 정부 덕분에, 그곳은 전임 사서가 있다. ⑭ 쓰레기 트럭을 이동 도서관으로 개조할 계획도 있는데, 이것은 시내와 근처 마을로 운행되어, 책이 필요한 사람들에게 책을 가져다 줄 것이다.
⑮ 이 모든 것은 책이 쓰레기가 되는 것을 보고 싶지 않았던 환경미화원들 몇 명으로 시작되었다. ⑯ 함께, 그들은 누구든지 행동을 취할 수 있고 그들의 지역 사회를 더 나은 곳으로 만들 수 있다는 것을 세상에 보여주었다.

구문해설

④ **As** their collection *grew larger and larger*, these kind-hearted workers decided to put the books to good use.
→ As는 '…함에 따라'의 의미를 나타내는 접속사
→ grow+비교급+and+비교급: 점점 더 …해지다
→ decide는 to부정사를 목적어로 취함.

⑭ There are even plans [**to convert** an old garbage truck into a mobile library], *which* will be driven around the city and to nearby villages, bringing books to people [who need them].
→ 첫 번째 [ ]는 plans를 수식하는 형용사적 용법의 to부정사구
→ which는 a mobile library를 부연 설명하는 계속적 용법의 주격 관계대명사
→ bringing 이하는 〈연속동작〉을 나타내는 분사구문 (= and it will bring....)
→ 두 번째 [ ]는 선행사 people을 수식하는 주격 관계대명사절

⑯ Together, they showed the world [that anyone can take action and make(V) their community(O) a better place(OC)].
→ [ ]는 showed의 직접목적어로 쓰인 명사절

04 Never Stop Running! P. 64

정답 1 ⑤ 2 ② 3 pain, signals

문제해설 1 ⑤ 다발성 경화증 환자인 케일라가 달릴 때 쓰러지거나 신체 조직이 상할 수 있다는 내용이다.
[문제] 이 글의 세 번째 단락의 주제로 가장 적절한 것은?
① 다발성 경화증 환자를 치료하는 방법
② 케일라의 코치가 그녀를 위해 하는 것

③ 케일라가 어떻게 다발성 경화증을 얻게 되었고 그것이 무엇인지
④ 다발성 경화증을 가지고 있는 것의 운동상 이점
⑤ 다발성 경화증 환자가 달릴 때 직면하는 위험들

2 '방해하다'를 의미하는 interrupt와 비슷한 뜻을 가진 단어는 ② disturbs이다.
[문제] 밑줄 친 interrupts와 의미가 가장 가까운 것은?
① 의도하다 ② 방해하다 ③ 지지하다 ④ 해석하다 ⑤ 구별하다

3 다발성 경화증의 특성상 달릴 때 통증을 느낄 수 없다고 하였고, 이는 신경이 신호를 제대로 보내는 것을 막기 때문이라고 하였으므로(⑧, ⑨번 문장) 빈칸에 알맞은 말은 각각 pain과 signals이다.
[문제] 빈칸에 들어갈 알맞은 말을 본문에서 찾아 쓰시오.
케일라는 달릴 때 다리에 통증을 느낄 수 없는데 이는 다발성 경화증이 그녀의 신경이 신호를 제대로 보내는 것을 막기 때문이다.

본문

① As a group of girls speeds across the finish line, / one girl seems to be having trouble. ② Her legs begin shaking, / making her lose her balance. ③ A moment later, / she falls into her coach's waiting arms. ④ The same thing happens / every time / she races.
⑤ Her name is Kayla Montgomery, / and she was diagnosed / with multiple sclerosis / at age fifteen. ⑥ Once, during a soccer game, / she started to feel something wrong / on her legs and back / and suddenly fell down. ⑦ After months of tests, / Kayla learned / that she had multiple sclerosis. ⑧ Known as MS, / it is a disease / that interrupts communication / between the brain and other body parts. ⑨ Because MS blocks her nerves / from properly sending signals, / particularly when she's warm, / she cannot sense the pain / that other runners feel.
⑩ This makes running dangerous for her / because she can't feel her legs / by the end of the race. ⑪ So, / she could fall / and hurt herself. ⑫ In addition, / she damages tissues in her body / when she keeps running. ⑬ Kayla gets help at every finish line, / where her coach catches her / and her parents put ice on her legs / to bring the sensation back.
⑭ Kayla won the North Carolina state title / in March 2014. ⑮ Her next goal is / winning the national title. ⑯ She has said / she was scared / that she might not be able to run / much longer. ⑰ Nevertheless, / she has decided to focus on / what she's able to do now. ⑱ MS may not have a cure, / but that isn't going to stop her from running.

해석

① 한 무리의 소녀들이 결승선을 빠른 속도로 통과할 때, 한 소녀는 어려움을 겪고 있는 것 같다. ② 그녀의 다리가 떨리기 시작하며 그녀의 균형을 잃게 한다. ③ 잠시 후, 그녀는 기다리고 있던 코치의 팔 안으로 쓰러진다. ④ 그녀가 경주를 할 때마다 같은 일이 일어난다.
⑤ 그녀의 이름은 케일라 몽고메리로, 그녀는 15살 때 다발성 경화증 진단을 받았다. ⑥ 언젠가 축구 경기 중에 그녀는 다리와 등에 무언가 잘못된 것을 느끼기 시작하면서 갑자기 쓰러졌다. ⑦ 몇 달간의 검사 끝에, 케일라는 자신이 다발성 경화증을 앓고 있다는 것을 알게 되었다. ⑧ MS라고 알려져 있는 다발성 경화증은, 뇌와 몸의 다른 기관 간의 의사소통을 방해하는 질병이다. ⑨ MS가 그녀의 신경이 신호를 제대로 보내는 것을 막기 때문에 – 특히 그녀의 몸이 더울 때 – 그녀는 다른 주자들이 느끼는 고통을 감지할 수 없다.
⑩ 이것은 그녀가 달리는 것을 위험하게 하는데, 경주 후반부쯤엔 다리의 감각을 느낄 수 없기 때문이다. ⑪ 그래서 그녀는 쓰러져 부상을 입을 수 있다. ⑫ 게다가, 계속해서 달리게 되면 그녀는 신체 조직에 손상을 입게 된다. ⑬ 케일

라는 결승 지점마다 도움을 받는데, 그곳에서 그녀의 코치가 그녀를 잡아주고 그녀의 부모는 감각이 다시 돌아오도록 그녀의 다리에 얼음을 대준다.
⑭ 케일라는 2014년 3월 노스캐롤라이나 주 대회에서 우승했다. ⑮ 그녀의 다음 목표는 전국 대회에서 우승하는 것이다. ⑯ 그녀는 오래 더 달리지 못할까 봐 두렵다고 말했다. ⑰ 그럼에도 불구하고, 그녀는 지금 할 수 있는 것에 집중하기로 결심했다. ⑱ MS는 치료법이 없을지는 몰라도, 그것이 그녀가 달리는 것을 멈추게 하지는 않을 것이다.

구문해설

① ..., one girl **seems to be** having trouble.
→ seem to-v: …인 것 같다 (= ..., it seems that one girl is having trouble.)

② Her legs begin shaking, [**making** her **lose** her balance].
→ [ ]는 연속동작을 나타내는 분사구문 (= and they make ....)
→ 사역동사(make) + 목적어 + 동사원형: (목적어)가 …하게 하다

⑬ Kayla gets help at every finish line, **where** her coach catches her and her parents put ice on her legs *to bring* the sensation back.
→ where는 every finish line을 부연 설명하는 계속적 용법의 관계부사 (= and there ...)
→ to bring은 〈목적〉을 나타내는 부사적 용법의 to부정사

⑰ Nevertheless, she decided to focus on **what** she's able to do now.
→ what은 선행사를 포함하는 관계대명사로 '…하는 것'이라는 의미임.

⑱ MS may not have a cure, but that isn't going to **stop** her **from running**.
→ stop + 목적어 + from + v-ing: (목적어)가 …하는 것을 그만두게 하다

Review Test

P. 66

A **1** ④ B **1** rescued **2** effective **3** inquired **4** convince C **1** ④ **2** ⑤ **3** ② **4** ④ D **1** 그녀의 다리가 떨리기 시작하며 그녀의 균형을 잃게 한다. **2** 그는 자신의 차량이 그 보트를 끌 만큼 충분히 강하지 않다고 걱정했다. **3** 그들의 수집품이 점점 더 방대해짐에 따라, 그들은 그 책들을 뜻있게 사용하기로 결정했다. **4** 나는 우리 리허설들에 불참한 모든 사람을 적어 두고 있었다. E **1** focus on what she's able to do now **2** who didn't want to see books go to waste **3** dozens of sales worth hundreds of dollars

해석

A

① 지역의: 당신이 살고 있는 지역에 속하는
② 이동하는: 이곳저곳 이동하거나 움직일 수 있는
③ 자신감 있는: 자신의 능력이나 생각에 대해 확신하는
④ 참석한: 당신이 있어야 하는 곳에 없는
⑤ 치료: 아픈 사람을 건강하게 만드는 의학적 치료

B

1 소방관은 불타는 건물에서 어린아이를 구출했다.
2 두통에 효과가 좋은 약이 있나요?

3 나는 비행기가 정각에 도착할지 물었다.

4 당신은 브라운 씨가 병원에 가보도록 설득해야만 한다.

C

1 다른 사람이 말하고 있을 때 끼어드는 것은 무례하다.
① 느끼다 ② 수반[포함]하다 ③ 손상을 주다 ④ 방해하다, 가로막다 ⑤ 상상하다

2 우리는 시끄러운 소리에 깜짝 놀라 그 소리가 어디서 나는지 보려고 밖으로 나갔다.
① 진단받아 ② 확장되어 ③ 지루해 ④ 던져져 ⑤ 깜짝 놀라

3 그들은 모두 다음 달에 오전 조로 근무를 할 예정이다.
① 부분 ② 교대 근무 (시간) ③ 균형 ④ 동료 ⑤ 직원

4 우리 딸은 돈을 모아서 동물 보호 센터에 기부하고 싶어 한다.
① 모으다 ② 풀어주다 ③ 구입하다 ④ 기부하다 ⑤ 개조하다

SECTION 06

유래

01 1 ① 2 ④ 3 ① 4 insult, English

02 1 ④ 2 ⑤ 3 protect, fighting

03 1 ② 2 it is believed that the question mark was created by early scholars
3 ④ 4 (1) T (2) F

04 1 ⑤ 2 ② 3 slips of the tongue

01 Dutch가 대체 뭘 어쨌길래 P. 70

정답 1 ① 2 ④ 3 ① 4 insult, English

문제해설

1 ① '더치라는 단어를 포함하는 표현'의 의미가 모두 부정적이며, 그 표현이 영국인들이 경쟁자인 네덜란드인들을 모욕하기 위해 만든 것이라는 본문의 내용을 통해 유추할 수 있다.
① 부정적인 느낌 ② 역사적 교훈 ③ 비용을 각자 부담하는 방법
④ 네덜란드인에 대한 정보 ⑤ 친구를 사귀는 방법에 관한 아이디어

2 ④ Dutch concert는 '큰 소음 또는 혼란'을 의미한다. (⑨번 문장)

3 When부터 콤마까지는 의미를 명확히 하기 위해 접속사를 생략하지 않은 분사구문으로, 주절의 주어 we와 refer(언급하다)는 능동 관계이므로 현재분사 referring이 되어야 한다.

4 해상 지배권을 놓고 네덜란드와 경쟁하던 영국의 선원들이 네덜란드인을 모욕하려고 이러한 표현을 만들었다. (⑫~⑭번 문장)
네덜란드인들을 모욕하려고, 영국인들은 네덜란드에 대한 나쁜 표현들을 만들었는데 이는 그들이 17세기에 경쟁자였기 때문이다.

본문

① When referring to people or things / from the Netherlands, / we use the word "Dutch." ② But did you ever notice / that many expressions containing the word "Dutch" / have a negative feeling? ③ A typical example / is "Dutch treat," / also known as "Dutch pay." ④ It is used / when you eat with someone at a restaurant / and split the bill. ⑤ The expression makes it seem / as if the Dutch are not generous, / even among friends. ⑥ There are many other examples. ⑦ A "Dutch bargain" is an agreement / made after drinking alcohol. ⑧ "Dutch courage" is / bravery / people show / when drunk. ⑨ "Dutch concert" means / a lot of noise or confusion. ⑩ And a "Dutch uncle" is a person / who ruins others' fun / by scolding them / over trivial matters.
⑪ Where did these expressions come from? ⑫ It is believed / that most of them were made by the English / in the 17th century. ⑬ At that time, / the English and Dutch were competing for power / on the seas. ⑭ So English sailors would make up these phrases / to insult their rivals.

해석

① 네덜란드 사람이나 사물들을 언급할 때, 우리는 '더치'라는 단어를 사용한다. ② 하지만 '더치'라는 단어를 포함하는 많은 표현이 부정적인 느낌을 갖고 있다는 것을 알고 있었는가? ③ 대표적인 예가 '더치 페이'라고도 알려진 '더치 트리트'이다. ④ 이 말은 어떤 사람과 식당에서 식사하고 돈을 각자 부담할 때 쓰인다. ⑤ 이 표현은 마치 네덜란드인들이 친구 사이에서조차도 후하지 않은 것처럼 보이게 한다. ⑥ 또 다른 많은 예가 있다. ⑦ '더치 바겐'은 술을 마시고 나서 맺어진 합의를 뜻한다. ⑧ '더치 커리지'는 사람들이 술에 취했을 때 보이는 용기를 의미한다. ⑨ '더치 콘서트'는 큰 소음 또는 혼란을 의미한다. ⑩ 그리고 '더치 엉클'은 사소한 일로 사람들을 꾸짖음으로써 다른 사람들의 즐거움을 망치는 사람이다.
⑪ 이러한 표현들은 어디에서 유래했을까? ⑫ 이들 대부분은 17세기에 영국인들에 의해 만들어졌다고 여겨진다. ⑬ 당시 영국인과 네덜란드인은 해상 지배권을 놓고 경쟁하고 있었다. ⑭ 그래서 영국 선원들이 그들의 경쟁자들을 모욕하려고 이러한 표현들을 만들어 내곤 했다.

구문해설

⑤ The expression **makes** it **seem** *as if* the Dutch are not generous, ...
→ make(사역동사)+목적어+목적격보어(동사원형): (목적어)가 …하게 하다
→ as if: 마치 …인 것처럼

⑦ A "Dutch bargain" is an agreement [made after drinking alcohol].
→ [ ]는 an agreement를 뒤에서 수식하는 과거분사구

⑧ "Dutch courage" is bravery [(that[which]) people show when (they are) drunk].
→ [ ]는 선행사 bravery를 수식하는 관계대명사절로, 앞에 목적격 관계대명사 that[which]가 생략됨.
→ when과 drunk 사이에 they are가 생략되었는데, 이렇게 주절과 부사절의 주어가 같은 경우 부사절에서 「주어+be동사」는 종종 생략됨.

02 마법에 걸린 세 자매 P. 72

정답 1 ④ 2 ⑤ 3 protect, fighting

문제해설 1 ④ 세 자매봉이 그 이름을 얻게 된 전설을 소개하는 글이다.

① 휴가 중에 갈 만한 멋진 곳들 ② 호주의 가장 유명한 전설
③ 세 자매봉이 인기가 많은 이유 ④ 세 자매봉은 어떻게 그 이름을 얻게 되었나
⑤ 아름다움의 상징: 세 자매봉

2 (A) 연속동작을 나타내는 분사구문으로 주어(the outraged brothers)와 능동 관계에 있으므로 현재분사 sparking이 적절하다.

(B) 주술사가 자매를 돌로 바꾼(turned them into stone) 것보다 그들을 사람으로 되돌려놓으려고 작정한 것이 앞서므로 대과거 had intended가 적절하다.

(C) '자매를 되돌려놓을 사람이 아무도 없었다'의 의미가 되어야 하므로 명사 no one을 수식하는 형용사적 용법의 to부정사 to change가 적절하다.

3 주술사는 세 자매를 그 모든 전투에서 보호하기 위해 그들을 돌로 변하게 했다. (⑦번 문장)
왜 주술사는 세 자매를 돌로 변하게 했나?
그들을 그 모든 전투에서 보호하기 위해서.

본문

① Among the many beautiful landmarks / in Australia's Blue Mountains, / the most iconic place is the Three Sisters. ② These sandstone peaks are / known for their great beauty. ③ But why are they called the Three Sisters?

④ According to aboriginal legends, / there were three sisters / named Meehni, Wimlah, and Gunnedoo / who lived in the Jamison Valley / as members of the Katoomba tribe. ⑤ These beautiful young ladies / fell in love with / three brothers from the Nepean tribe, / but marriage between the two tribes was forbidden. ⑥ The outraged brothers / decided to capture the three sisters, / sparking a great battle / between the tribes.

⑦ In order to protect the three sisters / from all of the fighting, / a witch doctor from the Katoomba tribe / turned them into stone. ⑧ He had intended to transform them / back into humans / when the battle was over, / but he was killed / during the fighting. ⑨ Since there was no one / to change the sisters back, / they remain to this day / as magnificent stone pillars / overlooking the valley.

해석 ① 호주 블루 마운틴즈의 많은 아름다운 지형지물 중에서, 가장 상징적인 장소는 세 자매봉이다. ② 이 사암(沙巖) 봉우리들은 뛰어난 아름다움으로 알려져 있다. ③ 그런데 왜 그 봉우리들은 세 자매봉이라고 불리게 되었을까?

④ 호주 원주민의 전설에 따르면, 자미슨 골짜기에서 카툼바 족의 일원으로서 살고 있었던 미니, 윔라, 구네두라는 세 자매가 있었다. ⑤ 이 아름다운 젊은 여성들은 네피안 족 출신의 세 형제와 사랑에 빠졌지만, 두 부족 간의 결혼은 금지되어 있었다. ⑥ 격분한 형제들은 세 자매를 납치하기로 결정했고, 이는 부족들 간에 큰 전투를 일으켰다.

⑦ 세 자매를 그 모든 전투에서 보호하기 위하여, 카툼바 족의 한 주술사가 그들을 돌로 변하게 했다. ⑧ 그는 전투가 끝나면 그들을 다시 사람으로 되돌려놓을 작정이었지만, 그는 전투 중에 죽고 말았다. ⑨ 그들을 다시 되돌려놓을 사

람이 아무도 없었기 때문에 자매들은 오늘날까지 골짜기를 내려다보는 아름다운 돌기둥으로 남아 있다.

구문해설 ④ ..., there were three sisters [named Meehni, Wimlah, and Gunnedoo] [**who** lived in ... tribe].

→ 첫 번째 [ ]는 three sisters를 뒤에서 수식하는 과거분사구

→ who는 three sisters를 선행사로 하는 주격 관계대명사

⑤ ..., but marriage (S) [between the two tribes] **was** forbidden (V).

→ [ ]는 marriage를 수식하는 전치사구

→ 주어인 marriage가 단수이므로 동사도 수 일치에 의해 단수형 was가 됨.

⑨ **Since** there was no one to change the sisters back, they remain to this day as magnificent stone pillars [overlooking the valley].

→ Since는 '…때문에'라는 의미의 〈이유〉를 나타내는 종속접속사

→ [ ]는 magnificent stone pillars를 뒤에서 수식하는 현재분사구

03 물음표? 느낌표! P. 74

정답 1 ② 2 it is believed that the question mark was created by early scholars 3 ④ 4 (1) T (2) F

문제해설 1 ② 물음표와 느낌표의 유래와 변천사를 설명하는 글이다.

① 빅토르 위고의 이상한 습관 ② 문장 부호의 역사 ③ 질문을 하는 다양한 방법들

④ 가장 가치 있는 고대 발명품 ⑤ 라틴어의 중요성

2 가주어 it, 진주어 that절을 활용하여 가주어 it을 맨 앞에 쓰고 that절을 뒤로 보낸다. believe가 수동태로 쓰여 that 이하가 '…라고 여겨지다'라는 의미가 된다.

3 본문의 transformed into는 '…로 변형된'이라는 뜻이므로 ④ changed (into)와 의미가 같다.

① …로 간 ② …으로 만들어진 ③ …에 빠진 ④ …으로 바뀐 ⑤ …으로 옮겨진

4 (1) 의문문을 뜻하는 *questio*를 문장 끝에 붙이다가 이것이 줄어든 *qo*를 쓰게 되었다. (⑨, ⑩번 문장)

(2) *io*는 라틴어로 '기쁨의 외침'을 뜻한다. (⑬번 문장)

본문

① There is a famous story / concerning the great author Victor Hugo. ② In 1862, / after completing *Les Misérables*, / Hugo sent the manuscript / to his publishers. ③ It was accompanied by a note / that simply read, "?". ④ The publishers understood / that Hugo was asking / what they thought of his latest work. ⑤ After reading it, / they sent a note / in reply. ⑥ It read, "!".

⑦ It's a funny story, / but did you ever wonder / about the origin of those two common punctuation marks? ⑧ No one is exactly sure / where they came from, / but it is believed / that the question mark was created / by early scholars. ⑨ When writing in Latin, / they would write *questio* / at the end of sentences / to indicate / that they were questions. ⑩ This was eventually

shortened to *qo* / to save space. ⑪ The lowercase *q* was written / atop the *o* / and over time / the two letters evolved / into the question mark.
⑫ As for the exclamation mark, / it is thought to have been created / through a similar process. ⑬ The Latin word *io* means / "an exclamation of joy." ⑭ The word was written / with one letter above the other / at the end of sentences, / and it was slowly transformed / into the punctuation mark / we know today.

해석 ① 위대한 작가 빅토르 위고에 관한 유명한 일화가 있다. ② 1862년에 『레미제라블』을 완성한 후, 위고는 그의 출판사에 원고를 보냈다. ③ 그것은 단순히 '?'라고만 쓰여 있는 쪽지와 함께였다. ④ 출판사에서는 그의 최신작에 대해 그들이 어떻게 생각하는지를 위고가 묻고 있다는 것을 이해했다. ⑤ 그것을 읽은 후, 그들은 답으로 쪽지를 보냈다. ⑥ 그것에는 '!'라고 쓰여 있었다.
⑦ 이것은 재미있는 이야기이지만, 당신은 그 흔한 문장 부호 두 개의 유래에 대해 궁금했던 적이 있는가? ⑧ 아무도 그것들이 어디에서 비롯됐는지 정확히 알지 못하지만, 물음표는 고대 학자들에 의해 만들어졌다고 여겨진다. ⑨ 라틴어로 글을 쓸 때, 그들은 질문이라는 것을 나타내기 위해 문장의 끝에 *questio*라고 쓰곤 했다. ⑩ 이것은 공간을 절약하기 위해 결국에 *qo*로 줄여졌다. ⑪ 소문자 *q*는 *o* 위에 쓰였고, 시간이 지나면서 두 글자는 물음표로 진화했다.
⑫ 느낌표에 대해 말하자면, 그것은 유사한 과정을 거쳐 만들어졌다고 여겨진다. ⑬ 라틴어 *io*는 '기쁨의 외침'을 뜻한다. ⑭ 이 단어가 문장의 끝에서 글자 하나가 다른 글자 위에 있는 채로 쓰였고, 그것은 우리가 오늘날 알고 있는 문장 부호로 서서히 변형되었다.

구문해설 ④ The publishers understood [that Hugo was asking {what they thought of his latest work}].
→ [ ]는 동사 understood의 목적어로 쓰인 명사절
→ { }는 의문사가 이끄는 명사절로, 동사 was asking의 목적어로 쓰임. 간접의문문의 형태로 「의문사+주어+동사」의 어순

⑨ [**When writing** in Latin], they *would* write ... to indicate that they were questions.
→ [ ]는 〈시간〉을 나타내는 분사구문으로, 의미를 분명하게 하기 위해 분사 앞에 접속사 when을 생략하지 않음.
→ 조동사 would는 과거의 불규칙적인 습관을 나타냄.
→ to indicate는 〈목적〉을 나타내는 부사적 용법의 to부정사

⑭ ..., and it was slowly transformed into the punctuation mark [(that[which]) we know today].
→ [ ]는 선행사 the punctuation mark를 수식하는 관계대명사절로, 목적격 관계대명사 that[which]가 생략됨.

04 What Did You Just Say? P. 76

정답 1 ⑤ 2 ② 3 slips of the tongue

문제해설 1 ⑤ 스푸너리즘이라는 용어는 스푸너가 50대일 때 공식적으로 영어에 편입되었다고 했다. (⑪번 문장)

[문제] 다음 중 스푸너리즘에 관한 이 글의 내용과 일치하지 않는 것은?

① 구절에서 소리를 바꿈으로써 만들어진다. (②번 문장)

② 일부러 또는 우연히 만들어질 수 있다. (②번 문장)

③ 뒤섞인 구절은 전혀 다른 것들을 의미할 수 있다. (⑤번 문장)

④ 그것은 옥스퍼드의 학장에게서 이름을 따왔다. (⑥번 문장)

⑤ 이 용어는 스푸너가 죽은 후 공식적인 단어가 되었다.

2 ②는 'feel like a fool'이 스푸너리즘에 의해 변형된 말이고, 나머지는 원래 하려던 말이다.

[문제] ①~⑤ 중, 스푸너리즘의 사례인 것은?

3 '그런 실수'는 ⑦번 문장에 언급된 이상한 말실수를 가리킨다.

[문제] 밑줄 친 such mistakes가 가리키는 것을 본문에서 찾아 쓰시오.

그것은 스푸너가 말할 때 저지른 이상한 말실수를 가리킨다.

본문

① Those who enjoy puns and word games / will also have fun with "spoonerisms." ② A spoonerism is / the mixing of sounds in a phrase / that makes the phrase itself sound funny, / either intentionally or by mistake. ③ Some spoonerisms involve / confusion of consonant sounds, / as in saying "fight a liar" / rather than "light a fire." ④ Others occur / when the vowel sounds are mixed up, / like when "feel like a fool" becomes "fool like a feel." ⑤ Spoonerisms often result in nonsense, / but the funniest are those / that change the meaning altogether, / such as saying "I'm a damp stealer" / instead of "I'm a stamp dealer."

⑥ Spoonerisms are named after Rev. William A. Spooner, / warden of New College in Oxford / around the turn of the 20th century. ⑦ Popular, kind, and intelligent, / Spooner was famous / for these peculiar slips of the tongue. ⑧ Hilariously, / he was seldom aware / that he was making such mistakes.

⑨ It is thought / that Spooner's classic mistakes included / "you've tasted two worms" / instead of "you've wasted two terms," / "a blushing crow" / for "a crushing blow," / and "our queer old Dean" / when he meant "our dear old Queen." ⑩ Although some doubted the authenticity / of these quotes, / the Spooner legend grew bigger and bigger. ⑪ The term "spoonerism" was officially incorporated / into the English language / while he was still in his fifties, / marking his amusing place in history / forever.

해석

① 말장난과 단어 놀이를 즐기는 사람들은 '스푸너리즘'으로도 재미있어 할 것이다. ② 스푸너리즘은 어구를 의도적으로 또는 실수로 재미있게 들리게 만드는 어구(語句) 내에서의 소리들의 혼합이다. ③ 어떤 스푸너리즘은 'light a fire(불을 붙이다)'라고 하는 대신 'fight a liar(거짓말쟁이와 싸우다)'라고 말하는 것에서와 같은 자음들의 혼동을 포함한다. ④ 다른 것들은 모음들이 뒤섞일 때 일어나는데, 'feel like a fool(바보같이 느끼다)'이 'fool like a feel'이 될 때와 같다. ⑤ 스푸너리즘은 자주 뜻이 통하지 않는 말로 귀결되지만, 가장 재미있는 것은 'I'm a stamp dealer(나는 우표 거래상입니다)' 대신에 'I'm a damp stealer(나는 축축한 도둑입니다)'라고 말하는 것처럼 뜻을 완전히 바꾸어 놓는 것이다.

⑥ 스푸너리즘은 20세기로의 전환기 즈음에 옥스퍼드 뉴 칼리지의 학장이었던 윌리엄 A. 스푸너 교수의 이름을 따서 명명되었다. ⑦ 인기가 많고 친절하며 명석했던 스푸너는 이러한 특이한 말실수로 유명했다. ⑧ 아주 재미있게도, 그는 자신이 그런 실수들을 하고 있다는 것을 거의 알지 못했다.

⑨ 스푸너의 전형적인 실수들에는 'you've wasted two terms(자네는 두 학기를 낭비했네)' 대신에 'you've tasted two worms(자네는 벌레 두 마리를 맛보았네)', 'a crushing blow(어마어마한 타격)' 대신에 'a blushing crow(수줍어하는 까마귀)', 그리고 'our dear old Queen(우리의 소중한 연로하신 여왕님)'을 의미할 때 'our queer old Dean(괴팍하고 연로하신 우리 학장님)' 등이 있었다고 여겨진다. ⑩ 비록 어떤 사람들은 이러한 인용의 진위성을 의심했지만, 스푸너의 전설은 점점 더 거창해졌다. ⑪ '스푸너리즘'이라는 용어는 그가 아직 50대였을 때 공식적으로 영어에 편입되어, 역사에 영원히 그의 유쾌한 자취를 남기게 되었다.

구문해설

① Those [who enjoy puns and word games] will also have fun with "spoonerisms."

→ [ ]는 선행사 Those를 수식하는 주격 관계대명사절

② ... in a phrase that makes the phrase itself sound funny, **either** intentionally **or** by mistake.

→ either A or B: A와 B 둘 중 하나

⑧ Hilariously, he *was* **seldom** *aware that* he was ....

→ seldom(좀처럼 … 않는)은 빈도를 나타내는 부사로 일반동사 앞이나 조동사, be동사 뒤에 위치함.

→ be aware that ...: …를 알다

⑪ ... in his fifties, [marking his amusing place in history forever].

→ [ ]는 〈연속동작〉을 나타내는 분사구문 (= and it marked ....)

Review Test P. 78

A **1** ⓔ **2** ⓓ **3** ⓐ **4** ⓑ **5** ⓒ B **1** transform **2** evolved **3** magnificent **4** overlooking C **1** ③ **2** ② **3** ④ **4** ⑤ D **1** 이 사암 봉우리들은 뛰어난 아름다움으로 알려져 있다. **2** 아주 재미있게도, 그는 자신이 그런 실수들을 하고 있다는 것을 거의 알지 못했다. **3** 이 표현은 마치 네덜란드인들이 친구 사이에서조차도 후하지 않은 것처럼 보이게 한다. **4** 출판사에서는 그의 최신작에 대해 그들이 어떻게 생각하는지를 위고가 묻고 있다는 것을 이해했다. E **1** that makes the phrase sound funny **2** transform them back into humans **3** by scolding them over

해석

A

1 인용: ⓔ 다른 누군가가 말하거나 쓴 것

2 꾸짖다: ⓓ 누군가를 그 사람의 행위 때문에 비난하다

3 의심하다: ⓐ 어떤 것이 사실이 아니라고 생각하다

4 망치다: ⓑ 어떤 것을 완전히 못쓰게 하거나 파괴하다

5 주요 지형지물: ⓒ 쉽게 알아볼 수 있는 건물이나 장소

B

1 그들은 이 지하실을 화랑으로 바꿀 예정이다.

2 새들은 공룡으로부터 진화했다고 여겨진다.

3 유럽 국가에서는 정말 아름다운 건물들을 볼 수 있다.

4 그 집은 언덕 위에 있어서 마을 전체를 내려다본다.

C

1 비록 그가 수잔의 감정을 상하게 하려고 의도하지는 않았지만, 그녀는 기분이 나빴다.
① 의심하지는 ② 문제되지는 ③ 의도하지는 ④ 신경 쓰지는 ⑤ 알아보지는

2 브라이언은 미국인이지만, 마치 그의 모국어인 것처럼 한국어를 말한다.
① 종교 ② 언어 ③ 전통 ④ 구절 ⑤ 어휘

3 잭은 나를 여러 번 모욕했지만, 나는 그를 용서하려고 애썼다.
① 끌어당겼지만 ② 인정했지만 ③ 궁금해 했지만 ④ 모욕했지만 ⑤ 대답했지만

4 나는 모리에게 다음 달 스페인 여행에 나와 동행해 달라고 부탁했다.
① 나누어 달라고 ② 경쟁해 달라고 ③ 억류해 달라고 ④ 권해 달라고 ⑤ 동행해 달라고

SECTION 07

의학 · 건강

01 **1** ⑤ **2** no matter how much you ate **3** ②
02 **1** ③ **2** ⑤ **3** ② **4** awake, hum, songs
03 **1** ⑤ **2** ③ **3** ② **4** rotten, infected
04 **1** ④ **2** to divers → for divers **3** ②

01 먹어도 먹어도 또 먹고 싶은 P. 82

정답 1 ⑤ 2 no matter how much you ate 3 ②

문제해설 1 ⑤ 마지막 문단에 성장 호르몬이 PWS 환자들에게 도움이 된다는 내용이 나온다. (⑪번 문장)
① PWS 환자는 허기를 전혀 느끼지 못한다. → PWS 환자는 끊임없는 배고픔을 느낀다. (③번 문장)
② PWS는 후천성 질병이다. → PWS는 유전적인 요인으로 발생한다. (⑥번 문장)
③ PWS 환자에게 체중 조절은 어렵지 않다. → 배고픔을 조절할 수 없어 체중을 조절하는 것이 어렵다. (⑧번 문장)
④ 환자의 부모는 과식을 조절하기 위한 엄격한 조치를 취해서는 안 된다. → 음식을 마구 먹으려고 하기 때문에 부모가 과식을 막기 위해 엄격한 조치를 취해야 한다. (⑩번 문장)
⑤ 성장 호르몬은 PWS 환자에게 도움이 될 수 있다.

2 '아무리 …해도'라는 의미를 가진 「no matter how ...」 구문을 써서 배열한다.

3 PWS는 뇌의 이상에서 초래된 것으로 끊임없이 배고파하는 증상을 보이는데, 이는 식욕을 조절할 수 없는 것이므로 (A)에는 '식욕'이란 의미의 appetite가 들어가야 한다. 또한 ⑧번 문장에서 PWS를 앓는 아이들은 항상 배가 고프기 때문에 체중을 조절하기가 어렵다고 했으므로 (B)에는 '비만'을 뜻하는 obesity가 적절하다.

본문

① When we feel hungry, / a good meal soon leaves us / full and satisfied. ② But imagine if, / no matter how much you ate, / the uncontrollable desire to eat / never left you. ③ Children with Prader-Willi syndrome (PWS) / actually suffer from this constant hunger. ④ Sometimes / it even causes them / to eat soil, paper, or almost anything / they can put into their mouths.

⑤ PWS is caused by a disorder / in a part of the brain / called the hypothalamus, / which controls appetite. ⑥ As PWS is a genetic disease, / it cannot be cured. ⑦ The greatest risk of PWS is obesity. ⑧ Since children with PWS are always hungry, / it can be particularly difficult / to control their weight. ⑨ They will do anything / to get food / whenever they can. ⑩ So parents are advised / to take strict measures / to prevent overeating.

⑪ Recent research has shown / that certain growth hormones / can help to reduce the proportion of body fat / and improve the physical strength and flexibility / of PWS sufferers. ⑫ This does not suggest a cure of the syndrome, / but it is certainly an encouraging discovery / for PWS patients and their families.

해석

① 우리가 배가 고플 때, 좋은 식사는 곧 우리를 배부르고 만족스럽게 해준다. ② 하지만 당신이 아무리 많이 먹어도, 제어할 수 없는 식욕이 절대 사라지지 않는다고 상상해 보라. ③ 프라더 윌리 증후군(PWS)을 겪는 아이들은 실제로 이런 계속되는 배고픔으로 고통받는다. ④ 때때로 그것은 그들로 하여금 심지어 흙이나 종이, 또는 입에 넣을 수 있는 그 어떤 것이라도 먹게 한다.

⑤ PWS는 식욕을 조절하는 시상하부라고 불리는 뇌의 한 부분의 이상에 의해 초래된다. ⑥ PWS는 유전적인 질병이기 때문에, 치료될 수 없다. ⑦ PWS의 가장 큰 위험은 비만이다. ⑧ PWS를 앓고 있는 아이들은 항상 배고프기 때문에, 몸무게를 조절하기가 특히 어려울 수 있다. ⑨ 그들은 할 수 있을 때는 언제나, 음식을 얻기 위해 무슨 일이든지 할 것이다. ⑩ 그래서 부모들은 과식을 막기 위해 엄격한 조치를 취하라는 조언을 받는다.

⑪ 최근의 연구는 특정 성장 호르몬이 PWS로 고통받는 사람들의 신체 지방의 비율을 줄이고, 체력과 유연성을 향상시킬 수 있도록 도울 수 있다는 것을 보여 주었다. ⑫ 이것이 증후군의 치료법을 시사하는 것은 아니지만, 이것은 PWS 환자들과 그 가족들에게 고무적인 발견임이 확실하다.

구문해설

② But imagine **if**, {no matter how much you **ate**}, the uncontrollable desire *to eat* never **left** you.

→ if+동사의 과거형: 가정법 과거 구문

→ { }는 〈양보〉를 나타내는 부사절

→ to eat은 앞의 the uncontrollable desire를 수식하는 형용사적 용법의 to부정사

④ ... to eat soil, paper, or almost anything [(that) they can put into their mouths].

→ 목적격 관계대명사 that이 생략된 경우로, nothing, anything과 같이 -thing으로 끝나는 대명사가 선행사일 때는 주로 관계대명사 that을 씀.

⑤ PWS is caused by a disorder in a part of the brain called the hypothalamus, **which** controls appetite.

→ which는 the hypothalamus를 부연 설명하는 계속적 용법의 관계대명사

02 수술실에 울려 퍼진 음악 소리

P. 84

정답 1 ③ 2 ⑤ 3 ② 4 awake, hum, songs

문제해설

1 ③ 파비오라는 음악가의 뇌종양 제거 수술에서 그의 음악적 능력을 지켜주기 위해 독특한 방식으로 수술을 했다는 내용이다.
① 뇌종양을 발견하기 위한 혁신적인 방법들
② 음악으로 뇌를 발달시키는 방법
③ 한 환자의 재능을 보존하기 위한 독특한 수술
④ 악기를 사용한 새로운 뇌 치료법
⑤ 의학과 예술을 결합시킨 위험한 기술

2 (A) 수식하는 앞의 명사 the part of the brain과 수동 관계에 있으므로 과거분사 involved가 적절하다.
(B) 사역동사 have의 목적어와 목적격보어가 능동 관계이므로 목적격보어로 동사원형인 play가 적절하다.
(C) 문맥상 종양이 '제거되는' 것이므로 수동태 was removed가 적절하다.

3 문맥상 뇌를 MRI로 스캔하는 동안 파비오가 노래를 흥얼거리면 뇌에서 음악과 관련된 부분의 '위치를 찾는' 데 도움이 될 것이므로 ② conceal(감추다)을 locate로 바꿔야 한다.

4 의사들은 수술 중 음악과 관련된 뇌 부위를 피하기 위해 환자를 깨어 있게 하고 그에게 콧노래를 불러달라고 요청했다. (⑨번 문장)
의사들은 음악과 연관된 환자의 뇌 부분에 영향을 주지 않고 종양을 제거하기 위해 무엇을 했는가?
그들은 환자가 수술을 받는 동안 환자가 깨어 있게 하고 그가 때때로 콧노래를 부르도록 시켰다.

본문

① While a team of doctors operates on his brain, / a patient hums songs / and plays the saxophone. ② This unusual situation actually happened / in 2016. ③ The patient was a 25-year-old musician / named Dan Fabbio.
④ Fabbio had a tumor / located in the part of the brain / involved in making and listening to music. ⑤ Doctors hoped to remove it / without affecting Fabbio's musical abilities. ⑥ They spent months / making a three-dimensional map / of his brain. ⑦ Fabbio would listen to songs / and then hum them / while the doctors performed MRI scans on his brain. ⑧ This helped the doctors / locate the parts of his brain / related to music.
⑨ Although the map was useful, / the cautious doctors decided / to keep Fabbio awake / during the surgery, / asking him to hum songs occasionally. ⑩ This activity showed the doctors exactly / which areas of the brain to avoid. ⑪ Toward the end of the operation, / they decided to give Fabbio a test. ⑫ They brought his saxophone into the operating room / and had him play a song on it. ⑬ He played the song perfectly, / and the doctors and nurses happily applauded his performance.
⑭ In the end, / the surgery was a great success. ⑮ The tumor was removed / and Fabbio didn't lose his musical talent!

해석 ① 의료진이 한 환자의 뇌를 수술하는 동안, 그 환자는 콧노래를 부르고 색소폰을 연주한다. ② 이 특이한 상황은 실제로 2016년에 일어났다. ③ 그 환자는 댄 파비오라는 25살의 음악가였다.

④ 파비오는 음악을 만들고 듣는 것과 관련된 뇌 부위에 종양이 생겼다. ⑤ 의사들은 파비오의 음악적 능력에 영향을 미치지 않고 그 종양을 제거하기를 바랐다. ⑥ 그들은 그의 뇌에 대한 3차원 지도를 만드는 데 수개월을 보냈다. ⑦ 파비오는 의사들이 그의 뇌에 MRI 스캔을 하는 동안 노래를 듣고 나서 흥얼거렸다. ⑧ 이것은 의사들이 음악과 관련된 뇌 영역을 찾도록 도와주었다.

⑨ 이 지도는 유용했지만, 신중한 의사들은 파비오가 수술 동안 깨어 있게 하기로 결정했고, 가끔 그에게 콧노래를 불러달라고 요청했다. ⑩ 이러한 활동은 의사들에게 정확히 뇌의 어느 영역을 피할지 보여주었다. ⑪ 수술이 끝날 무렵에, 그들은 파비오에게 테스트를 해보기로 결정했다. ⑫ 그들은 그의 색소폰을 수술실에 가져와 그가 그 색소폰으로 노래를 연주하게 했다. ⑬ 그는 그 노래를 완벽히 연주했고, 의사들과 간호사들은 그의 연주에 행복하게 박수를 쳤다. ⑭ 결국, 수술은 대성공이었다. ⑮ 종양은 제거되었고 파비오는 그의 음악적 재능을 잃지 않았다!

구문해설 ⑥ They **spent months making** a three-dimensional map of his brain.

→ spend+시간[돈]+v-ing: …하는 데 시간[돈]을 보내다[쓰다]

⑧ This **helped the doctors locate** the parts of his brain related to music.

→ help+목적어+동사원형[to-v]: (목적어)가 …하는 것을 돕다

⑨ **Although** the map was useful, the cautious doctors decided to keep Fabbio awake during the surgery, *asking* him to hum songs occasionally.

→ Although는 〈양보〉를 나타내는 종속접속사

→ asking 이하는 〈연속동작〉을 나타내는 분사구문 (= and they asked ....)

03 충치가 무서워! P. 86

정답 **1** ⑤ **2** ③ **3** ② **4** rotten, infected

문제해설 **1** ⑤ 충치를 치료하지 않고 무시했을 때 생길 수 있는 위험에 대한 글이다.

① 왜 우리는 치과의사를 무서워하나 ② 좋은 치과의사를 찾는 방법 ③ 충치가 있다는 징후

④ 무엇이 성인 충치를 유발하나 ⑤ 충치를 무시하는 것의 위험성

2 '너무 두려워서 치과에 갈 수 없다'를 의미하는 「too + 형용사 + to-v」 구문의 일부이므로 ③ going은 to go가 되어야 한다.

3 ② 앞서 소개된 남자의 사례를 통해, 충치를 방치하면 충치 때문에 다른 더 큰 질병을 얻어 수술을 받을 수도 있다는 의미임을 알 수 있다.

4 충치를 방치하여 박테리아 감염으로 인해 뇌에 암이 생긴 남자에 관한 내용이므로 빈칸에는 각각 rotten, infected가 알맞다. (⑪, ⑫번 문장)

남자의 썩은 치아가 박테리아에 감염되었고, 그것은 뇌에 암을 유발했다.

본문

① If you ever feel a pain / in your mouth, / don't ignore it. ② A toothache can be a sign / that you have a cavity. ③ And if cavities are left untreated / for too long, / they can become infected. ④ The problem is / that this kind of infection doesn't just affect your teeth. ⑤ It can have a serious impact / on your health, / leading to stomach problems, heart disease, diabetes, and brain disease.

⑥ A recent story of a man / highlights / the danger of ignoring a cavity. ⑦ The man had a severely rotten tooth, / but he was too scared / to go to the dentist / to have it pulled out. ⑧ So, / he just kept taking painkillers. ⑨ After some time, / he began feeling dizzy, / developed a fever, / and eventually collapsed. ⑩ He was taken to a hospital, / but the doctors couldn't figure out / what was wrong with him. ⑪ Finally, / they realized / that his rotten tooth had become infected. ⑫ Bacteria from the infection / had entered his brain, / causing cancer to form.

⑬ So even if you're afraid of / getting into dentist's chair, / be sure to make an appointment / if you think / you have a cavity. ⑭ If you don't, / you could end up lying down / on an operating table instead!

해석

① 입 속에 통증이 느껴진다면, 그것을 무시하지 마라. ② 치통은 충치가 있다는 것을 알려 주는 징후일 수 있다. ③ 그리고 충치가 치료되지 않은 채로 너무 오래 방치되면, 그것은 감염될 수가 있다. ④ 문제는 이런 종류의 감염이 단순히 치아에만 영향을 미치는 것이 아니라는 점이다. ⑤ 이런 감염은 여러분의 건강에 심각한 영향을 미쳐, 위장병, 심장 질환, 당뇨병, 그리고 뇌 질환에까지 이를 수 있다.

⑥ 최근의 한 남자의 이야기는 충치를 무시하는 것의 위험성을 강조하고 있다. ⑦ 그 남자는 심하게 썩은 치아가 있었지만, 너무 겁이 나서 그것을 뽑으러 치과에 갈 수가 없었다. ⑧ 그래서 그는 그저 계속 진통제만 복용했다. ⑨ 시간이 흘러, 그는 어지러움을 느끼기 시작했고, 열이 나다가 결국 쓰러졌다. ⑩ 그는 병원으로 실려갔지만, 의사들은 무엇이 문제인지 알아낼 수 없었다. ⑪ 마침내 그들은 그의 썩은 치아가 감염되었다는 것을 알게 되었다. ⑫ (충치의) 감염된 부위에서 생긴 박테리아가 그의 뇌 속으로 들어갔고, 암을 발생시킨 것이다.

⑬ 그러므로 치과의 진료 의자에 눕는 것이 두렵다 하더라도, 충치가 있다고 생각되면 반드시 예약을 하도록 하라. ⑭ 그러지 않는다면, 당신은 대신 수술대 위에 누워 있게 될 수도 있다!

구문해설

② A toothache can be a sign **that** you have a cavity.

→ that은 a sign과 동격을 이루는 명사절을 이끄는 접속사 (a sign = you have a cavity)

③ And if cavities(S) are left(V) untreated(C) for too long, they can become infected.

→ if cavities are left untreated는 5형식 문장 if you leave cavities untreated의 수동형으로, 5형식 문장의 목적격보어 untreated가 수동태에서는 주격보어가 됨.

⑤ It can have a serious impact on your health, **leading** to stomach problems, heart disease, diabetes, and brain disease.

→ leading 이하는 연속동작을 나타내는 분사구문 (= and it can lead ....)

⑩ He was taken to a hospital, but the doctors couldn't figure out **what was wrong with him**.

→ what was wrong with him은 figure out의 목적어가 되는 간접의문문으로 「의문사 주어+동사」의 어순

⑭ **If you don't**, you could *end up lying* down on an operating table instead!

→ If you don't = If you don't make an appointment
→ end up v-ing: 결국 …하게 되다

04 Is Scuba Diving Dangerous? P. 88

정답 1 ④ 2 to divers → for divers 3 ②

문제해설 1 ④ 작은 질소 방울들이 팽창하여 커져서 몸 속에 갇힌다고 하였다. (⑧번 문장)
[문제] 다음 중 이 글의 내용과 일치하지 않는 것은?
① 몇몇 잠수부들은 감압병을 겪은 적이 있다. (④번 문장)
② 감압병은 잠수부가 기본적인 안전수칙들을 무시할 때 일어난다. (⑤번 문장)
③ 잠수부의 몸에 갇힌 질소 방울이 감압병을 유발한다. (⑥번 문장)
④ 잠수부들이 잘못 떠오를 때 질소 방울은 몸 속에서 작아진다.
⑤ 질소 방울이 정맥 내에 있으면, 뇌로 이동하여 뇌졸중을 일으킬 수 있다. (⑩번 문장)

2 to부정사의 의미상의 주어 앞에는 전치사 for를 써야 하므로, to straighten의 주체인 divers 앞의 to를 for로 고쳐야 한다.
[문제] 밑줄 친 부분에서 어법상 틀린 부분을 찾아 바르게 고쳐 쓰시오.

3 (A) 앞 문장에서 감압병을 겪은 잠수부들을 만난 적이 있다고 했지만, 뒤에서는 이것이 드물다고 하고 있으므로 역접의 의미인 However가 적절하다.
(B) 앞 문장에서 질소 방울들이 관절 내에서 일으키는 고통에 대해 설명하고, 뒤에서는 질소 방울이 정맥 속에 생기면 뇌졸중을 일으킬 수 있다고 추가 설명하고 있으므로 Moreover가 적절하다.
[문제] 다음 중 빈칸 (A)와 (B)에 들어갈 말로 가장 적절한 것은?

본문

① **Q:** I've always wanted to try scuba diving, / but I've heard scary stories / about decompression sickness. ② Can you tell me / what this is / and how dangerous it is?
③ **A:** Thanks for raising / this important concern. ④ As a professional scuba instructor / based in Cebu, Philippines, / I have come across / other divers / who have experienced decompression sickness. ⑤ However, / I must emphasize / that it is rare, / and it only occurs / when divers ignore basic safety procedures.
⑥ The condition itself / involves nitrogen bubbles / becoming trapped in a diver's body, / normally in the joints or veins. ⑦ This happens / when divers don't surface properly / or surface too quickly. ⑧ When this happens, / the sudden decrease in pressure / causes tiny nitrogen bubbles / to expand into big ones / and get stuck inside the body. ⑨ When these bubbles are in the joints, / it becomes incredibly painful / for divers / to straighten their arms and legs / — the reason / why decompression sickness / is commonly called "the bends." ⑩ Moreover, / if the bubbles are in the veins, / they can travel to the brain / and cause a stroke.
⑪ As you can see, / decompression sickness can be very serious. ⑫ The good news is, / though, / that it is easily avoidable. ⑬ If you follow the safety precautions / and stay calm, /

you will have no such problems! ⑭ Please feel free to contact me / if you have any further questions.

해석 ① **Q:** 저는 늘 스쿠버 다이빙을 시도해 보고 싶었지만, 감압병에 대한 무서운 이야기들을 들은 적이 있습니다. ② 이것이 무엇이며 얼마나 위험한지 알려 주시겠습니까?
③ **A:** 이런 중요한 우려를 제기해 주셔서 감사합니다. ④ 필리핀의 세부에 기반을 둔 전문 스쿠버 강사로서, 저는 감압병을 겪은 다른 잠수부들을 만난 적이 있습니다. ⑤ 그러나, 저는 그것이 드물다는 점과 그것은 잠수부들이 기본적인 안전수칙들을 무시하는 경우에만 일어난다는 것을 강조하겠습니다.
⑥ 그 질환 자체는 질소 방울들이 잠수부의 몸 속, 보통은 관절이나 정맥 속에 갇히게 되는 것을 수반합니다. ⑦ 이것은 잠수부들이 올바르게 떠오르지 않거나, 혹은 너무 빨리 떠오를 때 발생합니다. ⑧ 이렇게 되면, 갑작스러운 압력의 감소로 매우 작은 질소 방울들이 큰 것들로 팽창되어 몸 안에 갇히게 만듭니다. ⑨ 이 방울들이 관절 내에 있으면 잠수부들이 팔다리를 뻗는 것이 너무나 고통스럽게 됩니다. 이것이 바로 감압병이 흔히 '벤즈(the bends)'라고 불리는 이유입니다. ⑩ 게다가, 만약 그 방울들이 정맥 내에 있으면, 그것들은 뇌로 이동하여 뇌졸중을 일으킬 수 있습니다.
⑪ 보시다시피 감압병은 매우 심각할 수 있습니다. ⑫ 그러나 희소식은 그것을 쉽게 피할 수 있다는 것입니다. ⑬ 만약 당신이 안전 예방책들을 따르고 침착함을 유지한다면, 그런 문제들은 없을 겁니다! ⑭ 질문이 더 있으면 주저 마시고 저에게 연락 주십시오.

구문해설 ⑤ However, I must emphasize [that it is rare, and it only occurs ...].
→ [ ]는 emphasize의 목적어로 쓰인 명사절

⑥ The condition itself involves **nitrogen bubbles** [becoming trapped in a diver's body, ...].
→ [ ]는 involves의 목적어가 되는 동명사구, nitrogen bubbles는 동명사의 의미상 주어

⑧ ..., the sudden decrease in pressure(S) **causes**(V) tiny nitrogen bubbles(O) **to expand** into big ones and **(to) get** stuck inside the body(OC).
→ cause+목적어+to-v: (목적어)가 …하게 하다

⑨ ..., it becomes incredibly painful ... — the reason [why ... "the bends."]
→ [ ]는 선행사 the reason을 수식하는 관계부사절

Review Test

P. 90

A ② B **1** instrument **2** concern **3** innovative **4** proportion C **1** ④ **2** ③ **3** ② **4** ④ D **1** 충치가 있다고 생각되면 반드시 예약을 하도록 하라. **2** 그것은 그들로 하여금 심지어 흙 또는 입에 넣을 수 있는 그 어떤 것이라도 먹게 한다. **3** 이러한 활동은 의사들에게 정확히 뇌의 어느 영역을 피할지 보여주었다. **4** 그들은 그의 색소폰을 수술실에 가져와 그가 그 색소폰으로 노래를 연주하게 했다. E **1** could end up lying down on **2** was too scared to go **3** are advised to take strict measures

해석 **A**
① 끊임없는: 늘 또는 매우 자주 일어나는

② 영향을 미치다: 어떤 사람이 성공하는 것을 쉽게 만들다
③ 조심스러운: 위험을 피하려고 주의하는
④ 감염: 박테리아나 바이러스에 의한 질병
⑤ 진통제: 통증을 완화해 주는 약

B

1 악기 하나를 완전히 통달하는 것은 시간과 노력이 든다.
2 마을 사람들은 극심한 가뭄에 대해 걱정을 했다.
3 그들은 혁신적인 치료법을 사용해서 암세포들을 파괴하는 것을 시도했다.
4 이 학교에서 높은 비율의 학생들이 명문 대학에 진학한다.

C

1 하나의 썩은 감자가 자루에 든 모든 감자를 손상시킨다.
① 신선한 ② 녹색의 ③ 달콤한 ④ 썩은 ⑤ 불에 탄[덴]
2 스트레스는 수면 장애의 원인이 될 수 있다.
① 식욕 ② 비만 ③ 장애 ④ 수술 ⑤ 위, 복부
3 의사들은 정기적인 검진의 중요성을 강조한다.
① 제거한다 ② 강조한다 ③ 비판한다 ④ 조직한다 ⑤ 결합한다
4 그 소프라노는 그녀의 공연으로 큰 박수갈채를 받았다.
① 욕구 ② 발견 ③ 폭력 ④ 공연 ⑤ 실수

SECTION 08

사회 · 환경

01 **1** ② **2** ① **3** ⑤ **4** (1) F (2) T (3) T
02 **1** ⑤ **2** ③ **3** ④ **4** humans in dealing with medical data in the healthcare system
03 **1** ④ **2** ③ **3** ③ **4** Beautiful wildflowers
04 **1** ③ **2** ① **3** ⑤ **4** tree-sitters

01 똑똑! 양말 한 켤레만 주세요 P. 94

정답 1 ② 2 ① 3 ⑤ 4 (1) F (2) T (3) T

문제해설 **1** ② 양말을 모아서 노숙자들에게 기부하는 아이디어를 시작으로 비영리 단체를 운영하게 된 한 대학생에 관한 내용이다.
① 노숙자들에게 집을 주자
② 큰 효과를 거둔 작은 아이디어
③ 뉴욕 시의 혹한

④ 여러분의 낡은 양말로 큰돈을 벌 수 있다
⑤ 집 없는 소녀가 어떻게 성공했는지

2 '나눠주다'라는 의미의 distribute와 유사한 의미를 가진 표현은 hand out이다.
① 나눠주다 ② …을 자랑하다 ③ …을 버리다 ④ …을 세우다 ⑤ …을 포기하다

3 릭트먼이 기숙사의 친구들에게 양말을 기부해 달라고 부탁해서 다음 날 아침까지 40켤레를 모았다고 하는 것이 자연스러우므로 주어진 문장은 ⑤에 들어가는 것이 적절하다.

4 (1) 릭트먼은 대학 친구에게서 KKGS에 대한 아이디어를 얻었다. → 릭트먼은 한 노숙자로부터 양말이 필요하다는 이야기를 듣고 나서 양말 기부를 하기 시작했다. (⑥, ⑦번 문장)
(2) KKGS는 지금까지 전국적으로 많은 노숙자들을 도왔다. → KKGS는 미국 전역의 노숙자에게 35만 켤레 이상의 양말을 기부했다. (⑨번 문장)
(3) KKGS 창립자는 이전에 양말 기부에 대해 생각해본 사람은 거의 없었기 때문에 이 단체가 특별하다고 생각한다. → 릭트먼은 노숙자에게 양말을 기부한 적이 있는 사람은 거의 없으므로 KKGS를 특별하다고 생각한다. (⑩번 문장)

본문

① Socks are just something / we pull onto our feet / every morning, / so they may not seem important / to you and me. ② But they can make a huge difference / in the lives of some people. ③ Adina Lichtman learned this / when she was a college student.
④ She had decided / to help homeless people in New York City / and was distributing free sandwiches on the street. ⑤ One grateful man thanked her for the sandwich, / but then he mentioned that winter was coming. ⑥ When the weather turns frigid, / he told her, / homeless people need socks / more than anything else. ⑦ That night, / after deciding to take action, / Lichtman started knocking on doors / in her dormitory, / asking her classmates / to donate one pair of socks. ⑧ By the next morning, / she had collected 40 pairs.
⑨ Today she runs a nonprofit organization, / called Knock Knock, Give a Sock (KKGS), / that has donated more than 350,000 pairs of socks / to homeless people all across America. ⑩ There are numerous organizations / that work to help the homeless, / but Lichtman explains / why KKGS is special: / "While many people donate clothing, / nine out of every ten clothing donors / have never donated socks." ⑪ Lichtman identified an important need / and found a way to fill it. ⑫ Thanks to her innovative thinking, / thousands of people will have warm feet / this winter.

해석

① 양말은 우리가 매일 아침 우리 발에 신는 것일 뿐이라서, 여러분과 내게는 중요하지 않아 보일지도 모른다. ② 하지만 양말은 어떤 사람들의 인생에는 커다란 영향을 미칠 수 있다. ③ 아디나 릭트먼은 그녀가 대학생이었을 때 이것을 알게 되었다.
④ 그녀는 뉴욕 시의 노숙자들을 돕기로 결심했고 거리에서 무료 샌드위치를 나눠주고 있었다. ⑤ 고마움을 느낀 한 남자가 샌드위치에 대해 그녀에게 고마워했지만, 그러고 나서 그는 겨울이 오고 있다고 말했다. ⑥ 날씨가 몹시 추워지면, 노숙자들은 다른 어떤 것보다 양말이 필요하다고 그가 그녀에게 말했다. ⑦ 그날 밤, 릭트먼은 행동을 하기로 결심한 후에, 그녀의 기숙사의 문들을 두드리기 시작해서, 그녀의 학과 친구들에게 양말 한 켤레를 기부해 달라고 부탁했다. ⑧ 다음 날 아침까지, 그녀는 양말 40켤레를 모았다.
⑨ 현재 그녀는 미국 전역에서 노숙자들에게 35만 켤레 이상의 양말을 기부해 온 Knock Knock, Give a Sock

(KKGS)이라고 불리는 비영리 단체를 운영하고 있다. ⑩ 노숙자들을 돕기 위해 일하는 수많은 단체들이 있지만, 릭트먼은 왜 KKGS가 특별한지 설명한다. "많은 사람들이 옷을 기부하지만, 옷을 기부하는 사람 열 명 중 아홉 명이 양말을 기부한 적은 없어요." ⑪ 릭트먼은 중요한 필요성을 찾아냈고 그것을 충족시킬 방법을 찾았다. ⑫ 그녀의 혁신적인 생각 덕분에, 수천 명의 사람들이 올겨울에 발이 따뜻할 것이다.

구문해설

① Socks are just something [(that) we pull onto our feet every morning], so they may not seem important to you and me.

→ [ ]는 선행사 something을 수식하는 관계대명사절로, 목적격 관계대명사 that이 생략됨. something, nothing, anything과 같이 -thing으로 끝나는 대명사가 선행사일 때는 주로 관계대명사 that을 씀.

⑦ That night, **after deciding** to take action, Lichtman started knocking on doors in her dormitory, *asking* her classmates to donate one pair of socks.

→ after deciding은 〈시간〉을 나타내는 분사구문으로, 의미를 분명하게 하기 위해 분사 앞에 접속사 after를 생략하지 않음.

→ asking 이하는 〈연속동작〉을 나타내는 분사구문(=and she asked ....)

→ ask+목적어+to-v: (목적어)가 …하도록 부탁[요청]하다

⑨ Today she runs a nonprofit organization, [called Knock Knock, Give a Sock (KKGS)], [that has donated more than 350,000 pairs of socks to homeless people all across America].

→ 첫 번째 [ ]는 삽입어구로 쓰인 과거분사구로 a nonprofit organization을 부연 설명함.

→ 두 번째 [ ]는 선행사 a nonprofit organization을 수식하는 주격 관계대명사절

⑪ Lichtman identified an important need and found a way to fill **it**.

→ to fill은 a way를 수식하는 형용사적 용법의 to부정사

→ it은 앞의 an important need를 가리킴.

02 AI: 역대 가장 똑똑한 의사 P. 96

정답 1 ⑤ 2 ③ 3 ④ 4 humans in dealing with medical data in the healthcare system

문제해설

1 (A) 빈칸 앞에서는 인간 뇌가 굉장하다고 하고, 빈칸 뒤에 이와 상반되는 내용이 이어지므로 역접을 나타내는 However가 적절하다.
(B) 빈칸 앞에서는 인간 의사의 한계에 대해 말하고 뒤에서는 AI가 인간 의사가 하기 어려운 일을 해낸다고 하므로 대조를 나타내는 on the other hand가 적절하다.

2 의사들이 훈련이 잘되어 있고 최신 장비에 접근할 수 있는데도 불구하고 의료 실수를 한다는 내용인 (B)가 이어지고, 이것이 의사의 잘못만은 아니라는 내용인 (C)가 오고, 그 근거로 의학 논문을 읽으려면 많은 시간이 필요하다는 내용인 (A)가 오는 것이 흐름상 자연스럽다.

3 AI는 인간 의사보다 실수를 덜 하지만 인간처럼 환자에 대한 배려와 보살핌을 보여줄 수 없다고 하므로 '이득, 혜택'을 의미하는 benefit은 '불리한 면'을 의미하는 downside가 되어야 한다.

4 AI가 의료 데이터를 처리하는 데 있어서 인간보다 일을 더 잘한다는 내용이 되어야 하므로, 「work(s)+better+

than+비교 대상+in v-ing」의 어순으로 배열한다.
AI는 인간과 비교해서 몇 가지 약점이 있지만, 그것은 분명히 매우 유용하고 의료 체계에서 의료 데이터를 처리하는 데 있어서 인간보다 일을 더 잘한다.

본문

① The human brain is an amazing thing. ② However, / there are some tasks / that are simply too complex / for our brains to handle well. ③ That's why artificial intelligence, / also known as AI, / plays many important roles, / especially in the field of healthcare.
④ Doctors in the US / are highly trained / and have access to / all the latest equipment. ⑤ (B) Despite this, / it is estimated / that American doctors make about 1.5 million medication mistakes / every year. ⑥ (C) This isn't / always the doctors' fault. ⑦ (A) If you wanted to read every new medical paper / that was published, / you would need 160 hours / of free time every week. ⑧ In reality, / most doctors spend five hours a month or less reading medical papers.
⑨ AI, on the other hand, / has the ability to analyze / and understand every medical paper / ever written. ⑩ All of these details can be stored in a database / and recalled instantly. ⑪ Using this information, / it can recommend medications and treatments / just as well as the best doctors, / and it is less likely to make mistakes.
⑫ Of course, / there is a downside. ⑬ AI cannot show concern and care as a human can. ⑭ Patients need proper treatments and medications, / but they also need compassion. ⑮ For this reason, / AI will never completely replace human doctors. ⑯ However, / we should still take advantage of AI / to reduce errors / within the healthcare system.

해석

① 인간 두뇌는 굉장한 것이다. ② 그러나, 그저 너무 복잡해서 우리의 뇌가 다룰 수 없는 몇 가지 일들이 있다. ③ 그것이 AI라고도 알려진 인공 지능이 특히 의료 분야에서 중요한 많은 역할들을 하는 이유이다.
④ 미국의 의사들은 훈련이 잘되어 있고 모든 최신 장비에 접근할 수 있다. ⑤ (B) 이에도 불구하고, 미국 의사들은 매년 약 150만 번의 의료 실수를 한다고 추정된다. ⑥ (C) 이것은 항상 의사의 잘못만은 아니다. ⑦ (A) 여러분이 발행된 모든 새로운 의학 논문을 읽기를 원한다면, 여러분은 매주 160시간이라는 여가 시간이 필요할 것이다. ⑧ 실제로는, 대부분의 의사들이 의학 논문을 읽는 데 한 달에 5시간 이하를 보낸다.
⑨ 반면에, AI는 지금까지 쓰인 모든 의학 논문을 분석하고 이해하는 능력이 있다. ⑩ 이 모든 세부 사항은 데이터베이스에 저장될 수 있고 즉시 불러와질 수 있다. ⑪ 이러한 정보를 사용하여, AI는 최고의 의사가 하는 것만큼 능숙하게 약물과 치료법을 추천할 수 있고, 실수할 가능성이 더 낮다.
⑫ 물론, 불리한 면이 있다. ⑬ AI는 인간이 할 수 있는 것처럼 배려와 보살핌을 보여줄 수 없다. ⑭ 환자들은 적절한 치료와 약물이 필요하지만, 또한 연민도 필요하다. ⑮ 이러한 이유로, AI는 인간 의사들을 결코 완전하게 대체할 수 없을 것이다. ⑯ 그러나, 우리는 의료 시스템 내의 실수들을 줄이기 위해 여전히 AI를 활용해야 할 것이다.

구문해설

① However, there are some tasks [that are simply **too complex** for our brains **to handle** well].

→ [ ]는 선행사 some tasks를 수식하는 주격 관계대명사절
→ too+형용사+to-v: 너무 …해서 ~할 수 없다

③ **That's why** artificial intelligence (S), [also known as AI], plays (V) many important roles, especially in the field of healthcare.

→ That's why: 그것이 …한 이유이다
→ [ ]는 삽입 어구로 쓰인 과거분사구로, artificial intelligence를 부연 설명함.

⑦ **If you wanted** to read every new medical paper [that was published], **you would need** 160 hours of free time every week.
→ If+주어+동사의 과거형..., 주어+조동사의 과거형+동사원형~: 만약 …하면[라면], ~할 것이다(가정법 과거)
→ [ ]는 선행사 every new medical paper를 수식하는 주격 관계대명사절

⑧ In reality, most doctors **spend five hours a month or less reading** medical papers.
→ spend+시간[돈]+v-ing: …하는 데 시간[돈]을 쓰다

⑨ AI, on the other hand, has the ability **to analyze and understand** every medical paper [ever written].
→ to analyze와 (to) understand는 the ability를 수식하는 형용사적 용법의 to부정사
→ [ ]는 every medical paper를 뒤에서 수식하는 과거분사구

03 도심 속 작은 오아시스 P. 98

정답 1 ④ 2 ③ 3 ③ 4 Beautiful wildflowers

문제해설

1 ④ 하이라인 공원은 버려진 철로를 재활용하려는 한 지역 디자이너의 아이디어로 만들어졌다. (⑧~⑫번 문장)
① (→ ①번 문장) ② (→ ③번 문장) ③ (→ ⑤번 문장) ⑤ (→ ⑯번 문장)

2 (A) 주어인 It(the High Line)은 '발견되는' 것이라는 의미의 수동태가 되어야 하므로 과거분사 found가 적절하다.
(B) '많은 …'을 뜻하는 「a number of+복수명사」는 복수 취급하므로 were가 적절하다.
(C) 문맥상 그것을 '사용하는 것을' 멈췄다는 의미이므로 동명사 using이 적절하다. stop to-v는 '…하기 위해 멈추다'라는 의미이다.

3 주어진 문장의 내용은 구조물의 활용 방법을 생각해내려고 했다는 것으로, They는 Friends of the High Line 단체의 사람들을 가리킨다. 따라서 주어진 문장은 철로를 어떻게 활용할 것인지 결정한 내용 앞인 ③에 들어가는 것이 가장 적절하다.

4 로버트 해먼드는 구조물 위에 올라가 그 위에 피어 있는 아름다운 야생화들을 본 순간 이것을 공원으로 바꿀 생각을 했다고 하였다. (⑪, ⑫번 문장)
무엇이 로버트 해먼드가 버려진 구조물을 공원으로 바꾸도록 영감을 주었는가?
구조물 위의 아름다운 야생화들이 그에게 영감을 주었다.

본문

① Unlike most parks, / the High Line in New York City / does not have sports fields, playgrounds, or a running track. ② It is not even found / at street level; / rather, it is located / high above the streets, / and passes between buildings.
③ The High Line was originally a train line / in Manhattan. ④ The street it ran along / became

known as "Death Avenue" / because a number of people were hit / by passing trains there. ⑤ To stop this, / the tracks were moved / onto a structure / that was 10 meters high. ⑥ Over time, however, / the line was used less and less, / and in 1980 / trains stopped using it altogether.
⑦ Some people complained / about the abandoned structure, / so the city decided / to tear it down. ⑧ But Robert Hammond, / a local designer, / wanted to keep it. ⑨ So he started an organization / called Friends of the High Line. ⑩ They tried to think of / a new use for the structure. ⑪ One day Hammond climbed onto it / and saw / that it was covered / in beautiful wildflowers. ⑫ At that moment, / he decided to turn it / into a park.
⑬ At first, / people opposed his idea, / because the park would cost a lot of money / to build. ⑭ But Hammond explained / that the park would be / beneficial to the city. ⑮ The city government finally decided / to support the project. ⑯ The park's first section / opened to the public / in 2009. ⑰ The next year, / more than two million people visited it. ⑱ With a little imagination and some hard work, / an old train line was turned / into a unique public space.

해석 ① 대부분의 공원과는 달리, 뉴욕 시의 하이라인은 운동장도, 놀이터도, 달리기 트랙도 없다. ② 그것은 심지어 거리와 같은 높이에 있지도 않다. 오히려 이 공원은 길 위에 높이 위치해 있어 건물들 사이를 지나가고 있다.
③ 하이라인은 원래 맨해튼의 철로였다. ④ 많은 사람들이 그곳에서 지나가는 기차에 치이는 바람에, 철로가 있던 길은 '죽음의 거리'로 알려지게 되었다. ⑤ 이를 막기 위해, 철로는 10미터 높이에 있는 구조물 위로 옮겨졌다. ⑥ 하지만 시간이 가면서, 이 노선은 점점 덜 사용되었고, 1980년에 기차는 이 철로를 사용하는 것을 완전히 중단했다.
⑦ 몇몇 사람들은 이 버려진 구조물에 대해 불평했고, 뉴욕 시는 그것을 철거하기로 결정했다. ⑧ 그러나 지역 디자이너인 로버트 해먼드는 그것을 보존하고 싶어 했다. ⑨ 그래서 그는 '하이라인의 친구들'이라고 불리는 단체를 시작했다. ⑩ 그들은 그 구조물의 새로운 용도를 생각해 내려고 애썼다. ⑪ 어느 날 해먼드는 구조물의 위에 올라가 보았고, 그것이 아름다운 야생화들로 뒤덮여 있는 것을 보았다. ⑫ 그 순간, 그는 그 구조물을 공원으로 바꾸기로 결심했다.
⑬ 처음에 사람들은 공원을 짓는 데 돈이 많이 들 것이라 그의 생각에 반대했다. ⑭ 하지만 해먼드는 공원이 시에 이익이 될 것이라고 설명했다. ⑮ 뉴욕 시 정부는 결국 그 프로젝트를 지원하기로 결정했다. ⑯ 공원의 첫 구획은 2009년 공공에 개방되었다. ⑰ 그다음 해, 이백만 명이 넘는 사람들이 이곳을 방문했다. ⑱ 약간의 상상력과 노고로, 낡은 철로가 독특한 공공장소로 탈바꿈했다.

구문해설 ⑤ **To stop** this, the tracks were moved onto a structure [*that* was 10 meters high].
→ To stop은 〈목적〉을 나타내는 부사적 용법의 to부정사
→ that은 a structure를 선행사로 하는 주격 관계대명사

⑦ Some people complained about the abandoned structure, so the city decided to **tear it down**.
→ 「동사+부사」로 이루어진 동사구의 목적어로 대명사가 올 때는 「동사+대명사+부사」의 어순으로 씀.
(*cf.* 목적어가 명사일 때는 「동사+명사+부사」와 「동사+부사+명사」 모두 가능)

⑭ But Hammond explained that the park **would** be beneficial to the city.
→ that절의 would는 주절의 동사 explained와 시제 일치를 이루어 과거형으로 쓰임.

04 A Unique Way of Demonstrating P. 100

정답 1 ③ 2 ① 3 ⑤ 4 tree-sitters

문제해설

1 ③ 트리 시팅을 하는 사람들은 정부 관리와 벌목꾼들과 대립한다고 했다. (⑧번 문장)

[문제] 다음 중 트리 시팅에 관한 이 글의 내용과 일치하지 않는 것은?

① 이것은 삼림을 베는 것에 대항하는 시위의 한 형태이다. (①번 문장)

② 줄리아 힐은 개인으로서 가장 오래 트리 시팅 운동을 한 기록을 가지고 있다. (⑤번 문장)

③ 정부와 몇몇 벌목꾼들이 이 운동을 후원한다.

④ 트리 시팅 시위자들은 날씨가 나쁠 때에도 나무에 머무른다. (⑩번 문장)

⑤ 몇몇 사람들이 트리 시팅을 하는 동안 죽었다. (⑪, ⑫번 문장)

2 (A) 트리 시팅은 위험한 일이라고 한 후에, 트리 시팅을 하는 사람들이 겪는 문제의 한 예를 언급하고 있으므로 For example이 적절하다.

(B) '기분 좋은 햇빛'과 '세찬 바람과 폭우'가 대조되고 있으므로 Though가 적절하다.

[문제] 다음 중 빈칸 (A)와 (B)에 들어갈 말로 가장 적절한 것은?

3 여러 가지 어려움에도 불구하고 오랫동안 트리 시팅을 한 줄리아 힐에게는 ⑤ strong-willed라는 말이 어울린다.

[문제] 줄리아 힐을 묘사하는 말로 가장 적절한 것은?

① 까다로운 ② 관대한 ③ 의존적인 ④ 감정적인 ⑤ 의지가 강한

4 they는 우리의 감사를 받을 자격이 있다고 언급된 tree-sitters를 가리킨다.

[문제] 밑줄 친 they가 가리키는 것을 본문에서 찾아 쓰시오.

본문

① "Tree-sitting" is one form of demonstration / that people use to stop loggers / from cutting down forests. ② Perhaps / the best known of these tree-sitting efforts / took place in a wooded area / of Northern California. ③ Here a young woman named Julia "Butterfly" Hill / showed incredible determination and strength / by sitting in a tall redwood / for 738 days. ④ Her efforts saved the tree / and brought worldwide attention / to the need to protect our forests / from loggers. ⑤ Julia holds the record / for the longest tree-sitting effort / by one person.

⑥ You may think / it is just sitting down, / but there is a lot more to tree-sitting / than that. ⑦ It is a dangerous activity / that requires lots of strength and courage. ⑧ For example, / tree-sitters are often confronted / by government officials and angry loggers. ⑨ The weather gives them a hard time, too. ⑩ Though some days are filled with pleasant sunshine, / others are filled with high winds and heavy rains, / so endurance is a key quality / of any tree-sitter. ⑪ And there is always / the danger of falling / from the tree. ⑫ Several tree-sitters have died this way / in recent years. ⑬ Clearly, / tree-sitters deserve our appreciation / for their efforts / because they are helping to save our forests, / which we can't live without.

해석 ① '트리 시팅'은 벌목꾼들이 숲의 나무들을 베는 것을 막기 위해 사람들이 사용하는 하나의 시위 형태이다. ② 이러

한 트리 시팅 운동 중 아마도 가장 유명한 것이 북부 캘리포니아의 한 삼림 지역에서 있었다. ③ 이곳에서 줄리아 '버터플라이' 힐이라는 이름의 젊은 여성이 높은 삼나무에서 738일을 앉아 있음으로써 놀라운 결단력과 힘을 보여 주었다. ④ 그녀의 노력은 그 나무를 구했고, 우리의 삼림을 벌목꾼으로부터 보호할 필요성에 전 세계의 관심을 가져왔다. ⑤ 줄리아는 개인으로서 가장 오랫동안 트리 시팅 운동을 한 기록을 보유하고 있다.

⑥ 그냥 앉아 있는 것뿐이라고 생각할지 모르지만, 트리 시팅에는 그것보다 훨씬 더 많은 것들이 있다. ⑦ 그것은 많은 힘과 용기를 필요로 하는 위험한 일이다. ⑧ 예를 들어, 트리 시팅을 하는 사람들은 종종 정부 관리나 화가 난 벌목꾼들과 대립한다. ⑨ 날씨도 그들을 힘들게 한다. ⑩ 어떤 날은 기분 좋은 햇빛이 가득하지만, 다른 어떤 날은 세찬 바람과 폭우가 엄습하기 때문에 인내심은 트리 시팅을 하는 사람 누구에게나 중요한 자질이다. ⑪ 그리고 언제나 나무에서 떨어질 위험이 있다. ⑫ 트리 시팅을 하던 몇몇 사람이 최근 몇 년 동안 이로 인해 사망했다. ⑬ 확실히, 트리 시팅을 하는 사람들은 그들의 노력에 대해 우리의 감사를 받을 만한데, 그들은 우리의 삶에서 없어서는 안 될 삼림을 구하는 것을 돕고 있기 때문이다.

구문해설

① "Tree-sitting" is one form of demonstration [that people use **to** ***stop*** loggers *from cutting* down forests].
→ [ ]는 선행사 one form of demonstration을 수식하는 목적격 관계대명사절
→ to stop은 〈목적〉을 나타내는 to부정사의 부사적 용법
→ stop + 목적어 + from + v-ing: (목적어)가 …하는 것을 막다

④ ... brought worldwide attention to the need **to protect** ....
→ to protect는 the need를 수식하는 형용사적 용법의 to부정사

⑬ ... because they are helping to save our forests, **which** we can't live without.
→ which는 선행사 our forests를 부연 설명하는 계속적 용법의 관계대명사

Review Test

P. 102

A **1** ⓒ **2** ⓓ **3** ⓐ **4** ⓑ **5** ⓔ B **1** Huge **2** deserves **3** instantly **4** opposed C **1** ④ **2** ⑤ **3** ④ **4** ③ D **1** 노숙자들을 돕기 위해 일하는 수많은 단체들이 있다. **2** 그것이 AI가 특히 의료 분야에서 중요한 많은 역할들을 하는 이유이다. **3** 이 모든 세부 사항은 데이터베이스에 저장될 수 있고 즉시 불러와질 수 있다. **4** 행동을 하기로 결심한 후에, 릭트먼은 그녀의 기숙사의 문들을 두드리기 시작했다. E **1** climbed onto it and saw that **2** to stop loggers from cutting down forests **3** a number of people were hit by

해석

A

1 많은: ⓒ 상당수로 존재하는
2 연민: ⓓ 동정심
3 혁신적인: ⓐ 새롭고 독창적인
4 고마워하는: ⓑ 감사를 느끼거나 표현하는
5 인내심: ⓔ 오랫동안 어려운 것을 하는 능력

B

1 공장에서 강한 바람을 만들어 내기 위해 커다란 선풍기가 사용되었다.

2 그는 세계 평화를 위해 열심히 일해 왔기 때문에 노벨 평화상을 받을 만하다.

3 자명종 소리가 그녀를 즉각 깨웠다.

4 대부분의 마을 사람들은 원자력 발전소의 건설이 마을에 미칠 수 있는 나쁜 영향 때문에 그것에 반대했다.

C

1 줄리는 며칠 동안 피로를 느껴 건강 검진을 받기로 결정했다.
① 매우 추운 ② 최신의 ③ 이전[옛날]의 ④ 의학[의료]의 ⑤ 공식적인

2 그녀는 그 버려진 집 옆을 지날 때마다 오싹함을 느낀다.
① 비영리적인 ② 사실상의 ③ 이용 가능한 ④ 인공의 ⑤ 버려진

3 어떤 전문가들은 그 무역 협정이 양국에 유익하다고 말한다.
① 꽁꽁 얼게[너무나] 춥다고 ② 지방이라고 ③ 추정된다고 ④ 유익하다고 ⑤ 적응할 수 있다고

4 나는 그녀가 이제는 변화를 만드는 것에 대한 두려움에 기꺼이 맞설 의향이 있다고 생각한다.
① 계획할 ② 기부할 ③ 맞설 ④ 포함시킬 ⑤ 나눠줄

SECTION 09

과학 · 우주

01 **1** ⑤ **2** ② **3** astronauts, spacewalk
02 **1** ④ **2** has a damaging effect on people's minds **3** ②
03 **1** ④ **2** told **3** ③
04 **1** ⑤ **2** ② **3** measures capsaicin levels

01 끈 떨어진 우주 비행사 P. 106

정답 **1** ⑤ **2** ② **3** astronauts, spacewalk

문제해설

1 ⑤ SAFER에 연료가 들어 있다는 언급만 하고 있다. (⑩번 문장)
① (→ ②번 문장) ② (→ ⑤번 문장) ③ (→ ⑥번 문장) ④ (→ ⑦번 문장)

2 '제공하다'를 의미하는 provides와 유사한 뜻을 가진 단어는 ② supplies이다.
① 허용하다 ② 공급하다 ③ 필요로 하다 ④ 나누다 ⑤ 진행하다

3 우주 유영 중에 우주선과 우주복을 이어주는 줄이 끊어져 우주를 표류하게 되는 것을 '오버보드에 처한다'라고 하였으므로 빈칸에 각각 알맞은 말은 astronauts와 spacewalk이다. (②, ③번 문장)
우주 비행사들이 우주 유영 중에 우주선과의 연결이 끊어지게 되는 것은 '오버보드에 처한다'라고 불린다.

본문

① In the film *Gravity*, / two astronauts accidentally drift off / into space. ② The rope / that attaches their spacesuits to their spacecraft / breaks / while they are on a spacewalk. ③ Among astronauts, / this situation is called / "going overboard."

④ If this really happened, / the astronauts would float away / helplessly. ⑤ Since they would be completely weightless, / kicking and waving wouldn't help them / change direction. ⑥ They wouldn't be able to go back / to their spacecraft / and might end up falling toward Earth, / eventually burning up / in the atmosphere.

⑦ For this reason, / NASA makes all astronauts wear / a special emergency jetpack / called SAFER. ⑧ First, / the jetpack stops the astronauts / from spinning around and around. ⑨ Then it provides them / with the ability to move / through space. ⑩ The jetpack has three pounds of fuel, / and astronauts carry enough oxygen / to breathe for seven and a half hours. ⑪ Using both of these, / they can return safely / to the spacecraft!

해석

① 영화 *그래비티*에서 두 명의 우주 비행사는 뜻하지 않게 우주를 표류하게 된다. ② 그들이 우주 유영을 하는 동안 그들의 우주복을 우주선에 부착해주는 줄이 끊어진다. ③ 우주 비행사들 사이에서 이런 상황은 '오버보드에 처한다'라고 불린다.

④ 만일 이런 일이 실제로 일어난다면, 우주 비행사들은 어찌할 도리 없이 떠돌아다니게 될 것이다. ⑤ 그들은 완전히 무중력일 것이기 때문에, 발차기를 하거나 팔다리를 흔드는 등의 행동은 그들이 방향을 바꾸는 데 아무런 도움이 되지 않을 것이다. ⑥ 그들은 우주선으로 돌아갈 수 없으며 결국 지구로 떨어져 마침내는 대기층에서 불타버리게 될 수도 있다.

⑦ 이런 이유로, 미국항공우주국(NASA)은 모든 우주 비행사들로 하여금 SAFER라고 불리는 특별한 비상 제트팩을 착용하게 한다. ⑧ 우선, 제트팩은 우주 비행사들이 계속해서 도는 것을 막아 준다. ⑨ 그러고 나서 제트팩은 우주 비행사들이 우주를 움직여 다닐 수 있는 능력을 제공해 준다. ⑩ 제트팩에는 3파운드의 연료가 있고, 우주 비행사들은 7시간 반 동안 호흡할 수 있는 충분한 산소를 가지고 다닌다. ⑪ 이 두 가지를 이용하여 그들은 우주선으로 안전하게 돌아올 수 있다!

구문해설

② The rope (S) [that attaches their spacesuits to their spacecraft] **breaks** (V) while they are on a spacewalk.

→ [ ]는 선행사 The rope를 수식하는 주격 관계대명사절

→ 문장의 주어는 The rope로, 주어가 단수이므로 동사도 단수형 breaks를 사용함.

④ **If** this really **happened**, the astronauts **would float** away helplessly.

→ 현재 또는 미래의 일과 반대되는 상황을 가정하여 나타내는 가정법 과거 문장으로, 「If+주어+동사의 과거형 ..., 주어+would[could/might]+동사원형 ~」의 구문

⑤ Since they **would be** completely weightless, *kicking* and *waving* **wouldn't help** them change direction.

→ 부사절의 would be와 주절의 wouldn't help는 「would+동사원형」의 형태로, 앞 문장에 이어 가정법 과거를 나타냄.

→ kicking과 waving은 주어로 쓰인 동명사

→ help는 목적격보어로 동사원형 또는 to부정사를 취함.

⑥ They wouldn't be able to go back to their spacecraft and might **end up falling** toward Earth, [eventually burning up in the atmosphere].

→ end up v-ing: 결국 …하게 되다

→ [ ]는 연속동작을 나타내는 분사구문 (= and they would eventually burn up in the atmosphere)

02 추운 것도 싫은데… P. 108

정답 1 ④ 2 has a damaging effect on people's minds 3 ②

문제해설 1 ④ 이어지는 문단에서 극지방의 날씨가 사람들의 정신에 어떤 영향을 미치는지 설명하고 있다.
① 비타민을 섭취하는 것의 중요성 ② 혹한을 극복하는 방법 ③ 극지방의 기후 변화
④ 극지방 기후가 사람들에게 끼치는 영향 ⑤ 사람들이 극지방을 여행하는 가장 안전한 방법

2 '영향을 주다'를 의미하는 표현 have an effect on과 분사가 명사를 앞에서 수식하는 용법을 활용하여 배열한다.

3 극지방에서는 혹한으로 인해 체내의 비타민이 부족하게 되어 정신 질환을 겪게 되고, 계속되는 긴 어둠으로 인해 우울증이 나타난다고 했다. (⑥, ⑨, ⑩번 문장)
극지방의 사람들은 체내의 비타민 부족과 오래 지속되는 어둠으로 인해 정신병 혹은 우울증을 경험한다.

본문

① Polar expeditions have contributed greatly / to our understanding of science. ② For instance, / we now know a lot more / about the effects / a polar climate has on people.
③ In the early days, / explorers often suffered / from some sort of mental illness. ④ One cause of the mental illness / was later discovered. ⑤ When people aren't used to living / in extremely cold conditions, / their bodies use up a lot of energy / to keep warm, / which gets rid of all the vitamins / in the body. ⑥ Deprived of vitamins, / the brain can't work normally, / and this can cause / depression, sleep disorder, or rage.
⑦ The time spent in total darkness / also has a damaging effect / on people's minds. ⑧ Winter in polar regions / is characterized by permanent night / and lasts several months. ⑨ It is not natural / for human beings / to spend long periods of time / in the dark. ⑩ In northern latitudes, / many people get depressed / during the dark winter months. ⑪ That is because / serotonin, / a chemical that is believed / to make people happy, / cannot be released / in the body / without sunlight. ⑫ This type of depression is known as SAD (Seasonal Affective Disorder).

해석 ① 극지방 탐험은 우리가 과학을 이해하는 데 있어 크게 기여를 했다. ② 예를 들어, 우리는 이제 극지방 기후가 사람들에게 끼치는 영향에 대해 더 많은 것을 알고 있다.
③ 초창기에 탐험가들은 종종 일종의 정신병을 앓았다. ④ 정신병의 원인 중 한 가지가 나중에 밝혀졌다. ⑤ 사람들이 극도로 추운 상태에서 사는 것에 익숙하지 않을 때, 그들의 신체는 몸을 따뜻하게 유지하기 위해 많은 에너지를 쓰게 되는데, 이는 체내의 모든 비타민을 소모하게 한다. ⑥ 비타민을 빼앗기면 두뇌는 정상적으로 작동하지 못하고, 이

는 우울, 수면 장애 혹은 분노를 초래할 수 있다.
⑦ 칠흑 같은 어둠 속에서 보내는 시간 또한 사람들의 정신에 해로운 영향을 끼친다. ⑧ 극지방의 겨울은 영원처럼 긴 밤이 특징이며 몇 달간 계속된다. ⑨ 인간이 어둠 속에서 오랜 기간을 보내는 것은 자연스러운 일이 아니다. ⑩ 북위도 지방의 많은 사람들은 캄캄한 겨울 동안 우울해진다. ⑪ 이는 사람들을 행복하게 만든다고 여겨지는 화학물질인 세로토닌이 햇빛이 없으면 몸에서 배출될 수 없기 때문이다. ⑫ 이런 종류의 우울증은 SAD(계절성 정서장애)로 알려져 있다.

구문해설 ⑤ ..., their bodies use up a lot of energy **to keep** warm, *which* gets rid of all the vitamins ....
→ to keep은 〈목적〉을 나타내는 부사적 용법의 to부정사
→ which는 앞의 절(their bodies use ... warm)을 받는 계속적 용법의 관계대명사

⑥ [Deprived of vitamins], the brain can't work normally ....
→ [ ]는 조건을 나타내는 분사구문 (= If it is deprived of vitamins, ...)

⑨ **It** is not natural **for human beings to spend long periods of time in the dark**.
→ It은 가주어, for human beings는 to부정사의 의미상의 주어, to 이하가 진주어임.

03 소똥의 향기로운 변신 P. 110

정답 1 ④ 2 told 3 ③

문제해설 1 ④ 연구원들이 소똥을 대량 처리하는 기계를 만들고 싶어 한다고 했지 이미 사용되고 있다는 언급은 없다.
① (→ ⑦번 문장) ② (→ ⑧번 문장) ③ (→ ⑪번 문장) ⑤ (→ ⑬, ⑭번 문장)

2 주절의 would를 통해 가정법 과거 구문임을 알 수 있다. If절의 동사에는 과거형이 쓰이므로 told가 알맞다.

3 (A) component는 '성분', compromise는 '타협'이라는 의미이므로 component가 적절하다.
(B) extract는 '추출하다', interact는 '소통하다'라는 의미이므로 extracting이 적절하다.
(C) affective는 '정서적인', effective는 '효과적인'이라는 의미이므로 effective가 적절하다.

본문

① Do you like the smell of vanilla? ② How about vanilla ice cream? ③ What would you think / if I told you / that the sweet smell of vanilla could be created / by using cow dung? ④ It may sound strange, / but it's true!
⑤ Researchers working with a chemical company in Japan / have found a way / to produce the chemical vanillin / from cow dung. ⑥ Vanillin is the main component / that's taken from vanilla beans. ⑦ But it can also be found / in the dung of animals / that eat grass. ⑧ The process of extracting it from cow dung / is a lot cheaper. ⑨ In fact, / the cost of making vanillin from cow dung / is less than half the cost / of making it from vanilla beans. ⑩ This process is also an effective way / of recycling cow dung. ⑪ After the vanillin is obtained, / the remaining dung can be used / as fertilizer for the soil.

⑫ Researchers hope to eventually create a machine / that will be able to process several tons of cow dung a day. ⑬ The vanillin these machines produce / will smell just like the real thing / and could be used in such products / as shampoos and candles, / though probably not in food. ⑭ Even though it's the same as the vanillin / that comes from vanilla beans, / consumers wouldn't be very interested in an ice cream / that gets its flavor from cow dung.

해석 ① 바닐라 향을 좋아하는가? ② 바닐라 아이스크림은 어떤가? ③ 만약 달콤한 바닐라 향을 소똥을 이용해서 만들 수 있다고 당신에게 말한다면 어떻겠는가? ④ 이상하게 들릴지 모르지만, 이것은 사실이다!
⑤ 일본의 한 화학 회사와 함께 일하는 연구원들은 소똥으로 화학물질 바닐린을 만들어내는 방법을 알아냈다. ⑥ 바닐린은 바닐라 콩에서 추출되는 주요 성분이다. ⑦ 그런데 그것은 또한 풀을 먹는 동물의 똥에서 발견될 수도 있다. ⑧ 소똥으로부터 바닐린을 추출하는 과정은 훨씬 더 싸다. ⑨ 사실, 소똥에서 바닐린을 만드는 비용은 그것을 바닐라 콩에서 만들어내는 비용의 절반도 되지 않는다. ⑩ 이 과정은 또한 소똥을 재활용하는 효과적인 방법이다. ⑪ 바닐린이 얻어진 후, 남은 똥은 토양을 위한 비료로 사용될 수 있다.
⑫ 연구원들은 궁극적으로는 하루에 수 톤의 소똥을 처리할 수 있는 기계를 만들고 싶어 한다. ⑬ 이 기계들이 만드는 바닐린은 진짜와 똑같은 냄새가 날 것이고 샴푸나 양초와 같은 제품에 사용될 수 있지만, 아마 음식에는 사용되지 않을 것이다. ⑭ 비록 그것이 바닐라 콩에서 나온 바닐린과 똑같다 할지라도, 소비자들은 소똥에서 그 맛을 얻어낸 아이스크림에 별로 관심을 갖지는 않을 것이다.

구문해설 ⑤ Researchers [working with a chemical company in Japan] **have found** a way to produce the chemical vanillin from cow dung.
→ [ ]는 Researchers를 뒤에서 수식하는 현재분사구
→ have found는 현재완료 시제로, 〈결과〉를 나타냄.

⑧ The process of extracting it from cow dung is **a lot** cheaper.
→ 비교급을 강조할 때는 much, still, even, far, a lot 등을 사용함.

⑭ **Even though** it's the same as the vanillin that comes from vanilla beans, ...
→ even though: 비록 …일지라도 (사실의 일)
cf. even if: 설령 …이라고 할지라도 (가상의 일을 가정)

04 How Hot Is It? P. 112

정답 **1** ⑤ **2** ② **3** measures capsaicin levels

문제해설 **1** ⑤ 오늘날에는 스코빌 척도보다 더 정확한 고성능 액체 크로마토그래피가 사용된다고 했다. (⑬, ⑭번 문장)
[문제] 다음 중 스코빌 척도에 관한 이 글의 내용과 일치하지 않는 것은?
① 이것은 고추의 매운맛 단계를 표시한다. (①~③번 문장)
② 한 화학자가 실험을 함으로써 그것을 처음 개발했다. (⑥~⑨번 문장)
③ 피망은 (스코빌) 척도에서 0이 나온다. (⑩번 문장)

④ 이것은 매운맛을 측정하기 위해 개별 시음자들을 이용한다. (⑧, ⑫번 문장)

⑤ 이것은 매운맛을 측정하는 가장 정확한 방법이다.

2 (A)의 앞에서 스코빌 척도가 매운맛의 정도를 잘 알려준다고 하고 뒤에서는 그 문제점에 대해 말하고 있으며, (B)의 앞에서 현재 매운맛을 측정하는 과학적인 방법에 대해 설명하고 뒤에서는 스코빌의 이름만은 그대로 사용한다고 하므로, (A)와 (B)에는 모두 역접을 나타내는 However가 적절하다.

[문제] 다음 중 빈칸 (A)와 (B)에 들어갈 말로 가장 적절한 것은?

3 앞에서 나온 measures capsaicin levels를 의미한다.

[문제] 밑줄 친 does so가 가리키는 것을 본문에서 찾아 쓰시오.

본문

① Anyone who enjoys hot food knows / that some peppers are / hotter than others. ② So, / is there any way / to measure their hotness? ③ The answer is: yes, / with the Scoville Heat Unit Scale.

④ Commonly known as the Scoville Scale, / it measures the amount of the chemical capsaicin / present in each pepper. ⑤ It then represents this number / in Scoville heat units (SHU). ⑥ The scale was first introduced / in 1912 / by a chemist / named Wilbur Scoville. ⑦ Here's the test: / peppers are ground up / and mixed with sugar water. ⑧ Testers then sip the solution, / which is gradually diluted / until it no longer burns their tongues. ⑨ Based on how much sugar water / is required to dilute each pepper / to this level, / an SHU number is assigned.

⑩ These numbers are given / in multiples of 100 SHU, / and the scores range from zero for sweet bell peppers / to over one million SHU / for an extremely spicy pepper / known as Naga Jolokia. ⑪ Scoville's system can give a good idea of / how hot a pepper is. ⑫ However, / the problem with it is / that it relies on the perceptions / of individual tasters.

⑬ These days, / when people want to measure levels of hotness / more accurately, / they use something / known as High Performance Liquid Chromatography. ⑭ Like the Scoville Scale, / it measures capsaicin levels, / but it does so / in a more scientific manner. ⑮ However, / in honor of Wilbur Scoville's work, / it also uses "Scovilles" / as its unit of measurement.

해석

① 매운 음식을 즐기는 사람은 누구나 어떤 고추들은 다른 것들보다 더 맵다는 것을 알고 있다. ② 그럼, 그것들의 매움을 측정할 어떤 방법이 있는가? ③ 대답은 '그렇다'로, 스코빌 매운맛 단위 척도로 할 수 있다.

④ 흔히 스코빌 척도라고 알려진 그것은 각각의 고추 안에 있는 화학물질인 캡사이신의 양을 측정한다. ⑤ 그런 다음 그것은 이 숫자를 스코빌 매운맛 단위(SHU)로 나타낸다. ⑥ 그 척도는 1912년에 윌버 스코빌이라는 이름의 화학자에 의해 처음 도입되었다. ⑦ 여기 그 실험이 있다. 고추는 갈려서 설탕물과 섞인다. ⑧ 그러고 나서 검사자들은 그 용액을 조금 마시는데, 그것은 더 이상 그들의 혀를 얼얼하게 하지 않을 때까지 점점 희석된다. ⑨ 얼마나 많은 설탕물이 각각의 고추를 이 정도까지 희석하는 데 필요한지를 바탕으로 하여, SHU 수치가 부여된다.

⑩ 이 수치는 100 SHU의 배수로 매겨지며, 피망에 해당하는 0에서부터 나가 졸로키아라고 알려진 엄청나게 매운 고추에 해당하는 백만이 넘는 SHU까지 다양하다. ⑪ 스코빌의 시스템은 고추가 얼마나 매운지 잘 알려줄 수 있다. ⑫ 그러나 이것이 갖는 문제점은 각 시음자의 인식에 의존한다는 것이다.

⑬ 오늘날, 사람들이 매운맛의 정도를 더 정확하게 측정하고자 할 때 그들은 고성능 액체 크로마토그래피(High Performance Liquid Chromatography)라고 알려진 것을 사용한다. ⑭ 스코빌 척도와 마찬가지로 그것은 캡사이신의 정도를 측정하지만, 더 과학적인 방법으로 그렇게 한다. ⑮ 그러나, 윌버 스코빌의 업적에 경의를 표하여,

그것 또한 측정 단위로 '스코빌'을 사용한다.

구문해설 ④ [Commonly known as the Scoville Scale], it measures the amount of the chemical capsaicin [present in each pepper].

→ 첫 번째 [ ]는 it(= the Scoville Heat Unit Scale)을 부연 설명하는 분사구문
→ 두 번째 [ ]는 capsaicin을 뒤에서 수식하는 형용사구

⑧ Testers then sip the solution, [which is gradually diluted until it **no longer** burns their tongues].

→ [ ]는 선행사 the solution을 부연 설명하는 계속적 용법의 관계대명사절
→ no longer: 더 이상 …않다

⑩ ..., and the scores **range from** zero for sweet bell peppers **to** over one million SHU for an extremely spicy pepper [known as Naga Jolokia].

→ range from A to B: (양 · 크기 등의 범위가) A에서 B까지 다양하다
→ [ ]는 an extremely spicy pepper를 뒤에서 수식하는 과거분사구

Review Test

P. 114

A ② B **1** flavor **2** measured **3** depressed **4** attach C **1** ④ **2** ② **3** ④ **4** ② D **1** 스코빌의 시스템은 고추가 얼마나 매운지 잘 알려줄 수 있다. **2** 인간이 어둠 속에서 오랜 기간을 보내는 것은 자연스러운 일이 아니다. **3** 만일 이런 일이 실제로 일어난다면, 우주 비행사들은 어찌할 도리 없이 떠돌아다닐 것이다. **4** 칠흑 같은 어둠 속에서 보내는 시간은 사람들의 정신에 해로운 영향을 끼친다. E **1** Since they would be weightless **2** use up a lot of energy to keep warm **3** have found a way to produce

해석 A

① 영구적인: 영원히 지속되는
② 분노: 극도의 행복감
③ 떠가다: 물이나 공기 중에서 천천히 움직이다
④ 탐사: 과학적 목적의 긴 여정
⑤ 소비자: 상품이나 서비스를 구매하는 사람

B

1 내 여동생은 딸기 맛 아이스크림을 아주 좋아한다.
2 우리 아버지는 우리 식탁의 크기를 쟀다.
3 심지어 반려동물도 집에 온종일 혼자 남겨지면 우울해질 수 있다.
4 앤드류는 사진 몇 장을 스캔해서 이메일에 첨부할 것이다.

C

1 나는 나뭇잎 하나를 강물에 놓고 그것이 떠가는 것을 지켜 보았다.

① 매달다 ② 해결하다 ③ 삼키다 ④ 떠가다 ⑤ 익사하다

2 이 기름은 올리브에서 추출되었다.

① 녹았다 ② 추출되었다 ③ 입증되었다 ④ 손상되었다 ⑤ 양조되었다

3 커피 맛이 너무 강해서, 나는 얼음을 더해서 그것을 희석했다.

① 허용했다 ② 기부했다 ③ 제한했다 ④ 희석했다 ⑤ 제공했다

4 그 노부인은 걸을 수 없어서 휠체어에 의존한다.

① 특징짓는다 ② 의존한다 ③ 빌린다 ④ 소통한다 ⑤ 빼앗는다

SECTION 10

생활

01 **1** ④ **2** enthusiastic and talented individuals to join our team **3** ④

02 **1** ③ **2** ③ **3** if, are **4** ②

03 **1** ⑤ **2** ① **3** dressed, buttons

04 **1** ③ **2** ⑤ **3** eggs, cheese, (ground) pepper

01 함께 일해요! P. 118

정답 **1** ④ **2** enthusiastic and talented individuals to join our team **3** ④

문제해설 **1** 전시실을 돌면서 관람객들을 응대하는 일이므로, ④ '전시실 직원'이 가장 적절하다. (⑨번 문장)

① 큐레이터 ② 통역사 ③ 경비원 ⑤ 자연사 전문가

2 to부정사의 형용사적 용법을 활용해 individuals를 to join 이하가 수식하도록 배열한다.

3 ④ 자연사에 관한 지식을 갖추면 우대한다고 했으므로 꼭 갖춰야 하는 것은 아니다. (⑮번 문장)

① (→ ④번 문장) ② (→ ⑩번 문장) ③ (→ ⑪번 문장) ⑤ (→ ⑰번 문장)

본문

① **Job Title:** Exhibit Hall Staff

② **Employer:** Houston Museum of Natural Science

③ **Location:** Houston, Texas

④ **Job Type:** Full Time, Temporary (Summer)

⑤ **Job Description:**

⑥ This summer / the Houston Museum of Natural Science will be hosting / one of the biggest prehistoric fossil exhibitions / ever held in North America. ⑦ This event will take place all summer, / from July 1 to September 15. ⑧ We are looking for enthusiastic and talented individuals / to join our team / and run this event. ⑨ Your duty will be to circulate / throughout the exhibition hall / and interact with visitors. ⑩ You will be responsible / for answering any

questions / they may have / and giving tours / in both English and Spanish. ⑪ The pay is $12.00/hr.

⑫ **Requirements:**

- ⑬ You must be outgoing and responsible.
- ⑭ You must possess excellent interpersonal skills / and be able to work well / in a crowded and noisy environment / with visitors of all backgrounds and ages.
- ⑮ Having a natural history background is an advantage.

⑯ **To Apply:**

⑰ Send your résumé/ by e-mail / to *mcohen@houstonmuseum.com.* ⑱ Only candidates selected for interviews / will be contacted.

⑲ Contact: Mark Cohen, Personnel Director

해석

① **직책:** 전시실 직원

② **고용주:** 휴스턴 자연 과학 박물관

③ **위치:** 텍사스 주 휴스턴

④ **근무 형태:** 전일제 임시직 (하계)

⑤ **직무 설명:**

⑥ 이번 여름, 휴스턴 자연 과학 박물관은 북미에서 열린 것 중에서 가장 규모가 큰 선사 시대 화석 전시회들 중 하나를 개최하려고 합니다. ⑦ 이 행사는 7월 1일부터 9월 15일까지 여름 내내 열릴 것입니다. ⑧ 저희는 저희 팀에 합류해 이 행사를 운영해 나갈 열의 있고 재능 있는 분들을 찾고 있습니다. ⑨ 업무는 전시장을 돌면서 관람객들과 교류하는 것입니다. ⑩ 관람객들이 하는 질문에 대답하고 영어와 스페인어로 안내를 해줄 책임이 있습니다. ⑪ 급료는 시간당 12달러입니다.

⑫ **자격 요건:**

- ⑬ 외향적이고 책임감이 있어야 합니다.
- ⑭ 대인 관계 능력이 뛰어나야 하고, 온갖 배경과 연령층의 관람객들이 있는 복잡하고 소란스러운 환경에서 일을 잘할 수 있어야 합니다.
- ⑮ 자연사와 관련된 지식이 있으면 우대합니다.

⑯ **응모 요령:**

⑰ 이력서를 이메일 mcohen@houstonmuseum.com으로 보내 주세요. ⑱ 면접에 뽑히신 분들에게만 연락이 갈 것입니다.

⑲ 연락처: 인사 관리자 마크 코헨

구문해설

⑨ Your duty will be **to circulate** throughout the exhibition hall and interact with visitors.

→ to circulate는 문장의 보어로 쓰인 명사적 용법의 to부정사

⑩ You will be responsible **for answering** any questions [(that) they may have] and **giving** tours in both English and Spanish.

→ answering과 giving은 모두 전치사 for의 목적어로 쓰인 동명사

→ [ ]는 선행사 any questions를 수식하는 관계대명사절로, 목적격 관계대명사 that이 생략됨. 선행사가 some이나 any 등 한정사의 수식을 받을 때, 관계대명사는 주로 that을 씀.

⑱ Only candidates [selected for interviews] will be contacted.

→ [ ]는 candidates를 뒤에서 수식하는 과거분사구

02 티켓을 예매하려면 P. 120

정답 1 ③ 2 ③ 3 if, are 4 ②

문제해설

1 book은 '예약하다'라는 의미로 ③ reserve와 동일한 의미이다.
① 빌려주다 ② 잡다 ③ 예약하다 ④ 기능하다 ⑤ 미리 보다

2 ③ 회원인 경우, 20-5800-1700이나 20-5800-4444로 전화하면 공휴일과 일요일을 제외하고 오전 9시부터 오후 6시까지 예매가 가능하다고 했다.

3 ⑥는 '표가 여전히 남아 있는 것이 아니라면 변경은 불가하다'라는 의미로, 바꿔 말하면 '표가 남아 있을 때에만 변경이 가능하다'는 뜻이다.
변경은 표가 아직 남아 있어야만 허용된다.

4 ② 공연 당일이라도 표가 남아 있으면 변경이 가능하며, 변경 시 10%의 추가 수수료가 부과된다. (⑦~⑨번 문장)
① (→ ⑤, ⑥번 문장) ③ (→ ⑩번 문장) ④ (→ ⑪번 문장) ⑤ (→ ⑫번 문장)

본문

Ticketing Information

① Welcome all art lovers / visiting the homepage / of the London AllArt Center. ② We provide useful ticketing information / on arts programs, performances, and exhibitions / in the London area. ③ You can book tickets / by phone or online (www.allarttickets.com). ④ For more details, / contact us at 20-7800-1400.

1 Reservation by Telephone

	Booking Office	Phone Number	Service Hours
Members	Service Plaza (On the 2nd floor of the Opera Center)	20-5800-1700 20-5800-4444	9 a.m. ~ 6 p.m. (Except holidays and Sundays)
Non-Members	AllArt ticket office	20-6402-1577 20-6402-1515	10 a.m. ~ 6 p.m. (Weekdays) 10 a.m. ~ 5 p.m. (Saturdays)

2 Ticket Changes

▶ ⑤ At least one day before the performance: ⑥ You can change dates or times (only for the same performance).

▶ ⑦ The day of the performance: ⑧ No changes are allowed / unless there are tickets still available. ⑨ There is an additional penalty fee of 10% / for each ticket / changed.

3 Refunds

▶ ⑩ At least one day before the performance (by 5 p.m.): / 90% refund (10% commission fee)

▶ ⑪ At least one hour before the performance: / 70% refund
▶ ⑫ Less than one hour prior to the performance: / No refund

해석 매표 정보

① 런던 올아트 센터의 홈페이지를 방문해 주신 예술을 사랑하는 모든 분들을 환영합니다. ② 저희는 런던 지역의 예술 프로그램, 공연, 전시회에 관한 유용한 매표 정보를 제공합니다. ③ 전화나 인터넷(www.allarttickets.com)으로 표를 예매하실 수 있습니다. ④ 더 자세한 내용을 알고 싶으시면 20-7800-1400으로 연락 주십시오.

1 전화 예매

	예약 사무실	전화번호	이용 시간
회원	서비스 플라자 (오페라 센터 2층)	20-5800-1700 20-5800-4444	오전 9시 ~ 오후 6시 (공휴일과 일요일 제외)
비회원	올아트 티켓 사무실	20-6402-1577 20-6402-1515	오전 10시 ~ 오후 6시 (평일) 오전 10시 ~ 오후 5시 (토요일)

2 티켓 변경

▶ ⑤ 공연 하루 전날까지: ⑥ 공연 날짜와 시간을 변경하실 수 있습니다. (같은 공연에 한함)
▶ ⑦ 공연 당일: ⑧ 표가 아직 남아 있는 경우가 아니라면 변경하실 수 없습니다. ⑨ 변경된 각 표에 대해서는 10퍼센트의 추가 수수료가 있습니다.

3 환불

▶ ⑩ 공연 하루 전날까지 (오후 5시까지): 90퍼센트 환불 (수수료 10퍼센트)
▶ ⑪ 공연 한 시간 전까지: 70퍼센트 환불
▶ ⑫ 공연(시작 전) 한 시간 이내: 환불 불가

구문해설 ① Welcome all art lovers [visiting the homepage of ... Center].

→ [ ]는 all art lovers를 수식하는 현재분사구

⑨ There is an additional penalty fee of 10% for each ticket changed.

→ changed는 each ticket를 수식하는 과거분사

⑫ Less than one hour **prior to** the performance: No refund
→ prior to: (시간 · 순서가) …보다 앞선, 이전의

03 단추에 그런 의미가? P. 122

정답 1 ⑤ 2 ① 3 dressed, buttons

문제해설 1 ⑤ 남성과 여성의 옷이 서로 다른 쪽에서 단추가 잠기는 이유에 대한 글이다.
① 누가 처음으로 단추를 발명했는가
② 언제 단추가 왼쪽에 달리는가
③ 의복이 과거에 얼마나 복잡했는가

④ 왜 여성들은 하녀에 의해 옷이 입혀져야 했는가
⑤ 왜 남성과 여성의 옷이 서로 다른 쪽에서 단추가 잠기는가

2 ① 남성과 여성의 셔츠 단추 잠그는 방향이 반대인 이유에 대해, 빈칸 앞에서는 대부분의 여자가 왼손잡이이고 대부분의 남자가 오른손잡이라면 타당할 것이라 하고, 빈칸 뒤에서는 단추 방향이 다른 이유를 재차 묻고 있다. 따라서 빈칸에는 앞의 가정을 부정하는 내용이 오는 것이 가장 적절하다.
① 하지만 대부분의 사람들은 오른손잡이이다.
② 그래서 모든 사람들은 양손을 사용해야 한다.
③ 그리고 몇몇 사람들은 그들의 오른손을 사용한다.
④ 또한, 그들은 더 이상 한 손만을 사용하지 않는다.
⑤ 하지만 오른손잡이인 재단사들이 더 많다.

3 여성들이 하녀에 의해 옷이 입혀지던 유럽 중상류층의 관습 때문에 여성의 옷 단추를 왼쪽에 달기 시작했다고 하였다. (⑪~⑬ 문장)
중상류층 가정의 여성들이 하녀들에 의해 옷이 입혀졌기 때문에, 일을 더 쉽게 하게 하기 위해 단추들이 왼쪽에 달리게 되었다.

본문

① Unless you work as a clothing designer, / you've probably never noticed / that women's and men's shirts button / from opposite sides. ② Men's shirts button on the right / and women's button on the left. ③ If most women were left handed / and most men were right handed, / this would seem logical. ④ But / most people are right handed. ⑤ So / why are men's and women's buttons / on opposite sides?
⑥ It's because of the history of fashion. ⑦ A few hundred years ago, / both women and men in Europe wore / a lot more clothes / than they do today. ⑧ Men wore shirts, vests, pants, and coats. ⑨ But / women had far more complicated outfits, / which included petticoats, bloomers, gowns, corsets, and bustles.
⑩ In middle and upper-class homes, / men usually dressed themselves, / since it was relatively easy / for them / to put on their clothing. ⑪ But for women, / things were not that simple; ⑫ they needed to be dressed / by their maids. ⑬ Tailors soon realized / that designing women's clothes / with buttons on the left side / made this process faster and easier. ⑭ Thus, / a custom was created / in clothes-making.
⑮ Most of us are not being dressed / by maids today. ⑯ However, / the clothing industry continues / to follow this tradition. ⑰ Since few people notice or complain, / no one has bothered / to change it.

해석

① 만약 당신이 의상 디자이너로 일하는 것이 아니라면 여성용과 남성용 셔츠가 반대쪽에서 단추를 잠그게 되어 있다는 것을 아마 알아채지 못했을 것이다. ② 남성용 셔츠는 오른쪽에서 잠그고, 여성용은 왼쪽에서 잠근다. ③ 만약 대부분의 여성들이 왼손잡이고, 대부분의 남성들이 오른손잡이라면, 이것은 타당한 것처럼 보일 것이다. ④ 하지만 대부분의 사람들은 오른손잡이이다. ⑤ 그럼 왜 남성과 여성의 단추들은 반대편에 있을까?
⑥ 그것은 패션의 역사 때문이다. ⑦ 몇백 년 전, 유럽의 여성들과 남성들 모두 그들이 오늘날 그러는 것보다 훨씬 더 많은 옷을 입었다. ⑧ 남성들은 셔츠, 조끼, 바지, 그리고 코트를 입었다. ⑨ 그러나 여성들은 훨씬 더 복잡한 옷을 입었는데, 거기에는 속치마, 블루머, 가운, 코르셋, 그리고 허리받이가 포함되어 있었다.

⑩ 중산층과 상류층 가정에서, 남성들은 그들이 옷을 입는 것이 상대적으로 쉬웠기 때문에 보통 그들 스스로 옷을 입었다. ⑪ 그러나 여성들에게는 일이 그렇게 간단하지 않았다. ⑫ 그들은 하녀들에 의해 옷이 입혀져야 했다. ⑬ 재단사들은 곧 단추가 왼쪽에 달리도록 여성의 옷을 만드는 것이 이 과정을 더 빠르고 쉽게 만든다는 것을 깨달았다. ⑭ 따라서, 의복 제작에서 하나의 관습이 생겨났다.
⑮ 오늘날 우리들 대부분은 하녀들에 의해 옷이 입혀지지는 않는다. ⑯ 그러나 의류업계는 이 전통을 따르는 것을 계속하고 있다. ⑰ 알아채거나 불평하는 사람이 거의 없기 때문에, 누구도 그것을 바꾸려고 애를 쓰지 않았다.

구문해설

⑦ ..., both women and men in Europe wore **a lot** more clothes than they do today.
→ a lot은 '훨씬 더'라는 의미로, 비교급을 강조하며 far, much 등과 바꿔 쓸 수 있음.

⑩ ..., since **it** was relatively easy **for them to put on their clothing**.
→ it은 가주어, for them은 to부정사의 의미상 주어, to 이하가 진주어

⑬ Tailors soon realized [that **designing women's clothes *with* buttons on the left side** made this process faster and easier].
→ [ ]는 realized의 목적어로 쓰인 명사절
→ designing ... side는 that절의 주어로 쓰인 동명사구
→ with: …이 달린

⑮ Most of us **are** not **being dressed** by maids today.
→ be동사+being+p.p.: 수동태의 현재 진행형

04 Can You Make Carbonara? P. 124

정답 1 ③ 2 ⑤ 3 eggs, cheese, (ground) pepper

문제해설

1 ③ 본래 '스파게티 알라 카르보나라'에는 크림이 들어가지 않으며(③, ④번 문장), 조리법의 재료 목록에도 크림은 없다.
[문제] 다음 중 조리법에 관한 이 글의 내용과 일치하지 <u>않는</u> 것은?
① 단 몇 가지의 재료만 있으면 된다. (⑤번 문장)
② 베이컨을 올리브 오일에 익혀야 한다. (⑪번 문장)
③ 파스타를 신선한 크림과 섞어야 한다.
④ 파스타의 열이 달걀을 익힐 것이다. (⑮번 문장)
⑤ 마지막 단계로, 약간의 후추와 간 치즈를 사용할 수 있다. (⑯번 문장)

2 뒤에 완전한 절이 이어지고 '베이컨을 익힌 팬에'라는 의미가 되어야 하므로 ⑤ what은 장소를 나타내는 선행사를 설명하는 관계부사 where나 「전치사+관계대명사」인 in which가 되어야 한다.
[문제] 밑줄 친 ①~⑤ 중, 어법상 <u>틀린</u> 것은?

3 조리법 1번에서 달걀과 치즈, 그리고 후추를 섞어 달걀 혼합물을 만든다고 했다. (⑦~⑨번 문장)
[문제] <u>달걀 혼합물</u>에 어떤 재료가 들어가는가?

본문

① *Spaghetti alla carbonara* can easily be found / in Italian restaurants / around the world. ② When people / outside of Italy / order this dish, / they expect a plate of pasta / covered in cream sauce / with mushrooms and pieces of ham. ③ However, / the original Italian recipe is a bit different. ④ There is no cream or mushrooms, / and its flavor is lighter. ⑤ This authentic version of *spaghetti alla carbonara* / is quick and easy / to make, / and it requires only a few ingredients.

⑥ **Ingredients**

500 g of spaghetti, 150 g of chopped Italian bacon, 120 g of grated Romano cheese, 5 eggs, olive oil, pepper

1. ⑦ Mix the eggs in a bowl. ⑧ Then slowly add the cheese / while stirring quickly. ⑨ Also, / add a little freshly ground pepper.
2. ⑩ Meanwhile, / start cooking the pasta. ⑪ In a saucepan, / heat a small amount of olive oil, / and cook the bacon in it. ⑫ Then about one minute / before the pasta is cooked *al dente*, / pour a couple of tablespoons of the water / from the pasta / into the egg mixture.
3. ⑬ After the pasta is cooked *al dente*, / drain the water from it, / and toss it / straight into the pan / where you cooked the bacon.
4. ⑭ Pour the egg mixture / into the pan / with the pasta and bacon, / and stir it. ⑮ The pasta is very hot now, / so it will cook the raw eggs.
5. ⑯ Finish off your *spaghetti alla carbonara* / with pepper and some grated cheese!

해석

① '스파게티 알라 카르보나라'는 전 세계의 이탈리아 식당에서 쉽게 찾을 수 있다. ② 이탈리아 밖의 사람들은 이 음식을 주문할 때 크림 소스로 덮이고 버섯, 그리고 햄 조각들이 든 파스타 한 접시가 나올 것으로 기대한다. ③ 그러나 원래의 이탈리아식 조리법은 약간 다르다. ④ 크림도 버섯도 없으며, 맛은 좀 더 가볍다. ⑤ '스파게티 알라 카르보나라'의 진짜 버전은 만들기에 빠르고 쉬우며, 단 몇 가지의 재료만 필요할 뿐이다.

⑥ **재료**

스파게티면 500g, 다진 이탈리아식 베이컨 150g, 갈아 놓은 로마노 치즈 120g, 달걀 5개, 올리브 오일, 후추

1. ⑦ 달걀을 큰 그릇에서 섞어라. ⑧ 그러고 나서 재빨리 젓는 동안에 치즈를 서서히 추가해라. ⑨ 또, 신선하게 간 후추를 약간 추가해라.
2. ⑩ 그동안에, 파스타 면을 요리하기 시작해라. ⑪ 냄비에 약간의 올리브 오일을 가열하고, 거기에 베이컨을 요리해라. ⑫ 그러고 나서 파스타가 알 덴테로 익기 약 1분 전에, 큰 수저 2~3개 분량의 파스타 삶은 물을 달걀 혼합물에 부어라.
3. ⑬ 파스타가 알 덴테로 익고 나면, 파스타 면에서 물을 따라 버리고, 파스타 면을 베이컨을 익힌 팬에 바로 옮겨라.
4. ⑭ 달걀 혼합물을 파스타 면과 베이컨이 있는 팬 안에 붓고, 저어라. ⑮ 파스타 면은 지금 매우 뜨거워서, 이것이 날달걀을 익힐 것이다.
5. ⑯ 후추와 약간의 간 치즈를 넣어서 당신의 '스파게티 알라 카르보나라'를 완성해라!

구문해설

② When people(S) [outside of Italy] order(V) this dish(O), they expect a plate of pasta [covered in cream sauce with mushrooms and pieces of ham].

→ outside of Italy는 people을 수식하는 전치사구
→ 두 번째 [ ]는 pasta를 뒤에서 수식하는 과거분사구

⑤ This authentic version of *spaghetti alla carbonara* is quick and easy **to make**, and it requires only *a few* ingredients.
→ to make은 앞의 형용사구 quick and easy를 한정하는 부사적 용법의 to부정사로, '…하기에'의 의미
→ a few+셀 수 있는 명사: 조금의 …

⑧ Then slowly add the cheese **while stirring quickly**.
→ while stirring quickly는 의미를 명확히 하기 위해 접속사를 생략하지 않은 분사구문으로 〈동시동작〉을 나타냄.

⑨ Also, add **a little** freshly ground pepper.
→ a little+셀 수 없는 명사: 조금의 …
cf. a few+셀 수 있는 명사: 조금의 …

Review Test

P. 126

A **1** ⓒ **2** ⓐ **3** ⓓ **4** ⓔ **5** ⓑ B **1** candidates **2** temporary **3** contacted **4** select C **1** ② **2** ③ **3** ⑤ **4** ④ D **1** 표가 아직 남아 있는 경우가 아니라면 변경하실 수 없습니다. **2** 이 행사는 7월 1일부터 9월 15일까지 여름 내내 열릴 것입니다. **3** 알아채거나 불평하는 사람이 거의 없기 때문에, 누구도 그것을 바꾸려고 애를 쓰지 않았다. **4** 파스타 면을 베이컨을 익힌 팬에 바로 옮겨라. E **1** Your duty is to circulate **2** a lot more clothes than they do **3** Unless you work as a clothing designer

해석

A

1 하녀: ⓒ 집이나 호텔의 여성 하인
2 날것의: ⓐ 조리되지 않은
3 환불(금): ⓓ 고객에게 반납된 돈
4 물을 빼내다: ⓔ 흘러 나가게 해서 액체를 제거하다
5 외향적인: ⓑ 다른 사람들과 만나고 얘기하는 것을 좋아하는

B

1 그 일자리에 적합한 후보들이 면접에 뽑힐 것이다.
2 이 웹사이트는 일시적인 문제가 있지만, 그것은 곧 해결될 것이다.
3 나는 신용카드를 잃어버려서, 신용카드 회사에 연락했다.
4 너는 여름 휴가를 보낼 장소를 선택했니?

C

1 선물을 주고받는 것은 크리스마스 관습이다.
① 조리법 ② 관습 ③ 휴일 ④ 묘사 ⑤ 배경
2 요리사가 이탈리아 출신이기 때문에 당신은 이 식당에서 진짜 이탈리아 음식을 즐길 수 있다.
① 상대적인 ② 사적인 ③ 진짜의 ④ 책임이 있는 ⑤ 자세한

3 그 문제는 너무 복잡해서 나는 그 문제를 푸는 방법을 설명할 수 없었다.
① 쉬워서 ② 논리적이어서 ③ 이용 가능해서 ④ 추가적이어서 ⑤ 복잡해서

4 노령화 인구는 의료 서비스에 대한 더 많은 지출을 필요로 할 것이다.
① 잡을 ② 재배할 ③ 제공할 ④ 필요로 할 ⑤ 생산할

SECTION 11

생물 · 동물

01 **1** ⑤ **2** ③ **3** hump, broad, feet

02 **1** ④ **2** ⑤ **3** (A) die (B) live

03 **1** ① **2** it was not humans who made these marks **3** ④

04 **1** ① **2** ② **3** ② **4** migration, hungry, hunt, birds

01 낙타가 이주를? P. 130

정답 1 ⑤ 2 ③ 3 hump, broad, feet

문제해설

1 ⑤ 낙타의 진화는 사막보다는 북극 지방에 의해 더 영향을 받았을 것이라고 하였다. (⑩번 문장)
① 낙타는 아마도 수백만 년 전에 눈 덮인 들판을 걸었을 것이다. (①, ②번 문장)
② 고대 낙타의 뼈가 북극 지방에서 발견되었다. (③번 문장)
③ 일부 낙타의 뼈는 낙타 종이 남쪽으로 이동했다는 것을 알려준다. (⑤, ⑥번 문장)
④ 북아메리카와 아시아는 수백만 년 전에 이어져 있었다. (⑦, ⑧번 문장)
⑤ 낙타의 진화는 사막에 의해 가장 많은 영향을 받았다.

2 '연결된'이라는 의미의 connected와 반대의 뜻을 가진 말은 ③ separated이다.
① 합쳐진 ② 연결된 ③ 분리된 ④ 통합된 ⑤ 붙은

3 밑줄 친 these features는 앞의 두 문장에서 언급한 낙타의 혹(hump)과 넓은 발(broad feet)을 가리킨다.

본문

① Can you imagine / camels walking across a snowy field? ② It sounds strange, / but this was probably / a normal sight / millions of years ago. ③ Scientists recently discovered / the bones of ancient camels / in the Arctic region of Canada. ④ Apparently, / this is / where they lived long, long ago.

⑤ Interestingly, similar camel bones have been found / about 1,200 kilometers / to the south. ⑥ This shows / that the species migrated south. ⑦ About seven or eight million years ago, / they crossed / from North America to Asia. ⑧ At that time, / the two continents were connected, / so they could simply walk across. ⑨ After a long journey, / they eventually made their way / to desert regions.

⑩ The fact that the camel migrated suggests / that its evolution may have been influenced / more by the Arctic / than by the desert. ⑪ Its hump would have allowed it / to store food / during the dark, frozen winter months. ⑫ And its broad feet would have made it easier / to walk across the snow / without sinking in. ⑬ Of course, / these features were extremely useful / when the camel switched / to a desert habitat.

해석 ① 당신은 낙타가 눈 덮인 들판을 가로질러 걸어가고 있는 것을 상상할 수 있는가? ② 그것은 이상하게 들리지만, 수백만 년 전에는 아마도 이것이 평범한 광경이었을 것이다. ③ 과학자들은 최근에 고대 낙타의 뼈를 캐나다의 북극 지방에서 발견했다. ④ 분명, 그곳이 낙타들이 아주 오래전에 살았던 곳이다.
⑤ 흥미롭게도, 비슷한 낙타 뼈가 남쪽으로 약 1,200km 떨어진 곳에서 발견되었다. ⑥ 이것은 낙타 종이 남쪽으로 이동했다는 것을 보여 준다. ⑦ 약 7, 8백만 년 전쯤, 낙타들은 북아메리카에서 아시아로 건너갔다. ⑧ 그 당시에는 두 대륙이 연결되어 있어서, 낙타들은 그냥 걸어서 건널 수 있었다. ⑨ 긴 여정 끝에, 낙타들은 마침내 사막 지역까지 오게 되었다.
⑩ 낙타가 이주했다는 사실은 낙타의 진화가 사막보다는 북극 지방에 의해서 더욱 영향을 받았을지도 모른다는 점을 암시한다. ⑪ 낙타의 혹은 어둡고 추운 겨울 동안 영양분을 저장할 수 있도록 해주었을 것이다. ⑫ 그리고 낙타의 넓은 발은 눈에 빠지지 않고 눈 속을 걷는 것을 더 쉽게 해주었을 것이다. ⑬ 물론, 이런 특징들은 낙타가 사막 지방의 서식지로 바꿔 갔을 때 매우 유용했다.

구문해설 ① Can you imagine **camels walking** across a snowy field?
→ camels는 imagine의 목적어로 쓰인 동명사 walking의 의미상 주어임.

④ Apparently, this is (the place) where they lived long, long ago.
→ 관계부사 where 앞에 선행사 the place가 생략되어 있음.

⑪ Its hump **would have *allowed*** *it to store* food during the dark, frozen winter months.
→ would have allowed는 「조동사 과거+have+p.p.」 구문으로 과거에 대한 추측을 나타내며, '…했을 것이다'의 의미임.
→ allow A to-v: A가 …하는 것을 허용하다

⑫ And its broad feet would have **made it easier to walk** across the snow *without sinking* in.
→ 「make+가목적어(it)+형용사(easier)+진목적어(to walk)」 구문으로, '걷는 것을 더 쉽게 해주다'의 의미임.
→ without v-ing: …하지 않고

02 해파리는 몇 살? P. 132

정답 1 ④ 2 ⑤ 3 (A) die (B) live

문제해설 1 ④ turritopsis nutricula라는 특정한 해파리가 불멸하는 방법에 대해 설명하는 글이다.
① 해파리가 짝짓기하는 방법 ② 곤충들의 생과 사
③ 일반 해파리의 생애 주기 ④ 특정 해파리는 어떻게 영원히 살 수 있는가

⑤ 번식에 있어 줄기세포의 역할

2 ⑤는 앞에 선행사가 없으므로 선행사를 포함하면서 관계사절 안에서 주어 역할을 하는 관계대명사 what을 써야 한다.

3 (A) 앞 문장에서 수천 년을 사는 나무와 몇 시간만 사는 벌레를 언급한 뒤, 역접의 접속사 But이 나왔으므로 모든 생물은 결국 '죽는다'는 내용이 나오는 것이 알맞다.
(B) 앞 문장에서 '죽음을 피할 수 없음(mortality)'에 대해 다시 생각하게 했다는 내용이 나오므로, 빈칸에는 live가 들어가는 것이 알맞다.

본문

① Some trees live / for thousands of years, / while some insects live / for only a few hours. ② But / every living organism will eventually die, / right? ③ Well, / a discovery in the Caribbean Sea / has made scientists / rethink the issue of mortality. ④ A rare jellyfish species / known as turritopsis nutricula, / might be able to live forever!
⑤ When ordinary jellyfish finish reproducing, / they begin to die. ⑥ But / turritopsis nutricula does something different / after mating. ⑦ It has an unusual process / whereby its cells don't decay. ⑧ Instead, / they change back / to their original form, / becoming similar to / what are known as "stem cells." ⑨ These cells join together / to form a polyp, / which is exactly what forms / when a male jellyfish's sperm fuses / with a female jellyfish's egg. ⑩ In this sense, / the jellyfish is literally born again; ⑪ it turns itself back into a baby / instead of dying. ⑫ Amazingly, / this cycle can repeat indefinitely, / making this jellyfish / one of the most unique organisms / on earth.

해석

① 어떤 나무들은 수천 년을 사는 반면에, 어떤 곤충들은 단지 몇 시간만을 살 뿐이다. ② 그러나 모든 생물은 결국에는 죽는다. 그렇지 않은가? ③ 카리브 해에서의 한 가지 발견은 과학자들로 하여금 죽는다는 것에 대한 문제를 다시 생각하게 했다. ④ turritopsis nutricula라고 알려진 한 희귀한 해파리 종(種)은 영원히 살 수 있을지도 모른다!
⑤ 일반 해파리들은 번식하는 것을 끝내면 죽기 시작한다. ⑥ 하지만 turritopsis nutricula는 짝짓기를 한 후에 뭔가 다른 것을 한다. ⑦ 그것은 세포들이 부패하지 않는 특이한 과정을 가진다. ⑧ 대신에, 그것들은 원래의 형태로 되돌아가서, '줄기세포'로 알려진 것과 비슷해진다. ⑨ 이 세포들은 한데 무리 지어 폴립을 형성하는데, 이것은 정확히 수컷 해파리의 정액이 암컷 해파리의 난자와 합쳐질 때 형성되는 것이다. ⑩ 이런 점에서, 해파리는 말 그대로 다시 태어난다. ⑪ 즉, 그것은 죽는 대신 자신을 새끼로 되돌려 놓는 것이다. ⑫ 놀랍게도 이러한 순환은 무한정 반복될 수 있는데, 이는 이 해파리를 지구에서 가장 특이한 생물 중의 하나로 만든다.

구문해설

③ Well, a discovery in the Caribbean Sea has **made** scientists **rethink** the issue of mortality.
→ make(사역동사)+목적어+목적격보어(동사원형): (목적어)가 …하게 하다

⑧ ... their original form, [becoming similar to **what** *are known as* "stem cells."]
→ [ ]는 〈연속 동작〉을 나타내는 분사구문 (= and they become ....)
→ what은 선행사를 포함하는 관계대명사로, what 이하는 전치사 to의 목적어
→ be known as: …로 알려져 있다

⑨ These cells join together **to form** a polyp, *which* is exactly what forms ....
→ to form은 〈결과〉를 나타내는 부사적 용법의 to부정사

→ which는 선행사 a polyp을 부연 설명하는 계속적 용법의 관계대명사

⑫... indefinitely, [**making** this jellyfish **one of the most unique organisms on earth**].
→ [ ]는 〈동시동작〉을 나타내는 분사구문
→ make + 목적어 + 목적격보어(명사): (목적어)를 …로 만들다

03 코끼리가 동굴로 가는 까닭은… P. 134

정답 1 ① 2 it was not humans who made these marks 3 ④

문제해설 1 ① 엘곤 산 근처의 우림에서는 비가 초목과 토양의 소금을 씻어내 버리기 때문에 코끼리들이 소금을 얻기 위해 소금이 풍부한 바위가 있는 엘곤 산의 동굴을 찾는 것이다. (두 번째 문단)
① 소금을 얻으려고 ② 식량을 저장하려고 ③ 포식자를 피하려고
④ 그들의 상아를 날카롭게 갈려고 ⑤ 강우로부터 대피하려고

2 「it ... that ~ (~한 것은 …이다)」 강조 구문이 되도록 강조하고자 하는 humans를 it was not과 that 사이에 두는데, 강조하고자 하는 대상이 사람이므로 that 대신 who를 쓸 수 있다. 따라서 it was not humans who made these marks로 배열한다.

3 (A) 빈칸 앞에는 우림의 장점인 많은 먹이에 대해 설명하고 빈칸 뒤에는 우림의 단점인 소금 부족에 대해 설명하고 있으므로, 빈칸에는 역접을 나타내는 However가 알맞다.
(B) 빈칸 앞과 뒤에 코끼리들이 동굴로 향하는 것의 위험성(포식 동물, 동굴의 틈새와 구멍)이 나열되어 있으므로, 빈칸에는 추가를 나타내는 In addition이 알맞다.

본문

① The caves at the base of Mount Elgon, / which is on the border of Uganda and Kenya, / are some of the most interesting caves / in the world. ② Inside, / there are long furrows with holes / that look / as if they have been made / by picks. ③ The first explorers of the site / assumed these / to be the sign of ancient Egyptians' mining activity. ④ But wildlife specialists / observing the caves / discovered that / it was not humans / who made these marks / but elephants, / which still visit the caves / to this day!

⑤ While most elephants live / on the plains of Africa, / the herds near Mount Elgon / live in the rainforest. ⑥ Because of the wet climate, / there is plenty of food for them. ⑦ However, / the problem is / that the heavy rainfall washes away the salt / from the plants and the soil. ⑧ As a result, / the elephants do not get / as much salt as they need / in their diet. ⑨ Thus, / they go to the caves of Mount Elgon, / where they can find / salt-rich rocks.

⑩ The elephants travel there / in family groups, / sometimes going as far as 150 meters / into the dark caves / to find salt in the rocks. ⑪ They use their tusks / to chip off rough bits of the cave wall, / which they then eat.

⑫ The elephants' journey is especially unusual / because it is very dangerous. ⑬ The elephants risk being attacked / by predators like hyenas and leopards / on the way to the caves. ⑭ In

addition, / the caves have big cracks and holes / that the elephants could fall into / since it is very dark inside. ⑮ In spite of all the danger, / they continue to wander / deep into the caves / to enjoy the tasty rewards!

해석 ① 우간다와 케냐의 국경에 위치한 엘곤 산 기슭에 있는 동굴들은 세상에서 가장 흥미로운 동굴들 중 일부이다. ② 그 안에는 마치 곡괭이로 만들어진 것처럼 보이는 구멍들이 있는 긴 고랑들이 있다. ③ 이 장소를 처음 탐험한 사람들은 이 고랑들을 고대 이집트인들의 광산 활동의 흔적이라고 추정했다. ④ 그러나 동굴을 관찰한 야생 동물 전문가들은 이 표시들을 만든 것은 바로 인간이 아닌 코끼리들이었으며, 그들이 오늘날까지도 여전히 동굴을 찾아온다는 것을 발견했다!

⑤ 대부분의 코끼리들이 아프리카의 평원에서 사는 반면, 엘곤 산 근처의 코끼리 무리는 우림에 산다. ⑥ 습한 기후 때문에 그곳에는 그들을 위한 먹이가 많다. ⑦ 그러나, 문제는 많은 강수량이 초목과 토양으로부터 소금을 씻어내 버린다는 것이다. ⑧ 그 결과, 코끼리들은 그들이 먹이에서 필요로 하는 만큼의 많은 소금을 얻지 못한다. ⑨ 그래서 그들은 엘곤 산의 동굴로 가고 거기서 소금이 풍부한 바위를 찾을 수가 있다.

⑩ 코끼리들은 가족 단위로 그곳으로 이동하며, 때때로 바위 속의 소금을 찾기 위해 어두운 동굴 속으로 150미터만큼 멀리 들어가기도 한다. ⑪ 그들은 동굴 벽에서 거친 조각들을 갈아내기 위해 그들의 상아를 사용하고, 그러고 나서 그 조각들을 먹는다.

⑫ 이 코끼리의 여정은 유난히 독특한데, 왜냐하면 그것이 너무 위험하기 때문이다. ⑬ 코끼리들은 동굴로 가는 길에 하이에나와 표범 같은 포식 동물에 의해 공격당하는 위험을 무릅쓴다. ⑭ 게다가, 내부가 매우 어두워서 코끼리가 추락할 수도 있는 커다란 틈새와 구멍들도 동굴 안에 있다. ⑮ 이런 모든 위험에도 불구하고, 그들은 계속해서 그 맛있는 보상을 즐기기 위해 동굴 안으로 깊이 들어간다!

구문해설 ② Inside, there are long furrows with holes [**that** look *as if* they *have been made* by picks].

→ that은 long furrows를 선행사로 하는 주격 관계대명사

→ as if: 마치 …인 것처럼 (as if 뒤의 내용이 가능성이 있을 경우, 가정법 동사가 아닌 직설법 동사를 사용함.)

④ But wildlife specialists [observing the caves] discovered that it was not humans who made these marks but elephants, **which** still visit the caves to this day!

→ [ ]는 wildlife specialists를 뒤에서 수식하는 현재분사구

→ which는 elephants를 부연 설명하는 계속적 용법의 주격 관계대명사 (= and they)

⑨ Thus, they go to the caves of Mount Elgon, **where** they can find salt-rich rocks.

→ where는 the caves of Mount Elgon을 부연 설명하는 계속적 용법의 관계부사 (= and there)

⑪ They use their tusks **to chip off** rough bits of the cave wall, *which* they then eat.

→ to chip off는 〈목적〉을 나타내는 부사적 용법의 to부정사

→ which는 선행사 rough bits of the cave wall을 부연 설명하는 계속적 용법의 관계대명사

⑬ The elephants **risk being attacked** by predators like hyenas and leopards on the way to the caves.

→ risk being attacked는 risk v-ing와 수동태 be attacked가 합쳐진 형태

04 The Amazing Sardine Run P. 136

정답 1 ① 2 ② 3 ② 4 migration, hungry, hunt, birds

문제해설

1 ① 정어리 떼 이동이 일종의 미스터리라고 하며 '정어리들이 왜 무리 지어 이동하는지'는 언급하지 않았다.
[문제] 이 글에서 언급되지 않은 것은?
① 정어리들이 왜 무리 지어 이동하는지
② 정어리 떼의 규모 (④번 문장)
③ 정어리의 다양한 포식자들 (⑥번 문장)
④ 돌고래들이 어떻게 정어리를 사냥하는가 (⑧, ⑨번 문장)
⑤ 사람들이 어떻게 정어리 떼의 이동을 즐기는가 (⑫~⑭번 문장)

2 ② 정어리 떼의 규모는 길이로 수 마일, 폭으로 1마일, 그리고 30미터 이상의 깊이에 달할 수 있다고 했으므로 '대수롭지 않은', '하찮은'을 의미하는 ⓑ insignificant는 '거대한'을 의미하는 enormous가 되는 것이 적절하다.
[문제] 밑줄 친 ⓐ~ⓔ 중, 문맥상 낱말의 쓰임이 적절하지 않은 것은?

3 주어진 문장의 They는 정어리를 사냥하려는 돌고래들을 가리키며, 이 문장은 정어리 떼를 둥글게 모으는 그들의 독특한 사냥 방식인 bait ball을 언급한 문장이다. 따라서 '일단 정어리들이 둥글게 모이면…'이라는 내용 앞인 ②에 들어가는 것이 가장 적절하다.
[문제] ①~⑤ 중, 주어진 문장이 들어가기에 가장 적절한 곳은?

4 정어리 떼의 이동이 시작되면, 배고픈 바다 동물들이 그 주위로 몰려든다. 돌고래는 정어리를 수면 위로 몰고 가고 이때 새들이 정어리를 사냥한다. (⑥~⑪번 문장)
[문제] 빈칸에 들어갈 알맞은 말을 박스 안에서 골라 쓰시오.
정어리의 이동이 시작될 때, 배고픈 바다 생물들이 흥분하게 된다. 돌고래들이 정어리들을 사냥할 때, 그들은 그것들을 수면 위로 몰고 가는데, 그곳에서 기다리고 있던 새들도 그것들을 잡을 수 있다.

본문

① Every summer / millions of little sardines swim / along the coast of South Africa / in a giant group. ② This amazing migration / is kind of a mystery, / but it certainly gets / all the animals nearby excited.

③ After laying their eggs / in the Agulhas Bank / off the southern coast, / the sardines swim / to the eastern coast of South Africa. ④ They travel in an enormous group / that can be miles in length, / up to a mile in width, / and over thirty meters deep. ⑤ Planes flying low over the ocean / can even see this gigantic group / of tiny fish. ⑥ Tens of thousands of animals / hungry for sardines / hurry to the area, / including dolphins, whales, gannets, sailfish, / and many kinds of sharks, / as well as orcas and seals / — making it earth's biggest event / for predators.

⑦ The dolphins have / an incredible hunting strategy. ⑧ They team up / to collect the sardines / into a round group, / called a "bait ball." ⑨ Once the sardines are rounded up, / it is easy / for the dolphins / to snatch them. ⑩ And when the dolphins push the sardines / to the top of the water, / flocks of birds waiting to catch them / can take advantage of the sudden opportunity. ⑪ Thousands of birds soar / and dive into the water, / creating another spectacle.

⑫ Many people come to watch the Sardine Run / from boats. ⑬ Some bring snorkeling equipment / to swim under the waves / among all the excited fish. ⑭ People enjoy the event / and they all agree / it's one of the most amazing sights / they've ever seen.

해석 ① 여름마다 수백만 마리의 작은 정어리들이 남아프리카 공화국의 해안을 따라 큰 무리를 지어 헤엄친다. ② 이 놀라운 이동은 일종의 미스터리지만, 확실히 주변의 모든 동물을 흥분하게 한다.
③ 남부 연안의 아굴라스 퇴(堆)에서 산란을 한 후, 정어리들은 남아프리카 공화국의 동부 해안으로 헤엄친다. ④ 그들은 길이로는 수 마일, 폭으로는 최대 1마일, 그리고 30미터 이상의 깊이에 달할 수 있는 거대한 떼를 이루어 이동한다. ⑤ 바다 위를 낮게 날아가는 비행기들은 아주 작은 물고기들의 이 거대한 무리를 볼 수도 있다. ⑥ 정어리에 굶주린 수만 마리의 동물들이 그 지역으로 서둘러 가는데, 여기에는 범고래와 물개뿐 아니라 돌고래, 고래, 부비새류, 돛새치, 그리고 많은 종류의 상어들이 포함되어, 그것이 포식자들을 위한 지구의 가장 큰 행사가 되게 한다.
⑦ 돌고래는 놀라운 사냥 전략을 가지고 있다. ⑧ 그들은 정어리들을 둥근 형태의 무리로 끌어 모으기 위해 협력하는데, 이것은 '미끼 덩어리'라고 불린다. ⑨ 일단 정어리들이 둥글게 모이면, 돌고래들이 그것들을 낚아채기는 쉽다. ⑩ 그리고 돌고래들이 정어리들을 수면 위로 몰고 갔을 때, 정어리를 잡기 위해 기다리던 새 떼는 이 갑작스러운 기회를 이용할 수 있다. ⑪ 수천 마리의 새들이 날아올랐다가 물속으로 다이빙하고, 이것은 또 다른 장관을 만들어낸다.
⑫ 많은 사람들이 배에서 정어리 떼의 이동을 보려고 온다. ⑬ 몇몇은 파도 아래에서 그 모든 흥분한 물고기들 가운데 수영을 하기 위해 스노클링 장비를 가져온다. ⑭ 사람들은 그 행사를 즐기며, 그것이 그들이 본 가장 놀라운 광경 중의 하나라는 데에 모두 동의한다.

구문해설 ② ... it certainly gets(V) all the animals nearby(O) excited(OC).
→ get + 목적어 + 목적격보어(형용사): (목적어)가 …하게 하다

⑥ Tens of thousands of animals [hungry for sardines] hurry to the area, including dolphins, whales, ..., **as well as** orcas and seals — [making(V) it(O) earth's biggest event for predators(OC)].
→ 첫 번째 [ ]는 Tens of thousands of animals를 뒤에서 수식하는 형용사구
→ A as well as B: B뿐만 아니라 A도
→ 두 번째 [ ]는 〈동시동작〉을 나타내는 분사구문

⑨ ..., **it** is easy **for the dolphins to snatch them**.
→ it은 가주어, for the dolphins는 to부정사의 의미상의 주어, to 이하가 진주어

⑭ ... and they all agree [(that) it's one of the most amazing sights {(that) they've ever seen}].
→ [ ]는 동사 agree의 목적어로 쓰인 명사절로, 접속사 that이 생략됨.
→ { }는 선행사 the most amazing sights를 수식하는 관계대명사절로, 목적격 관계대명사 that이 생략됨.

Review Test

P. 138

A ③ B 1 continent 2 habitats 3 reproduce 4 observe C 1 ② 2 ③ 3 ④ 4 ⑤ D 1 낙타의 넓은 발은 눈에 빠지지 않고 눈 속을 걷는 것을 더 쉽게 해주었을 것이다. 2 해파리는 죽는 대신 자신을 새끼로 되돌려 놓는다. 3 그들은 동굴 벽에서 거친 조각들을 갈아내기 위해 그들의 상아를 사용하고, 그러고 나서 그 조각들을 먹는다. 4 그것들을 잡기 위해 기다리던 새 떼는 이 갑작스러운 기회를 이용할 수 있다. E 1 as much salt as they need 2 becoming similar to what are 3 Planes flying low over the ocean

해석

A

① 부패하다: 자연 과정을 통해 분해되다

② 특징: 어떤 것의 중요하거나 전형적인 부분

③ 평원: 야생 식물들이 있는 매우 습한 땅의 지역

④ 국경: 두 나라를 나누는 공식적인 선

⑤ 장비: 특정한 활동을 위해 필요한 도구

B

1 아시아는 세계에서 가장 큰 대륙이다.

2 많은 동물들이 그들의 자연 서식지를 잃을 위기에 처해 있다.

3 초파리는 순식간에 번식하는데, 한 번에 약 500개의 알을 낳는다.

4 현미경은 우리가 아주 작은 살아 있는 것들을 관찰하는 것을 가능하게 한다.

C

1 연어는 산란하기 위해 바다에서 민물로 이동한다.

① 탈출한다 ② 이동한다 ③ 생산한다 ④ 유지한다 ⑤ 저장한다

2 나는 친구가 도착하기를 기다리면서 공원을 돌아다녔다.

① 넘어졌다 ② 전환했다 ③ 돌아다녔다 ④ 붙잡았다 ⑤ 나타났다

3 상어는 주로 작은 물고기와 오징어를 먹는 바다의 최상위 포식자이다.

① 먹이 ② 경쟁자 ③ 보상 ④ 포식자 ⑤ 생태계

4 지구는 한때 거대한 공룡들이 지배했다.

① 날카로운 ② 얼어붙은 ③ 희귀한 ④ 분명한 ⑤ 거대한

SECTION 12

연예 · 스포츠

01 **1** ④ **2** ③ **3** individuality

02 **1** ② **2** ① **3** ⓐ to get ⓑ to boast

03 **1** ③ **2** got in trouble for not sitting still **3** ③

04 **1** (1) T (2) T (3) F **2** ④ **3** ③ **4** blood, right

01 내가 모델이 된다고? P. 142

정답 1 ④ 2 ③ 3 individuality

문제해설 1 ④ 길거리에서 자신만의 스타일로 옷을 잘 입는 사람들을 찾아 사진을 찍고 블로그를 운영하는 패션 사진작가 스콧 슈만에 관한 글이다.

① 한 젊은 모델의 일상 ② 성공적인 블로거가 되는 방법
③ 옷을 잘 입는 사람들의 비결 ④ 길거리 스타일을 찍는 사진작가
⑤ 패션과 사진의 관계

2 (A) '…하면서 (시간)을 보내다'는 「spend+시간+v-ing」이므로 photographing이 적절하다.
(B) It은 가주어, 동사 matter 뒤가 진주어로 '…인지 아닌지는 중요하지 않다'라는 뜻이므로 명사절을 이끄는 접속사 if가 적절하다.
(C) '…하기 위해서'라는 목적을 나타내는 부사적 용법의 to부정사 to get이 오는 것이 적절하다.

3 스콧 슈만은 패션에서 가장 중요한 것은 자신만의 스타일을 갖는 것이라고 생각한다. (⑬, ⑭번 문장)
스콧 슈만이 패션에서 가장 중요한 것이라고 생각하는 것은?
그는 개성이 가장 중요한 것이라고 여긴다.

본문

① A stylish woman poses on the street, / and a man takes a picture of her. ② You might think / she is a model or celebrity, / but she is not. ③ She is just an ordinary, but fashionable woman / in her own clothes. ④ The photographer is Scott Schuman, / one of the world's most-famous fashion photographers.
⑤ After quitting his fashion sales job in 2005, / Schuman went to the streets / with his digital camera. ⑥ He spent four to five hours a day / photographing people's street wear. ⑦ His target was anyone / dressed attractively. ⑧ It didn't matter / if they were wearing / trendy clothes or expensive brands. ⑨ Then he posted the photos / to his blog, / *The Sartorialist*.
⑩ The blog gained international attention / because people found his pictures / different from typical fashion photos. ⑪ Millions of people of all backgrounds / started visiting his blog / to get style inspiration. ⑫ Soon famous brands began collaborating with him / on advertising campaigns, / and magazines started running his pictures.
⑬ Schuman believes / individuality is the most important thing in fashion. ⑭ To him, / a well-dressed person is one / who displays a personal style, / rather than a manufactured look / created by stylists.

해석 ① 한 맵시 있는 여성이 거리에서 포즈를 잡고 한 남자가 그녀의 사진을 찍는다. ② 당신은 그녀가 모델이나 유명인이라고 생각할지도 모르지만, 그렇지 않다. ③ 그녀는 자기 옷을 입은 한 평범하지만, 스타일 좋은 여자일 뿐이다. ④ 사진사는 스콧 슈만으로, 세계에서 가장 유명한 패션 사진작가들 중 하나이다.
⑤ 2005년 패션 세일즈 일을 그만둔 후, 슈만은 디지털카메라를 들고 거리로 나갔다. ⑥ 그는 하루에 네댓 시간을 사람들의 길거리 패션을 찍으면서 보냈다. ⑦ 대상은 누구든 매력적으로 옷을 입은 사람이었다. ⑧ 그들이 유행하는 옷을 입는지 비싼 브랜드 옷을 입는지는 상관없었다. ⑨ 그러고 나서 그는 그 사진들을 자신의 블로그인 '사토리얼리스

트'에 올렸다.
⑩ 사람들이 그의 사진을 전형적인 패션 사진과는 다르다고 생각했기 때문에 그 블로그는 국제적인 주목을 받게 되었다. ⑪ 수백만 명의 다양한 분야의 사람들이 스타일에 관한 영감을 얻기 위해 그의 블로그를 방문하기 시작했다. ⑫ 곧 유명 브랜드들이 광고 캠페인에서 그와 공동 작업을 하기 시작했고, 잡지들은 그가 찍은 사진들을 싣기 시작했다. ⑬ 슈만은 개성이 패션에서 가장 중요한 것이라고 믿는다. ⑭ 그에게 옷을 잘 입는 사람은 스타일리스트에 의해 만들어진 양산된 모습보다는, 자기 개인의 스타일을 보여주는 사람이다.

구문해설

⑤ [After quitting his fashion sales job in 2005], Schuman went to the streets with his digital camera.

→ [ ]는 의미를 명확히 하기 위해 접속사를 생략하지 않은 분사구문으로 〈시간〉을 나타냄.

⑦ His target was anyone [dressed attractively].

→ [ ]는 anyone을 뒤에서 수식하는 과거분사구

⑭ To him, a well-dressed person is one **who** displays a personal style, rather than a manufactured look [created by stylists].

→ who는 one을 선행사로 하는 주격 관계대명사

→ [ ]는 a manufactured look을 뒤에서 수식하는 과거분사구

02 최고의 운동 친구 P. 144

정답 1 ② 2 ① 3 ⓐ to get ⓑ to boast

문제해설

1 ② '라디오 듣기'는 Running Mate의 기능으로 언급되지 않았다.
① 자신의 진도를 확인하기 (④번 문장) ③ 달리는 거리를 기록하기 (⑤번 문장)
④ 위치 확인하기 (⑥번 문장) ⑤ 소셜 웹사이트에 올리기 (⑨, ⑩번 문장)

2 빈칸에는 긍정적인 의미의 '북돋다', '격려하다' 등의 말이 와야 하므로 '강요하다'를 의미하는 ① force는 빈칸에 들어갈 말로 적절하지 않다.
① 강요하다 ② 고무하다 ③ 동기를 부여하다 ④ 격려하다 ⑤ 격려하다

3 ⓐ try to-v: …하려고 노력하다[애쓰다] ⓑ in order to-v: …하기 위해서

본문

① Are you trying to get fit / by jogging? ② Well, / jogging can become lonely, boring, and repetitive, / so most people wind up quitting / after just a few weeks. ③ But now / there's new technology / that can help you stay interested and motivated.
④ A new smartphone application called / "Running Mate" / will allow you to map your runs / and check your progress / as you go. ⑤ Using the smartphone's GPS and accelerometer technology, / you're able to record the pace, the distance, and the route of your run. ⑥ While jogging, / you can hear voice feedback / on how you're doing, / tap the map to check

your location, / and see whether you're on track / to beat your record time. ⑦ If that doesn't inspire[motivate, stimulate, encourage] you / to keep going, / try listening to fun motivational messages / from famous athletes, / or play your favorite music / to lift your mood.
⑧ With Running Mate, / you'll never be lonely again / when out jogging. ⑨ You can send the details of your runs / to a community website / in order to boast about your fastest time, / set goals and challenges, / and stay in touch with friends. ⑩ The application is also compatible / with Facebook and Twitter, / so you can broadcast your achievements / to the world.
⑪ This application will help turn jogging / from a chore into a treat. ⑫ You'll get fitter and faster, / and you'll have a lot of fun, too!

해석 ① 당신은 조깅으로 건강해지려고 노력하십니까? ② 조깅은 외롭고, 지루하며, 반복적으로 될 수 있어서, 대부분 사람들이 몇 주만 지나면 그만두게 됩니다. ③ 하지만 이제 당신이 흥미를 느끼고 의욕을 가진 상태를 유지하게 도와줄 수 있는 새로운 기술이 있습니다.
④ '러닝 메이트(달리기 친구)'라 불리는 새로운 스마트폰 애플리케이션은 당신의 달리기 지도를 만들어 주고, 당신이 달리기를 함에 따라 진도를 확인하게 해줍니다. ⑤ 스마트폰의 GPS와 가속도계 기술을 사용하여, 당신은 속도와 거리, 그리고 당신의 달리기 경로를 기록할 수 있습니다. ⑥ 조깅을 하는 동안, 당신은 당신이 어떻게 하고 있는지에 대한 음성 피드백을 들을 수 있고, 지도를 가볍게 쳐서 당신의 위치를 확인할 수 있으며, 당신이 자신의 시간 기록을 깨기 위해 제대로 하고 있는지를 볼 수 있습니다. ⑦ 만약 그것이 당신이 계속하도록 격려하지 않는다면, 유명한 운동선수로부터의 재미있는 동기 부여 메시지를 들어 보거나, 당신의 기분을 좋게 해줄 좋아하는 음악을 트세요.
⑧ 러닝 메이트와 함께라면, 당신은 조깅하러 나갈 때 절대 다시 외롭지 않을 것입니다. ⑨ 당신은 자신의 최고 기록에 대해 자랑하고, 목표와 도전을 설정하며, 친구들과 연락하고 지내기 위하여 당신의 달리기에 대한 세부 사항들을 커뮤니티 웹사이트로 보낼 수 있습니다. ⑩ 이 애플리케이션은 페이스북과 트위터와도 연동되므로, 당신은 당신이 성취한 것들을 세계에 알릴 수 있습니다.
⑪ 이 애플리케이션은 조깅을 따분한 일에서 특별한 것으로 바꾸는 것을 도와줄 것입니다. ⑫ 당신은 더 건강하고 빨라질 것이며, 많은 즐거움도 느낄 수 있을 것입니다!

구문해설 ③ But now there's new technology [that can **help** you *stay* *interested* and *motivated*].
→ [ ]는 선행사 new technology를 수식하는 주격 관계대명사절
→ help + 목적어 + 동사원형[to-v]: (목적어)가 …하는 것을 돕다
→ stay + 형용사: 계속 …한 상태를 유지하다

⑥ **While jogging**, you can hear ..., and see *whether* you're on track to beat your record time.
→ While jogging은 의미를 명확히 하기 위해 접속사를 생략하지 않은 분사구문으로 〈동시동작〉을 나타냄.
→ whether: '…인지 아닌지'라는 의미로, 명사절을 이끄는 접속사
→ to beat는 〈목적〉을 나타내는 부사적 용법의 to부정사

⑧ ..., you'll never be lonely again when (you are) out jogging.
→ 주절의 주어와 때를 나타내는 부사절의 주어가 같을 때는 부사절의 「주어 + be동사」를 생략할 수 있음.

03 스타들의 숨겨진 과거 P. 146

정답 1 ③ 2 got in trouble for not sitting still 3 ③

문제해설

1 ③ 마이클 펠프스는 ADHD 때문에 학교에서 가만히 앉아 있지 못해서 곤란에 처했다고 했으므로(⑬번 문장) 학교에 다녔다는 것을 알 수 있다.
① (→ ⑦번 문장) ② (→ ⑧~⑩번 문장) ④ (→ ⑫번 문장) ⑤ (→ ⑯번 문장)

2 '…로 곤란에 처하다'는 'get in trouble for…'이고, 이유를 나타내는 전치사 for 뒤에 「not+동명사구(sitting still)」를 배열한다.

3 ③ 부모님이 읽는 법을 배우면 연기 에이전트를 구해 준다고 했는데, 현재 세계적으로 유명한 여배우가 되었으므로 난독증을 극복했다는 것을 알 수 있다.
① 키이라 나이틀리는 영화에 캐스팅되었다.
② 키이라 나이틀리는 재능 있는 여배우였다.
③ 키이라 나이틀리는 자신의 장애를 극복했다.
④ 키이라 나이틀리는 여전히 난독증을 앓고 있다.
⑤ 키이라 나이틀리는 장애 때문에 연기를 그만두었다.

본문

① At times, / it seems like / celebrities have no difficulties, / doesn't it? ② They're beautiful and charismatic. ③ But they sometimes face obstacles, too. ④ You may be surprised to know that / many celebrities have learning disabilities. ⑤ The following is / a list of inspirational stars / that have learned / to live with disabilities.
⑥ Bruce Willis is a skilled actor, / but he wasn't always natural / on camera. ⑦ Until he reached the age of twenty, / he had a stuttering problem. ⑧ In an interview, / he explained / that acting helped him beat his stutter / and work on his sense of humor. ⑨ By being funny, / Willis kept people's attention / off his disability / and on his acting skills. ⑩ In doing so, / he gained confidence.
⑪ American swimmer Michael Phelps / is fast and alert / in the pool. ⑫ But / Phelps' focus / wasn't always strong, / as he had ADHD. ⑬ In school, / Phelps sometimes got in trouble / for not sitting still / in class. ⑭ When he turned his attention to swimming, / however, / he was able to develop his concentration. ⑮ After years of training, / his hard work led to several Olympic gold medals.
⑯ When Keira Knightley was young, / her classmates teased her / because she could not read. ⑰ It turned out / she had dyslexia, / which causes people to read incorrectly. ⑱ To help her defeat her disability, / Knightley's parents made a deal with her. ⑲ They agreed to find her an acting agent / if she learned to read. ⑳ Well, you can probably imagine / how it turned out, / because Keira is now / one of the most famous actresses / in the world.

해석

① 때로, 유명인사들은 어려움이 없는 것 같이 보인다. 그렇지 않은가? ② 그들은 아름답고, 카리스마가 있다. ③ 하지만 그들도 가끔은 난관에 직면한다. ④ 많은 유명인사가 학습 장애를 가지고 있다는 것을 안다면 여러분은 아마 놀

랄지도 모른다. ⑤ 다음은 장애를 가지고 사는 법을 배운, 우리에게 영감을 주는 스타들의 목록이다.
⑥ 브루스 윌리스는 노련한 배우이지만, 그가 카메라 앞에서 항상 자연스러웠던 것은 아니다. ⑦ 스무 살이 될 때까지, 그는 말을 더듬는 문제가 있었다. ⑧ 한 인터뷰에서, 그는 연기가 그가 말 더듬는 것을 극복하고 유머 감각을 단련시키는 데 도움이 되었다고 설명했다. ⑨ 유머러스한 사람이 됨으로써, 윌리스는 사람들의 관심을 자신의 장애로부터 돌리고 연기 능력으로 향하도록 하였다. ⑩ 그렇게 하면서, 그는 자신감을 얻었다.
⑪ 미국 수영선수 마이클 펠프스는 물속에서 빠르고 기민하다. ⑫ 그러나, 펠프스는 ADHD(주의력 결핍 및 과잉행동 장애)를 앓았기 때문에 그의 집중력이 늘 강하지는 않았다. ⑬ 학교에서, 펠프스는 때때로 수업 시간에 가만히 앉아 있지 못하여 곤란에 처했다. ⑭ 그러나 그가 수영으로 주의를 돌리자, 그는 집중력을 기를 수 있었다. ⑮ 수년간의 훈련 끝에, 그의 고된 노력은 여러 개의 올림픽 금메달로 이어졌다.
⑯ 키이라 나이틀리가 어렸을 때, 그녀의 반 친구들은 그녀가 읽지 못해서 그녀를 놀려댔다. ⑰ 그녀는 부정확하게 읽게 만드는 증상인 난독증을 앓고 있다는 것이 밝혀졌다. ⑱ 그녀가 장애를 극복하도록 돕기 위해, 나이틀리의 부모는 그녀에게 조건을 걸었다. ⑲ 그녀가 읽는 법을 배운다면 그녀에게 연기 에이전트를 구해주기로 한 것이다. ⑳ 여러분은 아마 그 결과가 어떻게 되었는지 상상할 수 있을 것인데, 왜냐하면 키이라는 이제 세계에서 가장 유명한 여배우 중 하나이기 때문이다.

구문해설

① At times, it **seems like** celebrities have no difficulties, *doesn't it*?
→ seem like ...: …인 것 같다
→ 앞 문장의 주어는 3인칭 단수. 동사의 시제는 현재, 동사의 종류는 일반동사이므로, 부가의문문은 doesn't it?으로 씀.

⑨ By being funny, Willis kept people's attention **off his disability** and **on his acting skills**.
→ off his disability와 on his acting skills는 「동사(kept)+목적어(people's attention)+부사구」 구문의 부사구로 병렬관계를 이루고 있음.

⑫ But Phelps' focus was**n't always** strong, *as* he had ADHD.
→ not always: 항상 …인 것은 아니다 〈부분부정〉
→ as는 이유를 나타내는 접속사

⑰ It turned out (that) she had dyslexia, **which** causes people to read incorrectly.
→ she 앞에는 turned out의 목적어가 되는 명사절을 이끄는 접속사 that이 생략되어 있음.
→ which는 dyslexia를 부연 설명하는 계속적 용법의 주격 관계대명사

⑳ Well, you can probably imagine **how it turned out**, because Keira is now *one of the most famous actresses* in the world.
→ how it turned out은 imagine의 목적어가 되는 간접의문문으로 「의문사+주어+동사」의 어순
→ one of the+최상급+복수명사: 가장 …한 ~ 중의 하나

04 Why Runners Run Counterclockwise P. 148

정답 **1** (1) T (2) T (3) F **2** ④ **3** ③ **4** blood, right

문제해설 **1** (1) 오른쪽으로 돌 때 혈액이 왼쪽으로 밀린다고 했으므로 왼쪽으로 돌 때는 그 반대이다. (⑪번 문장)

(2) 반시계 방향으로 돌면 심장이 다른 기관에 혈액을 공급하기 쉬워져서 덜 지치므로, 시계 방향으로 돌 때는 반대의 효과가 난다. (⑨, ⑩번 문장)

(3) 본문에 따르면, 대부분의 사람들은 왼쪽으로 도는 것이 더 자연스럽다고 했다. (⑫번 문장)

[문제] 이 글의 내용과 일치하면 T에, 일치하지 않으면 F에 표시하시오.

(1) 당신이 왼쪽으로 돌 때, 혈액은 오른쪽으로 밀린다.

(2) 당신은 시계 방향으로 달릴 때 빨리 피곤함을 느낄 수 있다.

(3) 오른쪽으로 도는 것이 대부분의 사람들에게 더 자연스럽다.

2 '필수적인'이라는 의미의 vital과 가장 의미가 가까운 단어는 ④ essential이다.

[문제] 밑줄 친 vital과 의미가 가장 가까운 것은?

① 뻣뻣한 ② 치명적인 ③ 민감한 ④ 필수적인 ⑤ 독립적인

3 ③ 처음에 달리기 선수가 시계 반대 방향으로 돌 때 원심력을 겪게 된다는 내용인 (B)가 오고, 그래서 왼쪽으로 돌 때 원심력이 오른쪽으로 작용하여 신체 기관에 혈액 공급이 더 잘된다는 내용인 (A)가 이어진 후, 결국 이러한 혈액순환 덕분에 달리기 선수가 빨리 지치지 않는다는 (C)로 이어지는 것이 자연스럽다.

[문제] 글의 흐름에 맞게 (A), (B), (C)를 배열한 것을 고르시오.

4 심장의 중심이 왼쪽으로 더 치우쳐 있어 왼쪽으로 돌 때 원심력이 오른쪽으로 작용하여 다른 신체 기관에 혈액을 더 쉽게 공급한다고 했고, 대부분의 사람들이 더 강한 오른발을 가지고 있어 왼쪽으로 도는 것이 더 쉽다고 했다.

[문제] 왜 달리기 선수들은 시계 반대 방향으로 뛰는가? 빈칸에 들어갈 알맞은 말을 본문에서 찾아 쓰시오.

원심력이 심장이 혈액을 더 쉽게 공급하도록 돕고, 대부분의 사람들이 더 강한 오른발을 가졌기 때문이다.

본문

① Everyone enjoys / watching the track and field events / at the Olympics. ② Understandably, / the focus is / only on how fast the athletes are running. ③ But there's something else / most people probably don't notice. ④ In all the events, / the athletes run / in a counterclockwise direction. ⑤ Why is that?

⑥ Firstly, / it is related to the structure / of the human body. ⑦ Specifically, / the position of the heart, / which is the body's most vital organ, / is slightly to the left of the center. ⑧ (B) When a runner turns to the left / in a counterclockwise direction, / he or she encounters centrifugal force. ⑨ (A) On a left-hand turn, / centrifugal force pushes to the right / and helps the heart / to pump blood more easily / to the other organs in the body. ⑩ (C) This increase in blood circulation / means the runner does not tire / too quickly. ⑪ Turning to the right / has the opposite effect, / as blood is pushed to the left / and away from the other organs.

⑫ The other key point is / that turning to the left / is more natural / for most people. ⑬ The act of turning to the left / requires pushing harder / with the right foot. ⑭ Just as most people are right-handed, / most also have a stronger right foot. ⑮ Thus, turning left is an easier motion.

⑯ Next time you visit an athletics track, / try running around it / in a clockwise direction. ⑰ You'll feel / how much more difficult it is, / and understand / why we normally run the other way!

해석

① 모든 사람은 올림픽에서 육상경기를 보는 것을 즐긴다. ② 당연하게도, 초점은 선수들이 얼마나 빨리 달리고 있는지에만 맞춰져 있다. ③ 그러나 대부분의 사람들이 아마도 알아채지 못하는 다른 무언가가 있다. ④ 모든 경기에서, 선수들은 시계 반대 방향으로 달린다. ⑤ 왜 그럴까?

⑥ 우선, 이것은 인간의 신체 구조와 관련이 있다. ⑦ 구체적으로 말하면, 신체의 가장 필수적인 기관인 심장의 위치가 중심에서 약간 왼쪽에 있다. ⑧ (B) 달리기 선수가 시계 반대 방향으로 달리며 왼쪽으로 돌 때, 그 혹은 그녀는 원심력을 맞닥뜨리게 된다. ⑨ (A) 왼쪽으로 돌 때 원심력은 오른쪽으로 작용하고, 심장이 신체의 다른 기관으로 더 쉽게 혈액을 공급하도록 돕는다. ⑩ (C) 혈액순환에서의 이러한 증가는 달리기 선수가 너무 빨리 지치지 않는다는 것을 의미한다. ⑪ 오른쪽으로 도는 것은 반대의 효과가 있는데, 그 이유는 혈액이 왼쪽으로 밀려가서 다른 기관들로부터 멀어지기 때문이다.

⑫ 또 다른 요점은 왼쪽으로 도는 것이 대부분의 사람들에게 더 자연스럽다는 것이다. ⑬ 왼쪽으로 도는 행위는 오른발로 더 세게 미는 것을 필요로 한다. ⑭ 대부분 사람들이 오른손잡이인 것처럼 또한 대다수가 더 강한 오른발을 가지고 있다. ⑮ 따라서 왼쪽으로 도는 것이 더 쉬운 동작이다.

⑯ 다음에 당신이 육상 트랙을 방문하면, 그 둘레를 시계 방향으로 달리는 것을 시도해 보라. ⑰ 당신은 그것이 얼마나 더 힘든지를 느낄 것이며, 왜 우리가 보통 그 반대 방향으로 달리는지를 이해하게 될 것이다!

구문해설

③ But there's something else [(that) most people probably don't notice].

→ [ ]는 선행사 something else를 수식하는 관계대명사절로, 목적격 관계대명사 that이 생략됨.

⑦ ..., the position of the heart, [which is the body's most vital organ], is slightly ....

→ [ ]는 선행사인 the heart를 부연 설명하는 계속적 용법의 관계대명사절

⑫ The other key point is [that {turning to the left} is more natural for most people].

→ [ ]는 문장의 보어로 쓰인 명사절

→ { }는 that절의 주어 역할을 하는 동명사구

Review Test

P. 150

A **1** ⓓ **2** ⓐ **3** ⓑ **4** ⓔ **5** ⓒ B **1** pace **2** matter **3** collaborated **4** progress C **1** ③ **2** ③ **3** ② **4** ④ D **1** 사람들은 슈만의 사진들을 전형적인 패션 사진과는 다르다고 생각했다. **2** 조깅을 하는 동안, 당신은 당신이 어떻게 하고 있는지에 대한 음성 피드백을 들을 수 있다. **3** 많은 유명인사가 학습 장애를 가지고 있다는 것을 안다면 여러분은 아마 놀랄지도 모른다. **4** 대부분의 사람들이 아마도 알아채지 못하는 다른 무언가가 있다. E **1** inspire you to keep going **2** Next time you visit an athletics track **3** turning to the left is more natural

해석

A

1 놀리다: ⓓ 어떤 사람을 비웃거나 웃음거리로 만들다

2 가만히 있는: ⓐ 움직이지 않는

3 필수적인: ⓑ 매우 중요하거나 필수적인

4 장기: ⓔ 간이나 심장 같은 몸의 일부

5 반복적인: ⓒ 같은 일이 여러 번 일어나는 것을 수반하는

B

1 그 마라톤 선수는 경주 내내 빠른 속도를 유지했다.

2 네가 그 소식을 믿는지 믿지 않는지는 중요하지 않다.

3 공동의 목표를 달성하기 위해 전 팀이 협력했다.

4 과학 기술의 진보는 우리의 삶을 여러 면에서 변화시켰다.

C

1 이 책의 독자들은 삶의 장애물을 극복하는 방법을 배울 것이다.

① 혜택 ② 해결책 ③ 장애물 ④ 칭찬 ⑤ 업적

2 결승전에서, 마리아는 그녀의 라이벌을 물리치고 챔피언이 되었다.

① 놀고 ② 제공하고 ③ 물리치고 ④ 떨어뜨리고 ⑤ 자세를 취하고

3 나의 조카는 어렸을 때부터 농구에 대한 대단한 재능을 보였다.

① 안내했다 ② 보였다 ③ 가동했다 ④ 분석했다 ⑤ 지원했다

4 파키스탄 내전은 전 세계로부터 주목을 받았다.

① 무게 ② 접근 ③ 힘 ④ 주목 ⑤ 확신

MEMO

MEMO

MEMO

MEMO